Forbidden Fruit

Sin City's underworld
and the Supper Club inferno

By Peter Bronson

Forbidden Fruit

Sin City's underworld and the Supper Club inferno

ISBN: 978-1-7339955-7-3

For information, contact the author:

Peter Bronson
pbronson1253@gmail.com

Published by:

Chilidog Press LLC
pbronson@chilidogpress.com

Chilidog Press LLC
Loveland, Ohio
www.chilidogpress.com

Cover and book design:

Andy Melchers

Dedication

This book is dedicated to the victims and survivors of the Supper Club fire in 1977. Also to my family—especially my son, James, who encouraged me to write it because we share a love of local history. And to a surprising unsung hero who fearlessly took a stand against the mob in "Sin City," Judge Johnst Northcutt.

Contents

Part IV: 1960s

Part V: 1970s

Epilogue

Introduction

I was hooked on this story the first time I heard it from my barber Bill Gayheart, who was the unofficial Mayor of Milford, Ohio, and knew just about everything about everybody. As he cut my hair, he told me about a guy he met named Wayne Dammert, who saved 75 people the night the Beverly Hills Supper Club burned. Everyone who grew up in Cincinnati knew the story, but I was a tumbleweed transplant from Arizona so it was all news to me.

As we used to say in the newsroom, this one has it all: mobsters, hookers, murder and dice; dirty cops, crooked politicians, arson and cold-blooded hitmen. It has a surprising hidden back door to assassinations that shook the world. And then it comes home to a haunted hilltop where a nightmare tragedy scorched the earth. There's a colorful cast of gangsters, gamblers, strippers and mob bosses, and a few courageous citizens and lawmen who dared to fight back—as the best have done from Nehemiah to Elliot Ness.

There are dozens of books about the history of Northern Kentucky's "Sin City" underworld and the Supper Club fire of 1977. But as far as I can tell, none have put all the jigsaw pieces together. The regional and national impact of that vivid local history is the greatest story never told. It has been buried with the charred remains of the Zebra Room where the Supper Club fire started almost 50 years ago.

I wrote about it as an editor and columnist at *The Cincinnati Enquirer.* But I didn't know what I didn't know.

I didn't know my Freedom of Information Act requests to the FBI would take me back in time to the 1960s, to a room at the Desert Inn in Las Vegas where mob bosses divided their skim and talked about the old Beverly Hills Country Club that was their training wheels for Vegas.

I didn't know declassified transcripts of those illegal wiretaps would take a detour to Dealey Plaza in 1963 and a Los Angeles hotel kitchen in 1968, as gangsters plotted the assassinations of a President and his brother.

I thought I knew the story of the Kennedys—until I dove into those FBI tapes, declassified Kennedy papers and documents in the National Archives. Following the footprints of the underworld conspiracy, I was led right back to Newport.

Seasoned by my career as a newspaper reporter, editor and columnist, I thought I was pretty cynical about crime and corruption—yet I was still shocked to learn how Americans were deceived by the Warren Commission and corrupt FBI "Director for Life" J. Edgar Hoover. Unfortunately, political corruption of the FBI at the highest level is nothing new. I always took pride in the "first draft of history" created by the press—until I saw how that "first draft" has been manipulated to bury the truth and forge a counterfeit permanent record.

I didn't know Newport and Covington were such a dark and wild side of buttoned-down, Ivory-clean Cincinnati. I was surprised to learn the untold story of how hard Newport battled to leave it's notorious past behind, even leading the nation in a crusade against corruption and porn.

But the past refuses to stay buried. History is stubborn. It clings to the present like peeling letters on faded brick walls and empty lots where the brothels, bust-out joints and mob casinos have been scoured away. It heaves up from the ground the way shoes and broken dishes sprout in the woods where the Beverly Hills once lit the sky with the glow of its glamorous neon nightlife.

There is hardly anyone in the Cincinnati region who doesn't know someone who was singed by history when the Supper Club fire killed 165 people and at least two unborn children in 1977. The survivors still bear the scars, and many wonder if we will ever know the truth. Digging into the past for this book was like historical archeology, to brush away some of the accumulated dust of decades and reveal the clear outlines of that truth.

I used historical fiction for the opening scenes, the fictional characters in the Alibi Club and conversations by factual characters such as Charles Lester. But those are all rooted in research. Otherwise, all names, dates and stories are factual, based on books, academic research papers, government documents, newspaper stories, archives, FBI files and interviews with people who were there. Any mistakes are mine alone.

Stories take on their own lives. This one became a parable about human nature that's as old as the Garden of Eden. Humans just can't resist forbidden fruit, whether it's gambling, bootleg booze, hookers, porn or drugs. Wherever the government puts up a "Keep Off The Grass" sign, it is guaranteed that people will walk all over it. With Prohibition, the government made outlaws out of good, honest people and created an underworld market that made organized crime a national industry. And once that genie was out of the bottle, it could not be pushed back in.

My goal was to make a long-buried treasure of local history come alive—dramatic, entertaining, heartbreaking and meaningful, so readers can see how it has shaped the landscape we know today.

The word for this story is "fabulous." So extraordinary it is hard to believe. But that's the best part. It's true.

Part I — 1930s

1.
The Mob Lights a Match

A slender man in a long tweed topcoat came down the steps and stepped carefully over a mound of dirty, coal-dusted snow. A car idled at the curb, shrouded in steaming clouds of exhaust that were lit by the jaundiced glow of dim streetlamps.

"Did ya get the gas?" he asked as he climbed into the front seat of the rumbling Ford Deluxe sedan. "Never mind. Holy mother of God, I can smell it. It's like Mr. Rockefeller's Standard Oil refinery in here. Open a window, willya?"

"We tried that, Eddie, it's too damn cold," said a voice from the backseat. "Dave spilled some on his sleeve. It's his car, so he's driving."

"Is this how they do it in Detroit, Chick?" Eddie asked a man in back. "Take a bath in the stuff then light a match? How many cans you guys got in here? The way it's sloshin' around back there it sounds like my ma's washin' machine."

"We got three, which is more than enough, but Red—Mr. Masterson—he insisted," said Dave, pointing a thumb over his shoulder as he pulled away from a Newport rooming house that was pinched between a flashing neon bust-out joint and a gothic abandoned church. "Red's their man in Newport. He got the word from Cleveland. Ain't that right, Red?"

A second voice in the back said, "Uh-huh" in a surly croak that invited no more questions.

Edwin Garrison looked back at the man known as Newport's "Enforcer," and saw a slouched, stout, shadowy shape, hat brim pulled low, collar pulled high, hands jammed in pockets. He felt a chill and yanked the lapels and collar of his own coat up over his nose to block the gas fumes. Chick spoke again from the backseat.

"In Detroit they don't have to do this kinda fireworks. Everyone knows who's the boss. But this Schmidt guy—what the hell's a matter with him? I heard Moe D. told him personally that the club was for sale to Moe and nobody else, and Schmidt told him to take a flying leap. Is he bug-eatin' loony? You don't talk to Moe like that. He came up in the Purple Gang in Detroit. Those guys' idea of a second chance is another bullet in the head."

"Yeah, I feel bad about it myself," Dave Whitfield said. Sid Diehm, aka "Chick," was exhaling gusts of cheap scotch with every sentence, but he was right. "Pete was always solid when we worked for Remus. We drove bootleg for years together. When George went down, Pete did his time for running rum without rattin' anyone. Outside of he never left a tip and held onto a dollar until the green wore off, he was alright. I always liked him."

"Me too," said Eddie. Red just nodded.

"Well, it's not like we're burning him down personally," said Chick. "Right? I mean, nobody has to get hurt. We just build a bonfire inside the backdoor and Schmidt gets the message that Moe Dalitz and the Cleveland boys play for keeps. When they say sell, you put out the 'Sold' sign and pack your bags. We give Pete the hotfoot, he sells what's left at a fire-sale discount, Moe rebuilds the club, and all is back to beer and skittles. Even the cops gave up keepin' score on burn-outs in Newport. So, pretty soon the swells are back at the tables, maybe even the governor comes back again for a taste. They won't even smell the ashes when Moe gets done rebuilding it."

"Well I can sure as hell smell the gas," said Eddie. "It's givin' me a ass-ache. How far?"

"We're almost there, off Alexandria Pike, right up this hill," said Dave, downshifting to second gear as the Ford skidded in the slushy street. His Carolina drawl made it sound like "Rat up this heel."

At the top of the narrow two-lane track, the Beverly Hills Country Club loomed out of the darkness as a darker shape against the skyline glow of Newport's midnight neon. The long black car rolled to a stop behind the club. Dave set the brake and the men climbed out in their wool overcoats and high-topped, unbuckled rubber galoshes, wading through the snow and frozen tracks past a row of overstuffed garbage cans near the back door. They lugged heavy five-gallon cans of gas.

While the others stood back and waited, Eddie wrapped a snub-nosed .38 revolver in a handkerchief and used the butt to break a window in the backdoor, then reached in and turned the lock, kicking the door open with his foot.

They all went in quickly and began to dump the gas, splashing it against the walls as the cans glugged and gargled. Eddie went down into the dark basement, while Chick and Dave dumped gasoline in the kitchen. "Leave a couple of cans half full in the middle of the floor," said Red from the doorway, standing clear to avoid getting splashed.

"It's all set, let's go," Dave shouted toward the basement as he turned for the door. "Eddie, you're last out. Strike a match... Fire in the hole."

While Eddie was still fumbling in his coat pocket for a box of wooden matches, they heard a big thumping woosh as the fume-choked room ignited and a shock wave gave them a hard shove. As they stumbled into the snow, Eddie came out last, followed by two sharp explosions from the open cans.

"His sleeve was flaming like one a them shish-kabobs," Chick told his friends later. "Ya shouldda seen him running in circles, waving his arms like he was a floor show with fire swords. He musta splashed it on his coat while he was flinging it around. And on top of that he had flames shooting out of his feet where he walked through it. I can still see it. We threw him into a snowbank and rolled him around like a donut in sugar. His overshoes was half melted to his feet. Then we beat it the hell outta there. That place went up like the Chicago fire. It musta been the kitchen stove or maybe the furnace that set it all off."

As they raced back down the hill, Dave gunned the Ford into a fishtail slide at the bottom and slid into a fence, bounced off and kept going. The gas odor lingered, now mingled with the burned-rubber of Eddie's melted galoshes and the nauseating stench of fried human flesh, also coming from Eddie, who moaned, wept and cursed over his scorched arm and legs.

At least they didn't hear the screams anymore. "There were people in there," Chick said, panic in his voice. "One a them looked like a kid when they came falling out the window."

"Shut up. We saw it," Red said.

"But I thought it was supposed to be empty."

"I said shut up."

Chick was not too drunk to miss the menace in the voice. He shut up.

Earl Fillhart and his wife, Viola, were living on the second floor as caretakers. They woke to the sound of a dull explosion and soon felt the heat of flames rushing up the stairwell. Earl grabbed Viola and pushed her out the second story window into a snowbank, then ran back for his wife's five-year-old sister, Mary Lou Rardin, who was spending the night. He threw her out the window into the piled-up snow, then leaped out himself.

All three were burned. Viola was bruised and scorched, but saved from further injuries by the cushioning snowbank. Earl had burns and a twisted ankle. They were treated at a hospital in Dayton, Kentucky. The little girl got the worst of it. Mary Lou died two days later.

"TWO HURT, GIRL BURNED, IN RESORT BLAST," was the banner headline in the *Cincinnati Enquirer Kentucky Edition* the next morning, February 3, 1936. "Smith Place is Left in Ashes As Mystery Explosion Sets House Afire," said the stacked subheads in Western Union staccato. "Police Suspect Enemies of Owner. Family Leaps. Child's Injury Grave."

"Mrs. Fillhart said that just before the fire started she heard an automobile drive behind the building," the story said.

She would later describe the sound of breaking glass, then an explosion. Before her husband forced her out the second story window, she saw a man watching them from the ground. He stood by the long black car and just watched as she screamed for help. As the car pulled away, the Fillharts picked up Mary Lou and ran for a nearby house to get help. The neighbor took them to the highway where they caught a ride to the hospital. By the time the firemen arrived, there was nothing left to save.

2.
Gamblers' War Blamed

Owner Pete Schmidt insisted there was no gambling at his club and told police he had no idea why it was torched.
Kenton County Library archives.

The newspaper accounts were inconsistent and punctuated with errors. The little girl's name changed from "Raiden" to "Reiden" and finally to Rardin, and from Mary to Marion and finally Mary Lou. Her age fluctuated between 5 and 8 and settled on 5. But the newspapers made up what was lacking in accuracy with drama.

"INCENDIARISM," the headline yelled in the next day's paper, using the 1930s newsroom style for arson. "Gamblers' war blamed," it said, although the owner, Pete Schmidt, a former bootlegger and convict, insisted that gambling had never been permitted in his 14-room roadhouse, which was at that time already the most swank and successful "carpet-joint" casino in the Cincinnati area.

The local papers reported that the owner was "Pete Smith," unaware that Schmidt was using an alias.

The Cincinnati Post reported, "Mr. Smith reiterated that the blast had no connection with any quarrel with Northern Kentucky gambling interests." It was a curiously explicit denial.

The Kentucky Enquirer reported, "Smith said he knew no reason why his place should have been fired." He told the paper, "I will rebuild the place in time to operate next summer."

Police quickly picked up a Newport bartender, William Elrod, who worked in a York Street café owned by Dave Whitfield. At first, Elrod refused to talk. After a night in custody, he changed his mind.

Shooting on Monmouth Street

The brass-knuckle 1930s were long before Miranda rights and hands-off police questioning. They were the days when Cincinnati Detective Robert "Machine Gun" Meldon challenged a Newport mobster to a shootout in the street. Meldon waited with his trademark Tommy gun, which was invented in Newport by General John Thompson. The mobster never showed up, and Machine Gun Meldon's legend grew with his list of kills.

In wide open Newport, mob gunman Albert "Red" Masterson was also racking up kills that were rumored in the dozens. One verified score was a Chicago hitman from the Al Capone gang, John Rosen, who came to town in 1935, shoved a gun into the ribs of a Glenn Hotel manager and told him to find Red Masterson.

The manager and Rosen took an elevator upstairs, but the Newport Enforcer was out. Rosen left and caught a cab.

The cab driver told police he was ordered by Rosen at gunpoint to follow a car and run it off the highway. He refused to run it off the road, but followed the car back to the Glenn Hotel on Monmouth Street, where Rosen "leaped out and attacked the other man, leaving his victim lying on the sidewalk," the cab driver said.

Later, sitting in another cab at 609 Monmouth Street in Newport, Rosen finally spotted Masterson on the sidewalk, cursed him and called him out. Masterson walked up to the cab, yelled something that the newspapers translated to "Quit the fooling," and began firing two .38s into Rosen. He kept shooting until Rosen was entirely dead.

In court, Masterson testified that he had seen Rosen reach for a gun. No gun was found on Rosen, but Masterson's lawyer produced a witness who testified that he had reached into the cab while the gun smoke was still thick, took the gun from Rosen's lap and ran off to throw it in the river. Detectives from Louisville and Columbus, Ohio, told the court that Rosen was a well-known gangster who had served time for only a small fraction of his crimes and killings. They described a mob hitman who got what was coming.

"Acquittal of the 29-year-old defendant on the murder charge came at 13 minutes to 3 o'clock yesterday afternoon, Friday the 13th, and only half an hour after the jury had withdrawn for its deliberations," a newspaper report said.

The court ruled it was self-defense. Police said six of eight shots fired by Masterson hit Rosen. But the cause of death was "gambling war."

Masterson was also wanted in Cincinnati for violating parole in Ohio by carrying firearms. But the Kentucky judge set bond at $2,000, which was easily posted by Masterson. He walked away. His lawyer was Daniel Davies, the same attorney who would represent Garrison, Whitfield and Diehm.

Grand Jury To Investigate Murder And Arson Charge

Two prisoners, arrested Friday night in connection with a Campbell County resort fire last week that caused the death of a five-year-old girl, were held for the grand jury without bond by Judge William C. Buten, Campbell County Court, at a hearing for them yesterday in Newport Jail.

Edwin Garrison, 45 years old, 526 East Riverside Drive, Newport, was held on charges of murder and arson. David Whitfield, 32, cafe owner, 627 York Street, was held on charges of harboring a known felon and being an accessory before the fact of murder.

The hearing was conducted in the jail by Judge Buten because Garrison is so badly burned that it is necessary to carry him to and from his cot in the jail.

Police say Garrison admitted he was burned when he set the blaze that destroyed the rural resort of Pete Smith, Alexandria Pike, two miles south of Newport. This fire caused the death of Mary Lou Boiden, 5, sister of Mrs. Viola Fill-

DAVID WHITFIELD, lent when he appeared before Judge Buten yesterday. He fused to talk except to plead

Eruptions of violence in the streets and burn-outs of bars and nightclubs by the mob were as common as cops on the take in those days. And bent cops were so common in the 1930s that one of the biggest brothels in the county was owned and run by a local marshal, while Newport's police chief ran a casino.

But the "resort blaze" that made big headlines on both sides of the river in 1936 was different. It was not just mobsters killing each other. A little girl had been killed. The torching of

Schmidt's roadhouse had violated an unwritten code. Even crooked cops and a few gangsters wanted justice. There was no mercy to be found for men who would burn up a 5-year-old girl.

'First time I ever killed a child'

It took the police just four days to track down two of them.

After interrogating the bartender Elrod, detectives learned that Edwin Garrison and Sidney "Chick" Diehm were both burned in the arson, and had been taken to Dave Whitfield's café on York Street, which Whitfield had closed that night while Garrison and Diehm were given first aid.

Earl Fillhart identified Garrison's mugshot as one of two men he saw at the roadhouse when he went to investigate the fire.

Garrison and Whitfield were arrested on February 7.

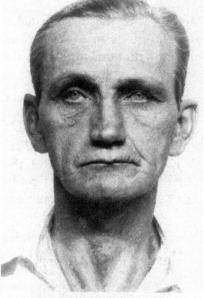

EDWIN SANFORD GARRISON

Mugshot from 1960

Whitfield said he had driven Garrison to a Covington doctor, Edward J. Nestley, and told the doctor that Garrison had been burned in a moonshine-still explosion. Garrison told the doctor it was a car wreck. The doctor apparently did not care which story was true or ask any questions. He gave Garrison some sedatives and followed up with a couple of visits over the next three days, without telling police.

When Garrison was finally found in the attic of a rooming house, thrashing and moaning in a fever of sweat, oozing burns and agony, police said he was half out of his mind.

"I see three people burning," he raved. "I still see them, especially the little girl."

He told the police, "It's the first time I ever killed a child."

He also boasted that he knew recently slain New York gangsters "Legs"

Diamond and Dutch Shultz, and had been working at Shultz's Coney Island Racetrack in Cincinnati. "Questioned about the blast and fire that is suspected of having its origin in a gambling war, Garrison kept his blistered lips tightly closed," the *Cincinnati Post* reported on February 12.

Whitfield and Garrison were charged with arson, murder and robbery during a hearing that had to be held in a cell at the Campbell County Jail. Garrison was too crippled by burns to be moved from his jailhouse cot without being carried to court.

Police launched a manhunt for the third man, Chick Diehm. Detectives tracked him through Detroit and several states, then finally found him hiding out in an apartment on West 45th Street in New York City on March 23.

All three men were described as hoodlums and "police characters."

Sidney Diehm, 34: For some reason, stories about Diehm showed no pictures of him. But he fit the "police character" portrait. He had been arrested for larceny a year before for trying to pay his bill at the Hotel Havlin in Cincinnati with a stolen adding machine. In 1927 he assaulted a federal prohibition agent "with intent to impede and obstruct justice."

Dave Whitfield, 33: Whitfield stares from his mugshot with a direct, defiant gaze. His lower lip is thrust out over a dimpled double chin. His dark eyes are sad but lifeless. He had grown up in North Carolina and served in the Navy, then served three terms in prison for robbery, embezzlement and violation of federal liquor laws. In court he said he once was a partner with Pete Schmidt, whom he had known for 10 or 15 years, going back to Prohibition when they made bootleg whiskey on a farm Schmidt owned on Tippenhauer Road in Campbell County, Kentucky.

Edwin Garrison, 35: In a newspaper photo borrowed from police files, Garrison wears a white shirt, tie and jacket. His thin lips are tight, his face as blank and cold as a snowdrift. The irises of his eyes are washed out, making the penetrating dots of his pupils stand out like bullet holes in glass. He was also a graduate of the George Remus College of Criminal Knowledge, and had been part of Pete Schmidt's crew. But lately he had been associated with the Meyer Lansky gang in New York. He was mathematics wiz who calculated racetrack odds. His police character friends called him "the human adding machine."

3.
Swift and Speedy Trials

Justice was a locomotive in those days, not the start-and-stop, lollygagging streetcar we know today.

Garrison was first to go to trial, on April 14, just two months after the fire and his arrest. He was still on crutches, healing from his severe burns. Stoic, betraying no emotion, he admitted he set the fire but "refused to enlarge on that statement," the *Enquirer* reported.

"DEATH PENALTY Is Aim of State," the headline said.

Viola Fillhart testified that she heard an explosion, woke her husband and saw a car outside as the house burst into flames. Earl Fillhart took the stand for two hours. He said he ran to the bedroom window to see a man carrying something into the house, and could clearly see the men, just 25 yards away. He identified Garrison during a lineup of suspects at the county jail.

Witnesses said Diehm, Garrison and Whitfield were in Whitfield's café together the night of the fire and left about 11 p.m. Then Diehm returned at 12:30, and Whitfield at 2:30. The Beverly Hills Country Club was torched at midnight. An empty gas can was found later behind Whitfield's café.

Garrison was described as sullen and silent in court. He did not take the stand, but his lawyer argued that the little girl may have been killed by a skull fracture from the fall, not her burns.

The jury didn't buy it. They took less than an hour to come back with a guilty verdict and sentenced Garrison to life in prison. One juror insisted on death, but the judge explained that the prosecutor had changed his mind, and a life sentence was the maximum allowed.

Diehm was next in court just two weeks later. After entering a guilty plea, he was sentenced to life in prison. His verdict might have been even quicker, but he refused to take the advice of two attorneys and both had to withdraw so he could get court-appointed lawyers. One of those who quit the case was the same lawyer who represented Garrison and Whitfield, Daniel Davies.

"Mrs. Mae Keller, Indianapolis, mother of Diehm, became hysterical during the jury's deliberation and had to be led from the courtroom," a news story said. There was no indication that Diehm showed any reaction—which was typical of the gangster code.

Garrison and Diehm were shipped off to the Kentucky State Reformatory, an intimidating turreted stone castle of punishment built in 1798, long since replaced by more modern repositories of reform and correction. The ancient penitentiary was medieval enough on the outside to suggest a Dark Ages dungeon within, but even that may have been too generous.

Whitfield was scheduled for trial a few weeks later, but in his case the speedy-trial train was derailed.

'Underworld figures depart'

Whitfield refused to confess and insisted he was innocent, that he had nothing to do with the fire. He was tried three times and spent three years in the Campbell County Jail while awaiting his appeals and life sentence.

His first trial started in mid-June. His old bootlegging friend Pete Schmidt took the stand and testified that Whitfield had threatened him in the cocktail lounge at Schmidt's Newport casino, the Glenn Hotel, and intended to do him "bodily harm" over an argument. But when the defense asked Schmidt about liquor deals, he took the Fifth and refused to answer "on the grounds it may incriminate me."

A waitress at Whitfield's café was caught changing her testimony and had to correct the record under threat of prosecution.

Then Whitfield took the stand. He claimed he was nowhere near the Beverly Hills Country Club that night, but was drinking with friends at the Blue Grass Inn in Southgate, a few miles down Alexandria Pike from Newport. He admitted buying three gas cans, but said they were for transporting liquor.

He claimed that when he heard about the fire from a waiter, "Red Masterson and I drove out ... near the spot where the resort was still burning."

When he got home around 2 a.m., Whitfield testified, Garrison was there waiting, badly burned from a "still explosion."

Garrison and Diehm were regulars in Whitfield's café and had known him for years, he said. As he mumbled and almost whispered his answers, the judge told him to speak up.

Another defense witness changed his testimony. Then the waiter who supposedly told Whitfield about the fire while he was drinking at the Blue Grass Inn was conveniently missing.

The jury took less than an hour to find Whitfield guilty and sentence him to life. But that verdict was overturned on appeal and he got another trial that began on November 20, 1937.

The first witness in the next trial was Earl Fillhart. He described visiting his wife's parents in Persimmon Grove, Kentucky, and bringing Viola's little sister home to spend the night. This time, Fillhart testified that he had seen Diehm and Garrison running away as he was lying on the ground with a sprained ankle, after leaping from the second-story window. He said another man was with them, but he was unable to identify him. He also said the automobile was there when they returned home from Persimmon Grove about 11 p.m., and he could tell that the men in the car were watching them.

Whitfield again testified and swore he was at the Blue Grass Inn with Red Masterson.

But the witnesses who drew a crowd were Diehm and Garrison, brought up from the penitentiary to vouch for Whitfield's innocence.

Garrison testified that he alone was responsible for the whole scheme. During a long day on the stand, he took credit for the plan to punish Schmidt, who had refused to pay "tribute for protection." Garrison said his only accomplice was Diehm.

He described using a one-gallon glass jug, which he filled from their car's gas tank with a rubber-tube siphon. "I carried the jug to the entrance of the clubhouse," Garrison testified. "There was heavy glass in the door, which I broke with the butt of my revolver, then I kicked in the door. I carried the jug into the basement and dropped it in the dark. Gasoline fell on my clothes. Before I could set it afire, there was an explosion.

"I ran out the door and behind our automobile where I smothered the flames with my gloved hands, which were burned, and climbed into the car."

Garrison said he knew the roadhouse was closed "because the grand jury was in session in February, which is a custom among the gambling proprietors (to shut down and leave town), not exactly out of respect but out of fear."

News reports on February 15, just 12 days after the fire, confirmed that much: "Numerous figures of Newport's underworld have departed for parts unknown. Authorities seeking to question some of them yesterday were told that the persons sought were in Florida."

Garrison claimed he never would have gone near the place if he knew there were people inside, because he loved children. But if Earl Fillhart's testimony was true, Garrison had watched the Fillharts and Mary Lou Rardin enter the farmhouse before setting it on fire.

As darkness fell outside the courtroom, the trial continued into an unusual night session while Diehm took the stand. He told the jury that he went to Garrison's apartment that night and woke him up by firing his revolver. Garrison took the gun away because "I was very drunk," Diehm said. He said Garrison invited him to go "burn a barn" that belonged to Schmidt and they left together.

Again, the jury wasted no time finding Whitfield guilty. His second life sentence was finally upheld by the state court of appeals and he was sent to prison on March 17, 1939.

Diehm and Garrison served just eight years. Both were paroled in mid-July 1944. "Diehm was paroled upon recommendation of a prison physician who stated that he had less than six months to live," the *Enquirer* reported. If the prison doctor's diagnosis was right, Diehm was dead by early January, 1945.

Garrison walked out of prison right into the waiting handcuffs and shackles of the state of Alabama. Detectives took him into custody and sent him back to state prison there for violating parole from a 15-year robbery sentence.

He escaped from prison several times. In 1952 he led an elaborate plan to break out of an Alabama prison farm by using a hydraulic jack to pry open a heavy iron door. In 1958 he escaped again, making him one of the few criminals who made it on the FBI's 10 Most Wanted List twice.

When the FBI caught up with him again in 1960, he was working in

St. Louis as a bookkeeper named "Mr. Crowe." The news stories said he was "as dangerous as a rattlesnake," but also such a math genius he could "instantaneously add up the lengthy serial numbers of 40 boxcars flipping by at a fast clip."

He was "mild mannered and talkative," when he was arrested and said, "I'm glad it's over with." He was sent back to prison at age 60 with a life sentence, so he may have died there—perhaps still having nightmares about a burning child.

Whitfield was paroled in mid-July 1947, after serving eight years. When he got out of prison, he found a job almost immediately—as manager of the Latin Quarter, a Newport casino owned by the Cleveland Four mob led by Moe Dalitz. Giving him a job at the Beverly Hills might have been too obvious.

'Seeking persons unknown'

The most feared and violent "police character" involved in the 1936 Beverly Hills Country Club "incendiary," Red Masterson, was not tried, convicted, named as a suspect or even questioned. He later went to prison on narcotics charges, returned to Newport to run the Merchants Club casino with mob backing for 20 years, and survived a shotgun blast in the face from notorious gangster and casino operator Buck Brady. The Enforcer died in 1972 at age 66 in a Cincinnati nursing home after a stroke.

In late 1937, separate lawsuits were filed: One by Earl and Viola Fillhart, and another by Ira Rardin, the father of the murder victim, Mary Lou Rardin. They targeted Pete Schmidt and "others," claiming Schmidt had received threats that something was going to happen to his roadhouse, and should have warned his caretaker. The suits alleged that the fire was "caused by person or persons unknown," implying that the three men in prison were not the only ones involved, and took orders from someone who remained in the shadows.

The $50,000 lawsuits by the Fillharts went nowhere, but Ira Rardin wouldn't quit. He was still fighting in court in 1941, when he was offered a judgment of $2,500 for the death of his 5-year-old girl. He refused and said he had never consented to the deal. His attorney, the only one he could find at the courthouse before the statute of limitations expired, turned out to be mob lawyer Charles Lester, a partner of Schmidt's, who cut the deal without Rardin's consent and pocketed the settlement.

If Ira Rardin was right, the Cleveland mob gave orders to start the fire that killed his daughter, then "settled" his lawsuit without consent and robbed him of even that small token of restitution.

Even after all the hundreds of news stories, court hearings, trials, investigations, police reports and guilty verdicts, the Beverly Hills Country Club fire of 1936 remains in some ways an unsolved mystery.

The testimony of Viola and Earl Fillhart doesn't make sense. They said they first saw a car and men approaching the roadhouse *after* an explosion. Then they changed that story and testified that they had seen men in a black car watching them when they got home.

Earl Fillhart said he saw the men in the house and confronted them, even kicking at one before they ran. But he also testified that he only saw them from the upstairs window. And then he said the first time he saw them was after he jumped from the window.

Viola's version also changed from trial to trial. They both told several different stories of the same events that should have been seared into their memories. But the prospect of naming names like "Red Masterson" was known to cause amnesia in many witnesses.

Who paid for the lawyer, Daniel Davies, who represented all three "police characters"? Davies was known around the courthouse to handle liquor cases for gangsters. After Davies withdrew from his case, Diehm could not afford a lawyer and needed court appointed lawyers. Who covered the bills before that? Who paid Davies to defend Garrison, then Whitfield through three trials and multiple appeals?

Davies was also connected to underworld attorney Charles Lester, who sat like a spider in the middle of a web of Newport graft, gambling, prostitution, murder, arson and police corruption.

Why did the prosecutor start out seeking death penalties, then drop the sentencing requests to life, requiring only eight years in prison? Gas chambers and electric chairs were in frequent use in those days. It's hard to imagine a case that deserved the death penalty more than burning a little girl to death over a gambling war.

Was Red Masterson involved? Newport legends say he was the one who bought the gas, but he was protected—or feared—enough to stay behind the scenes. He carried snub-nosed .38s—the same gun Garrison said was used to break the window.

The jury never believed Whitfield's alibi. So if he truly was with Masterson that night, as he claimed, they were together at the fire, not at the Blue Grass Inn. Nobody but Whitfield mentioned Masterson's name in court. Was Whitfield sending a message to others that he could drag the mob's Enforcer into the crime if the Cleveland gang did not do everything it could to keep him out of prison? Or was he signaling that the hitman was watching witnesses to make sure they stayed in line?

Whatever he was saying, it appears that Garrison and Diehm heard it clearly enough to volunteer testimony that might keep him out of prison. They had nothing to lose. They were already sentenced.

Most likely, Masterson was the boss and Whitfield was the leader of the arson crew that night. Whitfield kept Masterson out of it and was rewarded by the Cleveland mob with a nightclub job as soon as he got out of prison.

During Whitfield's final trial in November 1937, at the same time Ira Rardin filed a lawsuit naming "person or persons unknown," the trial coverage included this bold-faced news bulletin:

"Ira Rardin, father of Mary Lou Rardin, reported to Newport Police last night that he was followed by two automobiles containing several men after he and his wife left the Courthouse in their automobile for their home in Persimmon Grove, Kentucky. Police escorted them home, then began a search for the machines."

Someone wanted the Rardins to back off.

4.
The Morning After

Smoke-stained, weak winter sunlight struggled to enter the shadowy barroom through dirty windows. Neon lights that dazzled the eyes at midnight were turned off, their hot garish pinks, jungle greens and lurid purples replaced with a cold gray light that revealed crushed butts, scarred tables and ancient stains shaped like lost continents. The sawdust floor reeked of spilled booze, stale beer, tobacco-brown spit and urine. The jukebox slept off its nickel binge from the night before, and even the huddle of early—or very late—customers who were hunched at the rail looked colorless, nursing hair-of-the-dog shots and beers.

"... he comes into the Stork Club looking like Fred Astaire, says he's in town for the fellationalist society..."

"Philatelist. Stamp collectors," a phlegm-clogged voice corrected.

"Yeah, whatever you say," the first guy, Myron the Cabbie, continued. "Sounds more fun my way. So this guy asks, 'Sir, may I ask, why do they call this a bust-out joint?' And Jerry the bartender says, 'Because if you make any trouble you will go bustin' outta here without the aid of your feets.' He didn't get thrown out, but someone slipped him a lullaby highball and he sure did go out busted."

The laughs were half-hearted. Table-thumping "HAW-HAWs" from last night were stifled by headaches and bloodshot eyes. Phlegm-voice started a strangled chuckle then traded it for a wet, hacking cough like ripped canvas.

If a hangover had a color, it would be the cruel, mocking morning light that says whatever you intended to do on this day that the Lord has made is wasted, gone, burned away by liquor and lost words like the mangled butts in an overflowing ashtray.

If it had a smell, it would be the faint whiff of vomit tracked in from the sidewalk outside, where a sucker from Lansing, Michigan coughed up all the thrills of a night on the town in Newport, right after gagging up the last dollar he had brought along for a week of meetings and excitement in Cincinnati.

If it had a face, it would look like the reddened eyes and greenish pallor of Mr. Lansing as he woke up on dirty sheets in a room he struggled to recognize, his stomach lurching and his head splitting from the relentless hammers of shame, guilt, remorse and panic: Where's my wallet? How will I explain the meetings I missed today? What about my boss? What about my wife? What if someone finds out? Where am I? Please, God, get me out of this and I swear, never again…

That Monday morning at the Alibi Club, heads turned as one to greet an Alibi Club regular, a racetrack hand-book man, as he came through the battered door waving a newspaper, bringing along a tailwind of fresh, cold air like a strong cup of coffee. "You guys hear what they're saying about Red?" Gus the Bookie asked, approaching the bar.

He had too much energy, as jarring as laughter at a funeral, and it felt like a scolding finger-wag of rebuke to their fogged, stumbling brains. Nobody asked, so Gus continued.

"Sunday night he was filling up five-gallon cans of gas and this pump-jockey at the Texaco asks, 'Hey, Mr. Masterson, what's all the gas for?' So Red answers, 'You can read about it in tomorrow's paper.' So here it is, read all about it."

He whapped the paper on the bar-top with a pop that made a few of the men jump. It fell open to reveal a banner headline in bold letters as black as the cigarette burns in the bar, as tall as a shot glass:

TWO HURT, GIRL BURNED, IN RESORT BLAST

"Aw, not the Beverly Hills Country Club," one of the men said, wincing and shaking his head as the story sank in. "That place was beautiful. Best thing we had around here."

"Yeah, that's what Moe Dalitz thought when he come to visit," said another. "I guess if he can't have it, Schmidt can't neither."

"Don't anyone know the grand jury is in session? This could be bad for everyone," said a third. They all thought about that.

"They got some good tracks in Miami," said Gus almost to himself, as if it had just occurred to him. "And the money's even greener down there this time of year."

The cougher cleared his throat, spat into a wet bar napkin and wadded it with big hands that had rope-knotted knuckles, while the others looked at him and waited for him to speak. "Mr. Volstead's Prohibition has been very good to us. Hell, half the joints and all the business in Newport were bankrolled by bootleggers, and nearly all of them from the Remus outfit."

He paused to cough into his fist. "But now that hooch is legal, gambling is the game and gambling needs glamor to draw the swells. And that's what drew the big boys. We could all see it coming. New York. Detroit. Now Cleveland moving in. They already killed Dutch to take his racetracks at Coney and Latonia. This ain't our pond anymore, boys. Those guys are barracudas, and they will eat us minnows alive. Schmidt's just the first bite."

As they let that sink in, Myron the Cabbie muttered, "I ain't seen Knuckles string that many words together since never."

Brothers at the bar

The next day, a few blocks away in his quiet, dark-paneled law office, Charles Lester, Esquire, attorney at law, came to something like the same verdict in a hasty meeting with his corpulent "brother" at the Kentucky Bar, Daniel Davies.

"I'd like you to handle these guys," Lester said. He was a handsome man with a square jaw, regular features and combed-back, Brylcreemed hair over a high forehead. He could have been a smooth-tongued state senator or an up-and-coming executive at Procter & Gamble across the river. A dozen years younger and he could have been class president at Princeton.

Instead, he was one of the most powerful men in Kentucky and the Midwest. He was not one of the big mob bosses, but in Cincinnati, Newport, Covington and as far south as the Commonwealth capitol in Frankfort, he was known as the voice—some said "mouthpiece"—of the big bosses.

His office was decorated in what would now be recognized as Early Kentucky Colonel: portraits of hunting spaniels and thoroughbreds, handshake "grip and grin" snapshots with governors, congressmen and mayors, and various "Blue Grass State Chapter" awards hanging against hunter-green wallpaper above dark walnut wainscoting. All that was lacking was a framed certificate announcing that he was indeed an official Kentucky Colonel—an elite new club that already included W.C. Fields, Shirley Temple and J. Edgar Hoover.

Only the bags under his eyes hinted at the worry his voice would not betray. "We need to put a lid on this. Even Red had to admit that with the girl getting burned, it got out of hand."

"How many are we talking about and who are they?" Davies asked, frowning as if he smelled the foul odor of trouble.

"Dave Whitfield and two others, Ed Garrison and Chick Diehm. Diehm is a nobody. He will do whatever he's told. Garrison was working for Dutch Shultz before Schultz got killed. He probably would've been gunned down with the rest of Shultz's crew but he missed a train or a bus or something and showed up late for their dinner in New York. He was supposed to be making himself scarce here in Newport, but then he gets recruited and throws his hat in for this. Stupid. He will have to go down the same road as Diehm. But that road leads to prison, not the rope or the chair for any of them."

"That shouldn't be a problem," Davies nodded. "Kentucky put nine in the chair two years ago, but Campbell County hasn't had an execution this century, except that negro who was electrocuted for rape in 1916, if that counts. Maybe someday they will catch on that the crime capital of Kentucky has the least executions because it's *organized* crime. Anyway, the prosecutor can make all the noise he wants about sending them to the chair, but he knows it won't happen if we say it won't. What about Whitfield?"

"Somebody up there in Cleveland likes him. Moe Dalitz, Sam Tucker, I don't know who's on his side, but he and Red set it up. Red is off limits, of course, so Whitfield knows he will take the rap and probably do some time. But they want us to do everything we can for him."

"I don't like the looks of this. Representing all three in a spotlight case like this might raise uncomfortable questions. I've done a lot of this kind of syndicate work, as you know—hell, you sent me the cases. But it's always been quiet, like part of the background scenery. As long as I keep it that way, nobody cares if I own part of the Green Lantern with Buck Brady."

Lester's smile showed straight teeth but no spark of humor in his eyes. "Don't worry. I'll talk to anyone who makes trouble for you. They know where their sugar comes from. We're good as far up as the governor and maybe a lot farther than that. Everyone local wants it to fade away fast, just as much as Cleveland does. And you should too. I hear you're making good money from that bust-out joint. We all want to get back to normal."

"Amen to that. Buck says he wants to expand, maybe open up a new club like that Beverly Hills place, but not while the grand jury is extended over this fire." Davies paused to light a cigarette. "So where are these tough guys who play with matches?"

"I hear Diehm left town," Lester said. "Garrison was burned pretty badly and is holed up somewhere, too crippled to move. Whitfield is staying put, running his café on York Street like John Doe the unconcerned citizen. When things cool down a bit, so the cops don't shoot them on sight, we'll tell the chief where to find Garrison and he can pick up Whitfield. Finding Chick Diehm is their problem, but Lansky can probably help with that if Chick's in New York. Nobody wants this to get out of control."

"You mean like the fire?" Davies asked, leaning forward to tip his cigarette ash over a crystal ashtray on Lester's desk.

"I guess. Maybe Cleveland didn't want it to burn to the ground. I'm sure going to miss it. I took my wife to meet the governor there." Lester put his hands behind his head and leaned back in his padded desk chair, making it groan. "But then I wonder. Maybe they did want it this way. Maybe it's a message to all the other local casinos, to let them know that Cleveland is here to stay and takes no prisoners. I don't know. But Red said even he got a little sick when he stood there and watched the woman and kid falling out of that window."

"But not sick enough to do anything, right? That man's heart is as cold as a headstone in January. He gives me chills."

"Maybe you should tell him that next time you see him," Lester laughed, rocking forward to lean across the desk and signal the meeting was coming to an end. "That reminds me, you need to know. Red says Cleveland is also making a move to inherit Coney Island racetrack across the river, now that Dutch is out of the way. And I heard their fix went bad when the bagman died at the Arrowhead in Branch Hill, near Loveland. They're moving south, and that means Newport. We might be looking at more trouble than we've seen since the Atlantic City syndicate summit sliced up territory and put an end to the gang wars in 1929. The way I heard it, the Cleveland Four got Ohio and Northern Kentucky. Capone bragged that they even signed a contract. So it's surprising they haven't moved in on us before this. The only thing in their way was Dutch and the New York gang. And now... things could get hot."

"Pete Schmidt would say they already have," said Davies as he crushed out his cigarette and stood to leave.

As the door closed behind Davies, Lester went back to shuffling papers on his desk, but his mind was somewhere else. He was worried. Not about the fire and the burned kid. Red Masterson and Dan Davies could handle that. But what came after? What would happen to Charles Lester when the Cleveland Syndicate officially took over? Would he be only their errand boy? Another little bluegill in the Ohio River with the big catfish lurking below?

Trouble in Little Mexico

So far, Newport had been a strictly local business, Lester thought. Even going back to the Civil War, when soldiers crossed the Licking River and the Ohio to visit Newport brothels, it was a geographically isolated, conveniently close, three-ring sin circus for Cincinnati. Union General Joseph Hooker had two armies headquartered in Cincinnati— his Billy Yank soldiers and the platoons of prostitutes who swarmed around them, especially in Newport. No wonder they were still known as "Hookers," Lester smiled. Fate can be cruel to generals.

I suppose this land was always this way, he thought. Even before the white man came, the Shawnee called their sacred hunting grounds something like "Kentucky." And even then it was wild and untamed, shared by all the tribes the way gambling was now shared by all the big syndicates. Then along came Daniel Boone, followed by flatboats full of Philadelphia lawyers who filed claim after claim until Boone the bear-fighter was tied in knots by litigation, left with nothing but a quilt of overlapping lawsuits and jigsaw borders.

George Remus had spotted the advantages of geography in Northern Kentucky when he set up his empire in Newport. As soon as the Prohibition curtain fell in 1920, he used his pharmacy license to get permits to buy outlawed, quarantined, bonded whiskey for "medicinal purposes." Then he bought the Fleischmann's Distillery across the river in Cincinnati for less than $200,000, the story went, taking possession of warehouses that contained more than 3,000 gallons of whiskey.

Lester did the math in his head... five fifths in a gallon, 25 shots in a fifth... even at just $2 a shot in some Cincinnati speakeasy or Newport tiger blind, that's more than $750,000—a half-million-dollar profit. No wonder Remus claimed he could afford to spend a million a year just on bribes.

Remus could see that Newport was made for bootlegging. Only a handful of judges and cops had to be paid off. It was close to good roads, within easy reach for about 60 percent of the country. The same map-friendly convenience that brought corporate headquarters to Southwest Ohio made Newport a natural choice.

So when Remus ran out of bonded, bottled whiskey to buy and sell, he decided to make his own. Cleveland had cornered the market on smuggling from Canada; the East Coast mobs had the transatlantic imports; the West Coast had Mexico and Canada; and Miami had rum from Cuba. So Remus set up his own stills, put his pharmacy education to work and started making the best illegal "red" liquor a speakeasy could buy in the Midwest.

Soon he was known as "The King of the Bootleggers," and Newport was "Little Mexico," with more crooked cops than Tijuana and wilder than the dark side of a Mexican moon. Newport was on the national map as an "open-city," like Hot Springs, Arkansas, Biloxi, Mississippi and Saratoga Springs, New York.

Vice is like mice in a barn, Lester thought. If you see one, there are certain to be hundreds more behind the walls and in the haystacks. And outlawing alcohol made the whole nation into outlaw mice, scurrying to speakeasies, tiger blinds, cafes and nightclubs to buy a few bottles of bootleg liquor for a party, maybe pausing to play the slots or blackjack tables, noticing those pretty bargirls who seemed so friendly...

Once that door opened, all the rest of the mice came out of hiding, along with the big barn rats: gambling, prostitution, numbers, drugs, beatings, cops on the take and a highly refined network of graft that went all the way to the back doors of the White House.

Remus had conducted that sin symphony like a maestro. He became Robber-Baron wealthy like the Astors, Carnegies, Vanderbilts and Rockefellers. He liked to say, "I tried to corner the graft market, but there's not enough money in the world to buy up all the public officials who demand their share."

But he sure gave it a helluva try.

Unfortunately for Remus, the Newport-Cincinnati fix had limited range like a radio signal. It never reached the U.S. Treasury agents. If they couldn't get their tax revenues from legal booze, they would make sure nobody else got rich on it. So Remus was convicted and sent away in 1922. He lost everything, including the spectacular Cincinnati mansion with the indoor swimming pool and the lavish parties where he gave away new Fords and handed out diamonds like handfuls of peanuts.

He even lost his wife to one of the Treasury agents who helped send him to prison. While Remus did time, they spent his money and Imogene filed for divorce. But George Remus outsmarted everyone again.

Lester smiled, appreciating Remus's ingenious strategy with a professional, lawyerly eye. After he got out of prison in 1927, Remus tailed his wife's taxi to Eden Park in Cincinnati, then stepped out and shot her to death in the middle of the day, right in front of a whole jury pool of shocked witnesses.

Then he represented himself in court with a novel defense: He pleaded insanity. Whether because of well targeted bribes, his local popularity and generosity or his sheer legal creativity, he was acquitted of murder and sent to a state hospital for the criminally insane. Six months later he was released on a four-to-three vote of the Ohio Supreme Court.

But his law degree on top of the pharmacy education had not helped Remus when the Treasury agents first came knocking in 1922, Lester reminded himself. And Remus was much smarter than most. So smart he graduated from law school in 18 months. Even the smartest lawyers can go to prison. And most of the Remus bootlegging gang went with him, including Schmidt, Red, Whitfield and Buck Brady.

Buck and Schmidt had been pretty smart too. They stashed their profits from bootlegging, did their time, then came out and bought clubs in Newport as soon as they got paroled. Red continued to provide muscle for hire. Whitfield had his café and did odd jobs whenever Red needed help.

Lester thought about what Schmidt said when he was told Moe Dalitz liked the Beverly Hills Country Club. Schmidt said his swank club was worth $1 million. Dalitz offered him $30,000 in cash.

"Not for sale," said the tough ex-con and bootleg trucker who had hauled enough Remus liquor to fill the indoor pool at the Remus mansion.

"It could get rough. We'd hate to see you have a fire at that beautiful new club," he was warned.

"I can take care of myself," said Schmidt, who had already proved it by shooting a federal Treasury agent during a raid on his still that was making 1,000 gallons of shine a day. He did five years for that. Then he came out, went right back to work at his Glenn Hotel and soon bought the Old Kaintuck Inn in Southgate. He remodeled and upgraded the old roadhouse into the Beverly Hills Country Club, the premier casino this side of New York or Havana.

Pete's a hard-boiled egg, Lester thought. But if the tough ones don't bend, they get broken. And that could get messy. Why can't he just take the offer to sell out, stay on as the front man and take a generous share of the house?

Lester shook his head. It was going to get messy.

Rising from the ashes

A postcard of Pete Schmidt's rebuilt Beverly Hills Country Club.
Northern Kentucky Views

As Pete Schmidt began to rebuild his Beverly Hills Country Club on the blackened bricks and melted poker chips of the incinerated roadhouse, workers found a bomb on the construction site. They threw it into a nearby field on the 20-acre hilltop property, where it exploded. The gamblers' war was just getting started.

True to his word, Schmidt re-opened for business—bigger, better and brighter, although he still insisted that gambling was not allowed at his casino. At the grand opening, Kentucky Governor A.B. "Happy" Chandler and three other governors from nearby states joined the crowd to admire crystal chandeliers, deep carpets, gold-flocked wallpaper and polished oak paneling. Chandler's candid defense of gambling was, "If the people want it dirty, let them have dirty." Apparently, he liked dirty too. He was accused of investing state money with mob interests in Cuba. It was never proved, but he was just the first among many Kentucky governors who traded handshakes, back-slapping and dirty deals with mobsters at Newport-area casinos. He retired a very wealthy man.

The new Beverly Hills club rose from the ashes more swank and spectacular than anything seen before. But the sparks of public outrage had not cooled yet. While the Campbell County courthouse was busy sending the arsonists to jail in the spring of 1936, another courthouse across the Licking River in Covington was drawing public attention to a Kenton County judge who made headlines by making noise about reform.

5.
One Judge Takes a Stand

Gambling Is Assailed In Instructions To Jury By Kenton County Judge

BACKBONE

Called Vital Need

To Stiffen Enforcement Of Gaming Laws.

Constables Praised For Efforts Under Truck Statute —Fee System Approved.

More backbone is needed in the enforcement of law in Kenton County, Judge Johnst Northcutt told members of a grand jury when he impaneled that body in Kenton Circuit Court yesterday.

"Because of political ambition, or to be a good fellow, or for some other reason, the laws are not enforced," Judge Northcutt said.

Particular attention was given to the gambling situation by Judge Northcutt, who directed the jury to make a rigid investigation and to return indictments. In addressing the jury, Judge Northcutt said there

Lays Down The Law!

JUDGE JOHNST NORTHCUTT.
More backbone in law enforcement in Kenton County was demanded by Judge Northcutt yesterday in instructions to the grand jury. He referred specifically to gambling and whisky sales at unlawful hours.

THREE WOMEN

Of Covington Sue

For Return Of Pogue Distillery, Maysville.

Alice Delehanty And Two Others Demand Receiver Take Over Property.

SPECIAL DISPATCH TO THE ENQUIRER

Maysville, Ky., January 27.—A suit to obtain possession of the H. E. Pogue Distillery was filed late Monday afternoon in Mason Circuit Court by Alice Delehanty, Blanche Watson, and Cecil Lee Riggle, all of Covington.

The three women charge, through their attorneys, M. J. Hennessey and John A Shepard, of Covington, that they are the rightful owners of the distillery and its property.

The plaintiffs declare that on September 22, 1933, they, the owners of the entire capital stock of

Judge Johnst Northcutt made headlines by standing up against the mob.

"May it please the court, we'd like to request that Circuit Judge Johnst Northcutt vacate the bench for the remainder of this case because of his demonstrated public bias and prejudice against the defendants, including but not limited to participating in a raid on one of the defendant's place of business—"

"Motion overruled," the judge interrupted, rapping his gavel. "You may take your seat, Mr. King."

Covington attorney Bert King stacked his papers, aligned the edges carefully and took his time returning to his seat in the Kenton County courtroom, where he joined a flock of local lawyers lined up like birds on a telephone wire, representing Lookout House casino owner James Brink, former Chicago and Detroit mobster "Sleepout Louis" Levinson and a half-dozen others who operated, owned and managed gambling clubs in and around Covington.

It was May 1936, just a few months after the Beverly Hills fire that killed a 5-year-old girl. But the gangsters at the defendants' table did not look troubled at all. They made a show of looking bored and unconcerned, leaning back in heavy oak chairs that could have all been carved from the same "hanging tree" at about the same time the courthouse was built.

Their underworld friends lined the front rows of the gallery behind the railing, hats and a few overcoats on their laps. They wore dark suits in charcoal and navy blue, just like any gathering of businessmen at the exclusive Queen City Club in downtown Cincinnati. But there was something hard to define, just a little bit out of place for a boardroom. The suits were too stylish, too sharp, too tailored. The chalk-stripes were too bold. Some didn't even have the decency to take off their hats. And their faces had the unhealthy pallor of night people who don't see enough daylight. It reminded Judge Northcutt of the coloring he saw regularly on the faces of prisoners who were hauled into court after a few weeks in the county jail. The bailiffs called it "jailface."

There were also a few hard-eyed women in the crowd. They were pretty and fashionable, but again, something was just a little bit wrong. They were overdressed, with too much makeup, skirts too short, eyes red as if they had come directly from the smoke-fogged nightclubs. It was late spring, and the courtroom's tall narrow windows poured in bright sunshine that warmed the courtroom and made the gangsters tug at their tight collars and shift uneasily as sweat trickled down their backs under silk shirts and wool suits.

"That's rather an impertinence," the judge added, lifting his chin to glare coolly at the gangland defendants and their lawyers. He recognized a few local celebrities in the crowd. Red Masterson. Screw Andrews. Pete Schmidt. Just like roaches when you turn on the lights, he thought.

Judge Northcutt wore a high-collared white shirt and black bowtie under his robe, making him look almost priestlike. He was 43, but looked uncommonly youthful for a judge, as clean-cut as his University of Kentucky yearbook picture. His short dark hair could have been parted with a ruler and was combed close to the scalp. He had worked for and supported Governor Happy Chandler, so the underworld gangs figured the new judge's promises of reform were just the usual campaign mouthwash. But now the word on the street was that Chandler had given up trying to talk sense into Judge Northcutt, and Northcutt would not return the governor's calls. Apparently, the man was actually serious.

"The state can call its first witness," the judge said, turning to the smaller line of lawyers representing the Commonwealth of Kentucky.

"Elmer Ware," the bailiff called. The master commissioner of the Kenton Circuit Court came forward and raised a trembling right hand as he swore to tell the truth, the whole truth and nothing but the truth. As he took a seat in the witness box, he somehow managed to look officious and nervous all at once.

Commonwealth Attorney Ulie J. Howard stood, buttoned his jacket over his vest, and wasted no time. "Did anyone from the Lookout House ever approach you about gambling?" he asked. The spectators leaned forward and the courtroom fell so silent that passing traffic could be heard through the foot-thick walls.

"Yes, sir," Ware replied, straightening, looking more confident. "Ed Curd visited me three times." He nodded toward one of the men at the defendants' table. "He talked about the Lookout House and Judge Northcutt's attitude. He said he had been told that everything was all right in Kenton County, so he invested $15,000 to develop the Lookout House into one of the most elaborate and finest night clubs in the United States, outside of New York and Chicago."

"What else did he tell you?" Howard prompted, approaching the witness stand.

"He said that if Judge Northcutt would be reasonable in his conduct, we could all get along. He said he would go along with Judge

Northcutt politically, and the club would be run quietly and without embarrassment to the judge."

"Did he mention anyone else who is in the courtroom today?"

"Yes, he mentioned Jimmy Brink and said that if Judge Northcutt insisted on driving them out, he would be the heavy loser. He asked me to introduce him to Judge Northcutt, but I refused."

After a few more questions, the defense declined to cross examine and Ware was dismissed. The prosecutor next called Justice of the Peace John L. Cushing, who backpedaled and stalled until he was finally cornered and forced to admit that he had approached Judge Northcutt on behalf of the gambling syndicate. He shot a look to Brink and shrugged as if to say, "I did my best."

The judge leaned over toward the witness and interrupted: "Didn't you say to me, 'They want to know what you want. Political control or what?'"

Cushing was caught like a rabbit in a snare. "Yes, your honor," he mumbled.

'Machine guns were discussed'

B.H. Elierman of Covington testified next, and told the court that he had been asked to "persuade" Judge Northcutt "to let the Lookout House alone." The mob's messenger who asked him to help the judge "see the light" was a Kentucky State Trooper, he admitted.

Then Kentucky Constable J. C. Spicer testified about raids on the Lookout House: "The judge talked to us and told us he knew we weren't afraid to arrest the people at the Lookout House. The judge offered to help us with warrants and get us anything we needed, including a machine gun."

Again, Northcutt interrupted to clarify, acting as witness and judge. "Yes, let the record show that machine guns were discussed," he said, "but I dismissed the idea as unnecessary."

The case dragged on for weeks. Defense attorneys accused Northcutt of leading raids while carrying a gun. The judge insisted he had never left the car during a raid on the Lookout House, but did not deny being armed.

Finally, a permanent injunction against gambling at the Lookout House and other casinos in Kenton County was granted—and enthusiastically ignored. In June, Judge Northcutt had the Covington city manager, the police chief and the county sheriff in court. Each of them swore under oath, with his hand on a Bible, that they knew nothing about illegal gambling in the county.

During that court proceeding, a new attorney joined the defense table and objected strenuously to questions by the prosecutors. But when prosecutors and the judge challenged him and threatened to put him under oath, he refused to identify his client, then said he was only a spectator.

There was speculation that he came from Cleveland, or maybe Chicago or Detroit as a favor to Sleepout Louie, to keep an eye on the bosses' interests, or maybe send a message to the judge. But cars with out-of-state license plates were not unusual in downtown Covington near the courthouse—not with so many nearby brothels and tiger blinds to entertain visitors.

Frustrated by see-nothing politicians and do-nothing police, Judge Northcutt impaneled a "Blue Ribbon Grand Jury" of handpicked citizens whom he hoped were untouchable by the mob.

"Every man, woman and child of sufficient intelligence to keep out of the fire knows that gambling is rife in the county and city," the judge instructed them. "You will do nothing to minimize, whitewash, or evade the fixing of the direct and proper responsibility, if it is within your power, for conditions that have not merely become obnoxious, but putrid.

"If you fail, I shall not hesitate to say to you that you have done so, and other grand juries will be called who have the courage and will to drive these gamblers and their allies from the county."

It was the first serious talk of reform in 30 years, since The Rev. Robert Nelson at St. Paul's Episcopal Church had preached to Newport about driving out "the gambling element, whose profession is robbery," and warned that "public morals are, to say the least, threatened with falling into destruction and disgrace," earning "the contempt of every honest citizen."

Eureka Lodge No. 7 of the Knights of Pythias supported Rev. Nelson with a resolution demanding "strict enforcement of the laws prohibiting lawlessness in our city."

City leaders yawned.

But finally it looked like one judge might sober-up Newport's wild sister, Covington. The long mornings and hot afternoons of witnesses and testimony were over. Now the day had come for the grand jury to report its findings.

The deadline came... and passed. Minutes stretched into hours. There was no word from the jury room, no signal except that the grand jury was still in session, deliberating behind closed doors.

Northcutt feared the worst: after all the empty raids that netted bushels of poker chips and no arrests; after hearing public officials and police swear under oath that they had never heard the blaring speakers in cafes broadcasting race results while the handbooks took bets, and never seen dice bounce on a craps table; after all the threats and bribe offers and "friends" who brought him messages—even Kentucky state troopers—about how easy and profitable it would be to just go along and cooperate; after all that, once again, he would be blocked.

Then at last, a bailiff entered the courtroom carrying a folded note from the Grand Jury: They were ready to report. As crowds rushed in to pack the courtroom, the Blue-Ribbon Grand Jury members filed into the jury box.

"I understand that you have reached a conclusion?" the judge asked.

"That's correct," the foreman stood and reported.

"Please give the court your report," the judge said, his voice flat, hopeless.

"Your Honor, we report 196 indictments for illegal gambling..."

The courtroom erupted in shouts and a waterfall of babel as hundreds of voices talked over each other at once in a crescendo of unintelligible shock and surprise. Northcutt hammered his gavel and shouted, "Order in court! There will be order in this courtroom or the bailiff will clear the gallery..."

It was useless. Reporters were causing a tangled commotion, elbowing their way out the swinging doors as more people outside tried to wedge their way in. He noticed the faces of Levinson and Brink. They looked a bit paler. No longer bored. Angry. Threatening, like a gathering of darkening clouds.

He hardly heard the rest. But the Blue-Ribbon Grand Jury had done its job. Most of the major casinos, carpet joints, bust-out joints, tiger blinds, brothels and racetrack betting parlors were named and indicted. It was a who's-who list of local mobsters and a visiting gambler's guide to all the hotspots of vice in Kenton County that were wide open day and night… until today.

The indictments revealed testimony that bribes of more than $1,000 a day were being paid in Covington. "Perjury alone has prevented us from obtaining enough evidence to indict a number of these (police, judges and prosecutors) for flagrant if not criminal neglect of their duty," the grand jurors reported.

One young witness who testified to the grand jury had been beaten and almost blinded when gangsters knocked on his door and threw ammonia in his eyes when he answered.

A state officer had asked to have his name deleted from the reports. "I don't want to wake up some morning with a belly full of lead because lead is so hard to digest," he had testified.

'The lid is on'

As a result, gambling was briefly "shut down" in the Covington area, which ironically gave the mob bosses a windfall of new business in their Newport clubs. As gambling was suspended at Brink's Lookout House in Kenton County, the crowds took flight like startled starlings and settled across the county line in Campbell County, at the Merchants Club, the Yorkshire Club, the Stork Club and scores of other bars, lounges, nightclubs and casinos in Newport.

Then, as soon as the public spotlight shifted away, the local lawmen gave a wink and a nod, and the Lookout House and other Covington clubs were back in business.

In November 1939, as Judge Northcutt was running for re-election, the gamblers got their revenge. Another grand jury, this time hand-picked by friends of the mob, repudiated the work by Northcutt and his Blue-Ribbon Grand Jury reformers, dismissing 192 of their 196 indictments and calling their efforts "an emotional, hysterical crusade to enforce the law." The fix was fixed again.

Judge Northcutt replied, "The report is an excellent whitewash and the only way you could have improved upon it would have been to indict the witnesses and decorate the defendants."

Judge Northcutt later revealed that he had been offered $250 a week if he would back off. He was also threatened frequently. "You may not finish your present term," one anonymous letter said. "Who knows???"

He did finish his term, but lost his bid for re-election in 1940. "I'd rather be right than be judge," he said—a statement that became his obituary.

He died in his law office in 1947, at age 54. He was still fighting the gamblers. The last case he handled was a lawsuit by Frank Hope of Chicago, who sued three men at the Kentucky Club, 637 Scott Street, Covington, in an attempt to recover $8,000 in gambling losses.

Another case on the same docket shows how typical such lawsuits and losses were. Mrs. Willie Mae Carlson of Republic Street in Cincinnati claimed that her husband, Earl, a Navy veteran of World War II, had lost their family business by gambling away $9,540 at the Yorkshire Café at 518 York Street, Newport.

Both cases and three others that targeted five gambling clubs in Newport and Covington went to the Sixth Circuit Federal Court of Appeals in Cincinnati. The Kenton County Protestant Association supported the lawsuits in hopes of pushing underworld gambling out of the region. A school principal told the newspapers that even schoolchildren were playing slots. But before the cases went to trial, all but one were dismissed. "Payoffs to Plaintiffs Suspected," the headline said. The lawyer who arranged the payoff in at least one of the cases: Charles Lester.

In response to the headlines, the Kentucky Attorney General's office decided to revisit the Northcutt injunctions and launched an investigation to determine if they had been violated. But the Kenton County Attorney at that time had to recuse himself. He had been one of the lawyers for Brink's gambling gang in 1936.

Judge Johnst Northcutt's one-man stand was not in vain. As news of the courageous Don Quixote with the sainted first name spread, the *Louisville Courier Journal* sent a team of three reporters to visit Northern Kentucky during the summer of 1939, to investigate the judge's claims that illegal gambling was out of control in Newport and Covington.

Their report was splashed in a banner headline across Page One.

The Louisville reporters found gambling everywhere: slots in restaurants, handbooks to handle betting on radio broadcasts from racetracks that blared through cafes and into the streets; dice games, blackjack tables, roulette wheels and a dice game in nearly every bust-out club and café called "razzle dazzle," that was so rigged the mob bosses banned it in their classy carpet joints. Razzle Dazzle was so crooked it gave honest illegal gambling a bad name, they said.

At the new, rebuilt Beverly Hills Country Club, the reporters had their car parked by a "colored valet" and strolled through a luxurious bar to mingle with "perspiring and well-dressed persons, seeking to curry favor with Lady Luck" at long rows of 29 slot machines.

Under a neon sign announcing the "Club Room," they entered a Midwestern Monte Carlo of four roulette wheels, four dice tables, blackjack tables and other games that were thronged with high-rollers, including prominent Louisville police, prosecutors and politicians who mingled with the local Cincinnati and Northern Kentucky VIPs.

The reporters were surprised at the steep stakes: a $5 minimum purchase of 10-cent chips—about $100 in 2020 dollars. "We noticed players frequently threw $20 and $50 bills on the tables and asked for chips," they reported.

Business was booming.

And the "Jewish mob" from Cleveland was still determined to take it over the same way bust-out joints fleeced tourists—the easy way or the hard way, your choice.

6.
Nightclubs at War

When the bomb planted at the construction site of the new Beverly Hills Country Club failed to get results, the pressure from the Cleveland mob escalated.

One morning, as an accounting clerk opened the safe in the deserted back office, three men with guns walked in and cleaned it out, taking $9,000 in profits from the night before.

Pete Schmidt decided it would be wise to hire more security and make more frequent bank deposits. A few weeks later, he sent four members of his security team to the bank with $10,000 in cash from the previous night's take.

As they drove to Newport, a dark sedan followed, then pulled out as if to pass and overtook them. As it came alongside, gun barrels were suddenly thrust out the window. The unmistakable muzzle of a Thompson submachine gun was aimed at the driver and then pointed to the shoulder. The Beverly Hills crew had no match for the devastating firepower of the "Chicago Typewriter," which could riddle their car with 50 rounds of .45 caliber Automatic Colt Pistol slugs in the time it took to light a cigarette. They pulled over and stopped, got out with their hands raised and stood in the gravel shoulder and watched as the mob's "bankers" took the entire deposit.

No police report was filed. And nobody asked how come they had a $10,000 bankroll from a place that Schmidt insisted did not allow gambling.

It was just the beginning. Over the next months, local "police characters" working for Red Masterson and the Cleveland mob conducted a campaign of vandalism and intimidation at Schmidt's Beverly Hills carpet-joint, including "ding-donging," a local custom in which two or three guys would stroll into the plush lobby, unzip their pants and empty their bladders on the expensive new carpets. With best regards, from Moe.

Then on May 17, 1938, another bomb blew up a bridge and gate at the club. It was packed with enough TNT to wake up citizens who were sleeping miles away in Newport, Fort Thomas and Southgate. The blast was so loud, rumors circulated that the federal arsenal had exploded at Fort Thomas, which was headquarters of the U.S. Army's 10th Infantry from 1922 to 1940.

The window-rattling blast was not reported to police, either. Pete Schmidt denied that any bomb had even been detonated at his business. He said it must have come from a quarry a few miles away. The quarry owner scoffed. "Impossible," he said. No blasting had been done there for years.

"NIGHT CLUBS Reported at War," the front-page headline blared.

Schmidt, a hard man who had proved many times he could take care of himself, wanted nothing to do with police. But he was worried enough to hire even more gunmen for security, and even talked to a Toledo mob about forming a partnership. The Toledo gangsters tried on the idea of leasing the club from Schmidt, and even ran it for a while. But on second thought, they decided they wanted no part of a war with the Cleveland Four.

The Cleveland Four, sometimes called The Silent Syndicate, had the franchise for Ohio and Northern Kentucky, worked out and approved at an organized crime summit in Atlantic City in 1929, attended by mob leaders from Chicago, Kansas City, New York City, Florida, New Orleans and Cleveland, among others. It was hosted by Meyer Lansky, crime boss of New York. All the big names were present: Al Capone and Frank Nitti from Chicago: Dutch Shultz, Bugsy Siegel and Charles "Lucky" Luciano from New York and New Jersey; Abe Bernstein and his brother from the Purple Gang in Detroit. Moe Dalitz and Lou Rothkopf—later founders of the Cleveland Four—represented the "Little Jewish Navy" gang of smugglers who brought booze across Lake Erie from Canada.

As bootleg liquor flowed and the gangsters were entertained by girls and nightclub acts, they divided the nation into territories to reduce gang wars, such as the recent bloodbath in Chicago: Seven gangsters were machine-gunned in the St. Valentine's Day Massacre that year by the Al Capone gang, with help from triggermen sent by Detroit's Purple Gang.

The mob bosses also discussed plans to be ready when Prohibition ended. They agreed to move into legal liquor sales and distribution, and diversify into illegal gambling and racetracks.

As the territories were sliced up like a birthday cake, Dalitz and the Cleveland Four were anointed the kingpins of crime in the Heartland: Ohio and Northern Kentucky.

Schmidt soon realized that fighting the national syndicate was like trying to stop a freight train with a Cracker Jack whistle. On November 18, 1940, Schmidt finally surrendered and signed the papers to sell the Beverly Hills Country Club to Sam Tucker, who was one of the original members of the Cleveland Four along with Dalitz, Morris Kleinman and Lou Rothkopf. The papers were drawn up by Charles Lester. Schmidt got a $125,000 "down payment" and an ongoing share of the profits. Other nightclub owners took note, and said yes the first time they were asked.

Schmidt, who was built like a beer-barrel, with a large head on a thick neck, a bulbous nose and receding hair, gave up his glitzy, king-of-the-hill "showplace of the Midwest" and retreated to his dumpier Glenn Hotel casino on Monmouth Street in Newport.

Sam Tucker moved to Northern Kentucky to keep an eye on the Cleveland Four's new properties, which soon expanded to include another classy casino, the Lookout House.

But the Cleveland mob's jewel was the Beverly Hills Country Club, the classiest casino in the Midwest, perched on a hilltop in Southgate. There was nothing else like it between New York and Los Angeles. It was Las Vegas before Vegas was cool. And they were not about to let it go.

Postcards spread the word and made the new Beverly Hills Country Club one of the most popular nightclubs in the nation in the 1930s.
Kenton County Library archives

The original oval bar in the Beverly Hills Country Club.

Part II — 1940s

1.
Under New Ownership

Jimmy Brink's New Lookout House nightclub and casino competed with Beverly Hills as one of the finest "carpet joints." Northern Kentucky Views

As soon as he saw Red Masterson walk into his office, Jimmy Brink knew his days of owning the Lookout House were numbered in single digits. Business was good in 1941. Apparently, too good.

After the Beverly Hills Country Club burned, the Lookout House had become the No. 1 carpet joint in Northern Kentucky. It was a palace perched on a hilltop in Covington, with lots windows to frame the Cincinnati skyline. At night, with the city lit up like the magical kingdom of Oz, the view was better than any postcard. Everybody wanted a window table for special occasions, and the house was making money as if it owned the patent on legal tender.

"How's business at the Merchant's Club, Red?" he asked as Masterson pulled up a chair.

He knew how Red got that club from the Cleveland Four. It was his payoff for burning out Pete Schmidt. But even if everyone knew it, it was not something you could just bring up. Red might take offense. And when that happened, Red took offense with both hands, each filled with one of his trademark .38s. Stepping lightly around Red was a dance they all learned when they were working together for Remus.

"We're holding our own, but nothing like the nice set-up you got here," Masterson replied. "What're you clearing, about $94,000 a week?"

Jimmy blinked. That number was disturbingly accurate. They had done their homework. And that meant they were ready to move. He'd already heard rumors about a similar "offer" by Red to the owner of the Oasis, another country club casino outside the city limits, with a Casa Blanca theme of white stucco and a domed roof like a mosque for the mob. You could almost imagine the Oasis in a North African desert somewhere—if you ignored the pink neon and polished Cadillacs in the parking lot.

"Well, we have our own variety of problems," Brink said. "You guys are all set with Newport and Campbell County. Everyone who needed to be bought was bought by Remus a long time ago and they stay bought, from the beat cops to the judges and prosecutors. But we had to start from the ground up over here in Kenton County. That do-gooder judge Saint John Northcutt gave us heartburn like rotgut wine. We had to run up a lot of operating costs to take him outta office and elect the right people. The legal fees alone were killing us."

Brink was stalling. It was useless. If they knew what he was clearing, they knew what he was paying to the police, the sheriff, the judges, the politicians, all the way to Governor Happy.

"It must be working just fine," Red said, his face blank, hard to read. "We thought you were going to the can three years ago. What was it, 40 counts of illegal gambling?"

"Forty-five."

"The state was on your neck. And then they weren't. All the witnesses turned up in the hospital, unable to testify."

"And you got a nice payday for that."

"Yeah," Red said, thoughtful, as if he was working it out in his head, or maybe replaying the way he persuaded those witnesses to change their minds and forget they had ever seen gambling in the Lookout House. He scratched a kitchen match on the sole of his two-tone shoe, lit a plain-end Pall Mall cigarette and tossed the smoking match onto Brink's desk, missing the ashtray. It sat there, sending up a tiny trail like a smoke signal saying watch out, you're playing with fire.

Red squinted over the cigarette and continued. "And now you get to stay open when we're closed for a new grand jury across the county line. That would be a sweet deal to own such nice carpet joints in both counties. No waiting. Always open, here or there."

So that was the play. "They have grand juries on the west side of the Licking River, too," Brink said. "We close down when they're in session, just like Newport does."

Red just sat there, giving him that cold eye that made you wonder where your family was.

Pete Schmidt had sold out, Brink thought. And if Pete sold out, after surviving the burn-out, after the armed robbery, after the bombs and the ding-donging, the Lookout House was as good as gone. Better to sell out than to see it curl away into the sky on a cloud of black smoke. Or maybe not see anything but the dark side of a coffin lid.

Brink sighed, nodded and decided he would cut his best deal. He put his hands up, palms out, to signal surrender. Red just looked at him. Then finally he gave an almost imperceptible nod.

"Charles Lester will bring you the paperwork," he said, getting up to leave. "I think I'll stay for lunch."

"On the house," Brink said. "Hell, you own it now."

He paused, then just as Red was going out the door Brink said, "Hey, Red. How about one favor for old time's sake? Can I deal with Tucker instead of Lester? I don't trust that weasel and Sam is a gentleman among those boys."

"By now you should know better than to trust anybody," Red replied. "I'll talk to Sam and see what I can do."

Red was true to his word. Lester did the legal work, but Brink negotiated with Tucker.

He gave up 80 percent of the Lookout House for $125,000, plus a couple of side dishes: 10 percent of the take from the Beverly Hills Country Club and 10 percent of the take from what used to be his Lookout House.

It was a good deal, he kept telling himself. He would make out fine. They could have just muscled him out, he reasoned. but they had kept him on as manager, which was the Cleveland way. "Break it if it ain't fixed, but don't fix what ain't broke."

Jimmy Brink took his chips to another table and soon opened the more modest Yorkshire Club carpet joint in Newport later that year, approved and backed by both the Cleveland and New York mobs.

Brink stayed on as manager at the Lookout House until 1952, when it was raided. In August that year he was killed when his plane crash-landed in Atlanta, on his way to Florida. More than $7,000 was incinerated in the explosion, along with Brink's body, burned beyond recognition. Charles Lester went to court to claim the remaining $16,000 Brink was carrying.

As World War II loomed over the horizons off both coasts, the Cleveland Four had consolidated nearly all the premier casinos. The Beverly Hills Country Club was now under the new ownership of Moe Dalitz and the rest of the Cleveland Four.

It soon became known as the "Showplace of the Nation," not just the Midwest.

And somewhere underneath the footings of the posh club, the embers of arson still glowed, waiting to flare up again.

2.

'Nightclub Raid Finds Nothing'

"The war's been tough on us all," Charles Lester said with a wry grin.

"Which one?" Pete Schmidt replied. "Japan, Germany or Newport?"

It was late summer in 1943. Headlines that had shouted about gambling wars five years ago were now bringing news about a genuine bombs-and-tanks war, naming places like Guadalcanal, Sicily, Tarawa and Kursk, far away from Newport, Wilder and Covington.

Schmidt and Lester sat in a private corner of Schmidt's Glenn Hotel Rendezvous on Monmouth Street. Lester had asked for the meeting. Schmidt decided he would listen, but not without enough grains of salt to cure a Christmas ham. He reminded himself: This was the mob's operator, the same lawyer who drew up papers to take Schmidt's beautiful new Beverly Hills Country Club, and the same smooth-talking lawyer who orchestrated the defense of Red Masterson's stooges who had burned it down before that.

I'll listen, he thought. For now.

"You know, what with gas rationing, travel restrictions, all those men fighting in Europe and the Pacific, business could be better, right?"

Schmidt said nothing. Just stared at the dapper society-page lawyer with the clever eyes. Usually, Pete was as kind and caring as a funeral director. Not today. It was clear that the old scars were still not healed.

Lester twirled ice in his Jim Beam on the rocks and took a sip. This was not going to be easy, he thought, but nothing was ever easy with Schmidt. What kind of cement-head needs a fire, two bombs, several robberies and repeated yellow showers in the lobby to get the message? Only Pete. Stubborn Dutchman.

"You watch what's going on better than anyone in town. You've probably figured it out," he continued, applying a little flattery. "The boys in Cleveland think we need to make some wartime sacrifices like everyone else. They've decided there are too many independent rowboats drawing business away from their flagships. The bust-out joints don't have our volume of customers, so they chisel and cheat and load the dice until they bleed a man dry. They don't know enough to let the suckers win a little so they will keep coming back. And that draws heat to all of us. There's too many news stories and lawsuits about guys from Toledo who get rolled."

"You mean like those two dames that killed that guy by giving him enough knockout drops to put a polar bear in a coma? I can tell ya, those nitwits didn't come from this club, if that's what you're worried about."

"Yes, like that, but that's not what I'm here about. There's more."

"Like what?"

"Like what if someday Cleveland decides to run all the independents out of business and crush the small joints? The bust-out joints cause most of the headlines and headaches, and there are too many of them. We probably have more bust-out joints than voters in this town. Cleveland is talking about the kind of consolidation that happened at the big Atlantic City summit. It's already happening. And when they carve up the territory, there will be nothing left for us."

"Who's this 'us' you're talking about?"

"I mean men like you and me who built this town into what it is, who were here before New York, Chicago and Detroit got together and decided Newport belongs to Cleveland. I'm talking about a plan to protect what we built with our own two hands."

Schmidt leaned forward, putting his meaty forearms on the table. "I've never seen you do anything with your own two hands that didn't involve reaching in someone else's pockets. But if you got a plan to stop all that, let's hear it."

Lester took another drink, looked over his shoulders, and leaned in, keeping his voice low. "You know I'm wired to the inner circle. I know what they talk about. They're afraid of bad publicity and reform. So, I say, let's give them a double dose of both. Our own version of those knockout drops that left that guy from Toledo dead in a ditch."

Schmidt's stone face never showed a hint, but inside he was scrambling to keep up. Charles Lester? The mob's mouthpiece? Biting the hand that feeds him? What was this, some kind of razzle-dazzle game with crooked dice? Lester's a snake, he thought, but what if he's serious?

"We start with Red," Lester continued. "I think he needs some of that old-time religion I keep hearing about. The kind they sing about at the Church of Reformed Gamblers."

Now *that's* interesting, Schmidt thought. Nobody messes with Red unless they're dead serious—or soon to be just plain dead. "What about Cleveland? I fought 'em before, as you know damned well. Nobody fought harder than I did or stuck it out longer. But they hold all the high cards. You can't win."

"I'm not so sure," Lester smirked. "Moe Dalitz is in the Army now, learning the laundry business, I hear. Kleinman is busy running Cleveland. Rothkopf has his hands full managing booze supply for their joints, what with rationing and sugar so short. All hell is breaking loose up there. That leaves Tucker on his own in town here, with his attack-dog Masterson. And we've got a visiting judge in town who is not on the Cleveland fix list. I also know a Boy Scout in the state attorney general's office who is hot to clean up gambling. Sort of his patriotic duty for the war effort, I guess. If we play our cards just right..."

"How's that gonna work?"

"We get indictments and raid all the syndicate's places. Maybe toss yours in the mix to make it look good. You don't have to lose much of anything, because you know it's coming. But if we keep it quiet and move fast, it will hit them hard, starting with Red at the Merchant's Club."

Schmidt leaned back and rubbed his jaw. "Let me think it over."

"Don't take too long. We need to move fast, before they get wise that something's up."

Schmidt thought it over and decided to take a chance. It's a gamble, he said to himself, but playing the odds is my business. He called Lester the next day.

"I'm in. What's the ante?"

"Just let them take a couple of slots. We'll make sure you get them back in a week or two. You'll get some visitors tomorrow night."

"If you cross me..." He left the threat unfinished. As he hung up the phone, Schmidt realized what Lester meant about visitors tomorrow night. Why that slimy SOB, he thought. This raid was going off with me or without me.

On September 21, Newport Police raided nine nightclubs including the Beverly Hills Supper Club, the Merchant's Club and the Yorkshire Club. And, as an afterthought, they included Schmidt's Glenn Hotel Rendezvous. Five people were arrested on gambling charges. Schmidt was not one of them. About $100,000 worth of equipment was seized, almost none from Schmidt.

Charles Lester then teamed up with an assistant state attorney general to prosecute the county sheriff for allowing "open gambling" to flourish within a few hundred yards of the county courthouse, at the Merchant's Club run by Red Masterson for the Cleveland mob.

"Gambling devices have been exhibited and played and they were just as public as the magazine stand in a railroad station, the resorts just as public as a post office, and the pastimes were advertised in the public press," said the mob lawyer without irony.

Among the evidence seized in the September raid were 41 slot machines taken from the Beverly Hills Country Club. But they all mysteriously disappeared from police evidence storage. A few months after the raid, a visiting judge held two men in contempt and ordered them to return the slots. They were Beverly Hills boss and Cleveland Four founder Sam Tucker, and the Newport Police Chief.

"The equipment disappeared when under police guard," the *Cincinnati Enquirer* reported on February 1, 1944.

Judge John L. Vest said, "The testimony has shown that Chief J. Len Plummer called Patrolman Walter Sweeney into the office while the patrolman was guarding the seized equipment. Patrolman Sweeney arrived at about 8:15 that morning and remained there talking to Chief Plummer until about 9:35. In that interval, all of the equipment was moved..."

The setback for the mob's clubs was very temporary, but the problems stirred up by Lester and Schmidt lingered and spread across the Licking River to Covington and Kenton County.

Police chief declares war

The following July, in 1944, Covington Police Chief Alfred F. Schild declared war on gambling by saying his police were "sick and tired of being made fools of by gamblers and any of their kind."

He ordered the Covington Police to get tough on anyone connected to open gambling, but also called out the courts. "When the case enters a high court—boom!—all the police work goes for naught and it makes us look like 'suckers' in the eyes of the public." Former Judge Northcutt probably nodded.

But then Chief Schild's "crackdown" began to falter and grind to a halt. Disgusted Covington Police officers called an off-duty meeting to protest that they were not allowed to enforce gambling laws because Chief Schild had turned all authority over to the department's crooked vice squad, where gambling complaints crawled off to die.

Another curious item was reported after the September 21, 1943 raid in Newport orchestrated by Schmidt and Lester. As the gamblers' war spilled out of the nightclubs and into politics at City Hall, city officials were accused of offering protection to mob gambling "resorts." Among those caught in the scandal was attorney Daniel Davies, attorney for 0the arsonists who burned the Beverly Hills Country Club in 1936. He was accused of being a partner in the Merchants Club with Sam Tucker, Red Masterson and other gangsters.

"I defy them to prove I am associated as a partner in the Merchants Club," Davies objected, parsing his words with lawyerly precision.

Schmidt and Lester lost the first battle, but launched a new attack in the late 1940s. Schmidt backed Robert Sidell, a bandleader at the Beverly Hills Country Club, for mayor. Sidell lost to James Deckert. The new mayor promptly threatened to "make it damned hot" for Schmidt's Glenn Rendezvous unless he paid $6,000 to Deckert. Sure enough, Schmidt's casino was the only one of the Big Six in Newport that was raided immediately after Mayor Deckert took office. The Beverly Hills Country Club, the Yorkshire Club, the Merchants Club, the Yorkshire Club and the Flamingo were untouched.

When the raiders showed up at Schmidt's nightclub, the door to the downstairs gambling hall was locked. They read their search warrant to Pete's son Glenn Schmidt, who said, "You'd better read this to Pop."

He sent someone to find his father and they read their search warrant again to Pete Schmidt.

"Well, there it is boys," Pete grinned when they were done. "You don't see nothing and there is nothing there."

"We are interested in what is behind that door," City Commissioner Charles Eha said, stepping forward.

"I don't have a key," Schmidt said, giving a shrug.

The raiders stood there, shoulders sagging, ready to turn and leave. Eha, elected as a reformer, could see that it was all going nowhere— another empty raid because someone had tipped off Schmidt. He looked for the biggest cop in the crowd, grabbed him by the sleeve and ordered, "Break down the door!"

Newport Police Sgt. Carl Ape smiled. He was the kind of man who embraced his unhappy surname and even enjoyed the jokes and hazing because he had the size and strength to back up the "Ape Man" jokes. He stepped forward and gave the door two hard, jarring kicks that rattled the walls and began to split the brass hardware from its frame. He was winding up for a third kick when Schmidt, the famous tightwad who tossed around dimes like they were manhole covers, shouted, "Wait!"

He reached into his pocket and produced a key. "This is what you want, I guess."

When they burst through the door, Eha was deflated. There was not much left to find. The raid netted just three slot machines and a dice table. A disappointment, but not a total failure.

Schmidt was indicted and prosecuted, but his lawyer Charles Lester won an acquittal, by branding Eha as a liar and a "Carrie Nation," a withering insult in those post-Prohibition times—comparing him to the hatchet-swinging radical who attacked taverns and smashed beer-barrels in her crusade to outlaw the simple freedom of a cold glass of ale on a hot afternoon.

Schmidt retaliated by giving the press an affidavit prepared by Lester, revealing Mayor Decker's attempted $6,000 shakedown.

Newport didn't know which side to believe: the crooked politician, or the gangster and his crooked lawyer? Most figured they were all crooks, and they were right.

But a month later Schmidt folded again. He sold his Glenn Rendezvous to the Levinson brothers, Ed and "Sleepout Louis," who were affiliated with gangs in Chicago and New York. At least it was not the Cleveland Four again. Then again, the Cleveland mob and the Detroit boys were as tight as dots on dice.

Meanwhile, the Cleveland mob was spreading out like spilled blood to take over another Newport carpet joint, the Flamingo Club.

Eight million soldiers were coming home from the war. Hundreds of thousands would come through the huge Art Deco Union Terminal train station, just a short taxi ride across the river in Cincinnati. They would be primed and ready for the wild, wide-open nightlife in Newport and Covington, their pockets stuffed with military "mustering out" paychecks.

The mob was primed and ready too.

By 1948, the Yorkshire Club was making $750,000 a year and the Beverly Hills Country Club was hauling in $975,000.

But there were still a few clubs on the mob's shopping list.

3.
'Gangland Guns Bark'

Shotgun Blast Is Fired Into Auto In Newport; Buck Brady Arrested

Gangland's guns barked again in Newport last night.

This time a shotgun blast was fired on crowded Third Street from one moving car into another, with both cars going out of control and striking four other automobiles.

But when the smoke had cleared and the commotion had subsided, Albert "Red" Masterson, Newport underworld character, was found in Speers Hospital, Dayton, Ky., with his face and neck riddled with buckshot pellets and Ernest "Buck" Brady, widely known police character who once drove the car of Bootleg King George Remus, was telling Newport police that he "ran for dear life and hid in an outhouse when he heard shots being fired."

Brady is known as a former owner of the Primrose Club on Licking Pike, now being operated as the Latin Quarter.

It all began when Masterson, said to be one of the operators of the Merchants Club, 15 E. Fourth St., Newport, was driving slowly along Third Street between York and Monmouth Sts.

Another car drew alongside and a volley was fired into Masterson's car. Crazed by pain, Masterson leaped or fell from his moving car, which did not stop until it had collided with an automobile parked

ALBERT 'RED" MASTERSON.

at Third and Monmouth Sts. and owned by Earl Behringer, 317 View Pl., a Covington Police Sergeant.

After ducking momentarily behind another automobile Masterson ran back to his car, climbed inside and drove north on York Street to Speers Hospital. Physicians there sewed 14 stitches in his shoulder

Continued On Page 6, Column 6.

August in 1946 was hotter than a waffle iron, Red thought. Steamy enough to wilt a plastic flower. He loosened his tie and took off his damp jacket as he left his Merchants Club, conveniently located a block north of the courthouse on East Fourth Street, where he and the local police and politicians could keep an eye on each other. On any given day, you could easily find judges and politicians at the Merchants Club, but that traffic was one-way only. Red and his gang seldom went to court, he reflected with a smile.

As he pulled into traffic on Third Street, a black sedan pulled alongside on his left. He glanced over and briefly recognized Buck Brady's face behind a hat pulled low, looking down the black tunnel of a shotgun muzzle pointed straight at him.

Red Masterson's Merchants Club was close enough to the courthouse to almost hear a banging gavel over the noise of craps games and slots.
Kenton County Library archive

As he ducked away, he caught the blast of buckshot in the left side of his face and shoulders. The shotgun sounded unreasonably loud, ringing in his ears as the sedan tires squealed, followed by a crash as the gunman's car swerved out of control, bounced off two parked cars on Third Street and slamming into a third.

Masterson slid out of his own moving car as it rolled on and crashed into parked cars. While all hell was breaking loose, with gunmen running down the street, cars crashing and steaming, people shouting, he slowly got to his feet, stumbled back to his car and drove himself to Speers Hospital. Doctors gave him 14 stitches in his shoulder and neck and removed a dozen buckshot pellets from his chin and face. He was listed in "fair condition," and refused to talk to police.

Ernest "Buck" Brady was another George Remus alumnus, a longtime friend and partner in crime with Red. In 1922, Brady and seven other bootleggers had been caught near Perryville, Kentucky, hauling 410 gallons of whiskey in five trucks. A gun battle broke out as the gangsters fired on the federal agents who blocked them at a bridge. Nobody was killed. Brady was out on bond at the time, for prohibition violations car theft.

After running whiskey with Remus, he opened the Green Lantern, one of the nicer clubs that catered to blacks.

With profits from the Lantern, he bought a derelict 1895 slaughterhouse that was said to be haunted. According to local legend, it was visited by the ghost of Pearl Bryan, a pregnant young woman who was murdered and dismembered 1896 by two Cincinnati dental students. Her headless body was found in a ravine in Fort Thomas. National news reports called it the "crime of the century." Her identity was traced by shoes she wore. The father of her child and his boardinghouse roommate were convicted and hanged in front of the courthouse on York Street—the final public hangings before the county gallows were torn down. Her head was never found, but her headless ghost was seen at the slaughterhouse, searching for it near the pit where animal parts had been dumped for years.

Buck Brady figured that was bushwa, folderol, patented bunkum. But ghost stories might be good for business. So he remodeled the building and turned it into the Primrose Club, which opened in 1933.

Business was very good. Wilder's town marshal, Big Jim Harris, had his own well-known casino and brothel called the Hi-De-Ho, so there was no worry about too much rectitude from the local law.

The Primrose Club in Wilder was one of the last independent competitors for the Beverly Hills Supper Club and the Lookout House, meaning Brady was alone against the Cleveland Four. Brady knew that Sam Tucker and the other bosses in Cleveland would not allow that for long. The underworld network was buzzing with rumors that Red would visit soon to make an "offer."

So Buck fired the first shot. He was not the kind of man to back down to anyone. Not even Red. Not even Cleveland.

After shooting Red point blank, he figured the Enforcer was dead. But then things went sideways. His getaway driver crashed their stolen car and witnesses saw three men get out and run. Two of the gangsters waved pistols and fired shots at bystanders as they ran for the Central

Bridge toward Cincinnati. Buck ran the other way.

Police found him a few blocks away hiding in an outhouse. In the weeds nearby was a .32/20 Winchester varmint rifle. Shotgun shells were found on the seat of the crashed getaway car.

"Gangland's guns barked again in Newport last night," the *Kentucky Enquirer* reported on August 6. "But when the smoke had cleared and the commotion had subsided, Albert 'Red' Masterson, Newport underworld character, was found in Speers Hospital, Dayton, Kentucky, with his face and neck riddled with buckshot pellets, and Ernest 'Buck' Brady, widely known police character who once drove the car of Bootleg King George Remus, was telling Newport Police that he 'ran for dear life and hid in an outhouse when he heard shots being fired.'"

To anyone reading the papers, it looked as open-and-shut as a slamming jail door. They had one of the shooters seen fleeing the scene: gangster Buck Brady. They had the shooting victim, who was another notorious gangster. They had witnesses who saw everything.

But Lady Justice in Newport peeked out from under her blindfold and winked. When Masterson was subpoenaed to testify, he took the stand and swore Buck Brady was not the gunman. The prosecutor said he had no choice but to drop the charges against Brady.

"Masterson, who is recuperating at his Fort Thomas home at 1027 Highland Ave., from a shotgun blast that riddled the right side of his face and neck, has denied that he recognized any of the occupants of an automobile that drew alongside his car just before the shotgun blast was fired," it was reported on August 25, 1946.

The godfather of local gangsters and king of bootleggers, George Remus, even vouched for his former driver Brady as a character witness. Although initial reports said Brady would be charged with "shooting to kill and aiding and abetting in the ambush and shooting of Masterson," he was not even fined for disturbing the peace.

Like Pete Schmidt and Jimmy Brink, Brady considered the odds against him and folded. The Cleveland Four sent word that he had two options: give them the Primrose Club and get out of town, or stay and face the wrath of Red. He moved to Florida.

His Primrose Club was taken over by Moe Dalitz and the Cleveland Four, renamed the Latin Quarter with a new manager: arsonist Dave Whitfield, fresh out of the Kentucky Penitentiary.

4.

Gambling vs. The Law

Without his fedora and matched revolvers, Red Masterson looked like a moon-faced, clean-cut, middle-aged, dyspeptic shoe salesman. By the time he was shot in 1946, he had the beginnings of a double chin, neatly combed black hair and a hard-eyed, wary stare. It was the coal-black eyes that told the rest of the story. In rare newspaper pictures, he stares directly at the camera, giving it the same stony look that was probably the last thing seen by John Rosen and others who fatally crossed the Enforcer.

"You look like hell," Daniel Davies told Masterson.

"Double-ought buckshot ain't exactly Pepsodent," Masterson replied. "It's not good for your smile. Ten out of ten doctors don't recommend it."

They sat in a corner of the darkened Merchants Club, which they shared as partners with Cleveland Four boss Sam Tucker. "You know Ulie Howard," Davies said, more a statement than a question.

"Sure I do. He was the Covington prosecutor teamed up on that do-gooder crusade with the Judge Northcutt, may he not rest in peace."

"He was commonwealth attorney for Kenton County for 20 years," Davies replied. "But now he's dead too. He took his own life after the reformers got him disbarred."

"Aw, that's too bad," said Red, shaking his head as if he cared. "All that because he got kicked out of the lawyers' sorority or whatever you guys call it."

"It's serious," Davies said. "The Kenton County Protestants Association said he winked at gambling. And I guess they backed it up, because he lost his license to practice law in a federal court."

"Like I said, too bad for him. But what's that got to do with us."

"It could mean more trouble," Davies said, looking worried as he crushed a cigarette in an overflowing glass ashtray that had a Merchants Club poker chip stenciled in the bottom. "What if this KCPA crowd goes after me? What would you do without your... what do the Italians call it in New York? 'Consigliere.' What would you do without your friendly neighborhood attorney and business partner?"

"I guess I would manage somehow when I got done crying," Red said, looking around as if he wanted to be somewhere else. "And there's always Charles Lester, right? But like I said, what's it got to do with me?"

"Just this," Davies said. "We've always had reformers come and go. Guys like Northcutt and Chief Schild in Covington. Some can be bought or scared into seeing it our way, and some can't. But this new group, they have convictions, and I don't mean the kind you get from a judge and a jury. They believe that God is on their side and they are hellbent to clean up their county. If John Doe and his missus ever wake up and decide they've had it with whores, booze and gambling, there will be no stopping the politicians who run on that ticket."

Red thought about it. "So who do we burn, buy or bury?"

"You don't get it, that's the point," Davies said. "This is not like a police chief or a mayor or even a governor, for that matter..."

Davies froze as Red's right hand reached under his coat and pulled a .38 from his shoulder holster. Suddenly, those blank eyes were boring into his.

Red held the gun in his big hand the way a plumber holds a wrench, familiar, almost a part of him. The stubby muzzle was pointed casually, just over Davies' right shoulder. Then he laid it down on the table with a hard knock of steel on wood.

Davies frantically wracked his memory for something he might have said or done to bring down the wrath of the Enforcer. Was the meeting a set-up? Was Red sent to kill me? Did I insult him? Is he insane?

"What's that?" Red said, pointing a thumb at the pistol as if he was surprised to see it lying there and honestly didn't know.

Davies started to speak, had to clear his throat, and answered, "It's a gun."

"Wrong," Red replied. "That's a stick."

He let that sit for a while, as Davies tried to think of a way to get help. He wanted to look around but he was mesmerized by Red's glare, afraid to move. A stick? What the hell?

Red reached in his pants pocket this time and brought out a fat wad of rolled up bills. He tossed that on the table next to the gun.

"What's that?" he asked again.

"It looks like a bankroll big enough to choke a hog," Davies said, forcing a chuckle that made his jowls wobble as he felt a trickle of sweat roll down his back.

"Wrong again," Red said. "That's a carrot."

Later, Davies reassured himself that he would have been quicker to figure out where Red was going if only he had not been so damned frozen with fear. All he could think of at the time was how many others had spent their last moments on earth trying to figure out one of Red's riddles.

"That's all it takes," Red said finally. "Show them the stick, then offer the carrot. Sometimes we skip the carrot so everyone knows we're serious, see?"

He put the gun back in his holster the way other men would put away a wallet, then picked up the cash and put it back in his pocket and shook out a cigarette from Davies' pack of Pall Malls. "And sometimes we use the little stick, like this," he said, lighting a kitchen match with his thumbnail.

"I get it," Davies said, feeling his pounding heart begin to slow down. "Believe me, I'm not trying to tell you how to do your business. Nobody's better at it than you. Nobody gets results the way you do. But maybe we can do this the easy way, so nobody has to get hurt."

Red seemed disappointed, as if Davies had somehow let him down and spoiled the fun. The lawyer hurried on to make his point as if he were trying to beat the gavel in court: "I'm just saying this could be the kind of brushfire that you can't put out once it gets started. We need to start thinking about how to get behind it so we can make sure it blows in the right direction."

"What's Sam Tucker say about it?" Red asked, squinting through a cloud of smoke.

"Sambo's the one who told me to talk to you."

They were right to be worried. The sparks of reform were floating on the breeze, looking for a place to land and flare up. In the summer of 1944, the Campbell County Baptists Association asked the state to step in and enforce injunctions against open gambling. Kentucky Attorney General Eldon S. Dummit replied by telling the Baptists to go to hell. At least that's how they heard it.

Dummit said he would not help prosecute gambling because most people in Campbell County *wanted* things just the way they were.

"The tragedy of the whole situation in Campbell County is that gambling has been permitted for many, many years and today it is recognized by the business community as one of the important economic institutions, and its elimination will throw hundreds of people out of employment," the attorney general said.

It was the mortal sin of politics: He spoke the truth.

Dummit said he would help only "when the citizens of that county evidence a real and actual desire on their part to aid in the effort.

"The office of the attorney general cannot go into any community and change the moral standard. The people create their own moral standards (that) are not going to change until the people make the change themselves."

Whether he meant it that way or not, it was taken as an insult and a challenge to Northern Kentucky, which was scorned by the most of the state as a morally stunted, uncivilized carbuncle of corruption.

Most of the state was not far wrong.

But the good citizens of Northern Kentucky were incensed.

The Rev. Leo Drake, moderator of the Baptist Association representing 20 churches and 6,000 members, replied with hellfire and brimstone in an open letter to Attorney General Dummit.

He started by saying it was "absurd" to say the people in Campbell County wanted gambling. "Passing the buck is a chronic habit of not only Campbell County officials but state officials as well, and your office has a pretty good case of the disease," his letter said.

"I have lived all my life in Campbell County and I can testify to you that the people of this county do not want this ugly situation and have never wanted it, for the good people of this county like every other county are always in the majority.

"Show me where gambling ever has benefited any community. It can't be important business to tear down the morals of our youth and create such a state of affairs that not only local but state officials are a laughingstock."

The Reverend Drake's letter was published in the *Kentucky Enquirer* on August 21, 1944, two days after the story quoting Dummit's statement. The pastor listed chapter and verse of open gambling, taxis shuttling gamblers from Cincinnati, sham trials and widespread cynicism and distrust of mob-owned local government, courts and law enforcement. He also described how the investigator sent by Dummit to report on gambling in Newport instead went on a drinking tour of casinos as a guest of mob attorneys, and got so drunk he had to be carried to a Cincinnati hotel to sleep it off.

"Your office will do nothing about it," he wrote. "Why? Do these Newport and Campbell County officeholders know that they have the goods on you men at Frankfort?"

Residents of Campbell County and Kenton County read that letter and shook their heads, asking the same question: Does the mob own everyone in Kentucky?

In January of 1949, the Kenton County Protestant Association's leader made headlines: "Gambling to End in Kenton, Protestant Group Predicts."

But asked to back up his prediction, KPCA leader W. Sharon Florer said all he had was hope. "I said that just to be facetious."

As the 1940s came to a close, that slender stick of jaded hope was all the reformers had to lean on, while victims of the mob-run nightclubs, resorts and supper clubs leaned on the presumably uncorrupted federal courts and the gangsters leaned on anyone who got in their way.

In 1948, Jack Bundman and his wife, Mildred, of Cincinnati, sued the Yorkshire Club for $28,000 in gambling losses and $15,000 in injuries. Bundman said that after losing $2,700 one night, he asked the manager for $800 back.

Yorkshire boss Morris Nemo invited Bundman into his office to discuss it, then gave the unlucky gambler a severe beating instead.

In the U.S. District Court in Covington, local papers reported that "a bizarre tale unfolded" in late 1949, described in a federal lawsuit by

Margaret Cutler against the Beverly Hills Country Club. She claimed that her husband had gambled away his car dealership in Cincinnati and even pawned her jewelry.

"Mr. Cutler testified that as a result of losing from $300 to $1,800 from day to day at the club, he ran through a used car business that had grossed $1 million a year and was finally forced out of business," the *Cincinnati Enquirer* reported.

His wife testified that they had lost their $22,000 home, two automobiles, $10,000 worth of furniture and their business, Norbert Motors on Reading Road. They eventually recovered $15,000.

The attorney representing the Beverly Hills Country Club: Daniel Davies.

A month later, in November 1949, another breathless banner headline in the *Cincinnati Enquirer* fanned hopes for reform. "Bust-Outs Must Close, Thiem Reiterates." Sgt. Jack Thiem, head of the Newport Police Vice Squad, was waging a "one-man war on gambling and vice."

His enthusiasm was beyond question. But it was not exactly clear which side he was on.

Finally, a crackdown... on bingo

Sgt. Thiem was accused of roughing up a small-time hood and racetrack jockey, who filed a complaint claiming that Thiem threatened "to break my legs and throw me in a sewer."

In April, Thiem provoked public protests by raiding bingo games at the Newport Elks and the Knights of Columbus. He even arrested a Newport city commissioner during one of his raids on dive-bars, bust-outs and clip joints.

As reformers geared up for the next city elections, Thiem seemed determined to remind them of the old adage, "Be careful what you ask for." His raids posed an uncomfortable question: "You want to eliminate gambling? Fine, how about if we start at your church?"

The citizens were irate. Long, convoluted debates examined how many angels could play bingo on the head of a pin without really "gambling." The Catholic Diocese decided to cast the first stone and split with the Protestant reformers to protect its cash flow from bingo.

But while Thiem was tipping over tables in the bingo halls and bust-out joints, the Big Six mob casinos went curiously untouched. A raid on the Flamingo Club netted nothing; not even a pair of dice. Thiem's vice squad got only taunts from "police characters" in otherwise empty rooms that had been cleaned out card tables, roulette wheels and slots.

When Thiem was arrested for threatening to murder another street thug, the city manager disbanded the vice squad but promised, "It should be made clear that this is not just another sporadic shutdown" of gambling.

Surprisingly, he was correct. A grand jury selected from outside Newport backed up court orders that shut down the Newport clubs for 16 months.

Small, independent clubs that competed with the mob's carpet joints were put out of business, while mob casinos outside Newport—the Beverly Hills Country Club and the Lookout House—sponged up the business.

As the lid stayed on in Newport through the following August, the mob was so secure it used the police to enforce its monopoly.

As part of a newspaper crusade against illegal gambling, the *Louisville Courier Journal* teamed up with the *Cleveland Plain Dealer* to investigate and report on the Newport gambling moratorium.

"It began with the formation of the Newport Civic Association in preparation for last fall's election of a new City Council," they reported in 1950. "Ordinarily, 'reform' movements aren't taken seriously in Newport. But at the time, the situation was out of the ordinary. That is, it is worse than usual. 'Bust-out' joints—the cheaper dives that resort to crooked dice, drugged drinks or even blackjacks to part customers from their money—had become so flagrant that even the operators of the swanky places were embarrassed. Besides, it was casting reflections on their own operations. In addition, prostitutes, their pimps, drunks, hoodlums and other unsavory characters were everywhere. Each day brought a new batch of incidents.

"One thing led to another until the community's businessmen, politicians, church leaders and the bigger gamblers decided something would have to be done to save Newport's fair name. They (and that includes even the Cleveland kings of gambling who control six of the biggest joints in this two-county area) got behind the Civic Association."

Four Republican reformers were elected on promises to "clean up, but don't close up" gambling in Newport. They named a new city manager and imposed a 2 a.m. curfew that targeted bust-outs, where crowds swelled after the big six casinos had closed for the night.

The mob's nightclubs were inoculated by bribery, immune from the crackdown flu. The newsmen reported $250,000 in bribes to city officials by the Cleveland Four. "reform" meant the wild and raunchy bust-outs were busted out of business.

To set an example, Sgt. Thiem came down hard on the Dogpatch, "a particularly notorious place" that had wallpapered Newport with handbills promising "Fifty beautiful girls for hostesses. Bring your sweetheart. If you have no girl, we'll furnish one. Take your pick."

A vanload of gambling equipment was seized from the Dogpatch.

The next night Sgt. Thiem and his squad raided bingo parlors, to remind reformers that a little religion can be more than enough.

"What's going on?" angry voters asked as they crowded into a Newport City Commissioners meeting. "If you're going to raid bingo, why not go after the big casinos?"

Thiems raids could have been designed by the Cleveland Four. In fact, the "clean up, not close up" campaign was engineered by Red Masterson, who had taken the advice of Dan Davies to get behind the locomotive of reform so as not to get run over by it.

Sgt. Thiem's one-man war on gambling was eventually rewarded with a job in security at a Las Vegas casino owned by Moe Dalitz.

The grand opening of Glenn Schmidt's new $700,000 "Playtorium" on Fifth Street was delayed. But mob-owned casinos outside Newport drew bigger crowds than ever. And that was fine. Moe Dalitz was busy investing in a new wide-open casino, the Desert Inn in Las Vegas, where Nevada had legalized gambling in 1931. Sam Tucker was in Miami, then Havana, setting up new casinos and hotels. It was left to Louis Rothkopf to visit the Cleveland Four's Newport properties and assure them things would work out fine.

After all, there was growing talk in Washington and all over the country about this guy Senator Kefauver and his investigation into organized crime. The last thing the mob wanted was for the traveling Kefauver Circus to put up a tent in Newport.

The Beverly Hills was a jewel for the Cleveland mob. Guests arrived at the "country club" entrance and stepped into a dazzling oval bar that glowed under ultramodern recessed lights. Kenton County Library archive

Downtown Newport nightlife in the 1940s. During the high times of Sin City, more than 300 prostitutes were counted in one mile. Cab drivers were paid a commission to deliver soldiers and convention visitors to Kitty's, Mabel's and the Hi-De-Ho Club. Kentucky Views

Part III — 1950s

1.
Estes in Plunderland

"...a suit was filed to recover the gambling losses. The day for the trial approached and this butcher, who lost his life savings and his two butcher shops gambling in the Harvard Club, was visited by a black, large sedan, filled with men."

The man on the television loomed over the microphone, seated at a heavy oak table that held a bouquet of microphones perched on stands, each as big as a blooming rose. He had a kind face and graying, curly hair that always looked uncombed. He looked like a man who laughed easily, but with the kindly, mannered dignity of a judge, which is exactly what he had been in Cleveland, where he worked alongside Cleveland Public Safety Director Elliot Ness, the legendary "Untouchable" who put away Al Capone in Chicago. But the grandfatherly charm was deceiving. Ohio Governor Frank Lausch was no stranger to crime and the underworld.

It was January 17, 1951. Five senators faced Governor Lausch that day on a raised, dark wood dais like supreme court justices, flanked by a half-dozen staffers. Their chief counsel sat in the middle, also in front of a microphone. They were riveted as the governor continued.

"They went upstairs to his house, and they said, 'If you love your wife and child, you had better not appear in that courtroom and testify...'"

"Turn it off," said the fat man at the bar nursing a boilermaker.

"Yeah, I'd rather watch a soap opera," said the one in the checkered sportscoat three stools down.

"Leave it alone," said the tall man with big hands. He was known as "Knuckles," but it was not his nickname, it was the surname he was born with. Hardly anyone knew that his first name was Darwin. "That's the governor of Ohio," he growled. "It's a big deal. And I want to hear what happens to the butcher guy."

The rest of the men fell silent and decided they were very interested in the television after all. In fact, they reconsidered, it was better than a soap opera. Didn't everyone say these hearings were the greatest thing on TV? Millions were watching. The newspapers pictures showed women at the beauty parlor, glued to the TV set as they sat under those torpedo-shaped hairdryers; huddles of college students gathered around a TV in a classroom; and whole offices of insurance agents, downtown shoppers and newsrooms, all bowing in front of those little glowing boxes like some new Space Age religious ritual.

And here *they* were, too, all staring at the little screen behind the bar.

The Judge Hardy governor looked angry.

"Could he go to court and testify and have protection of his body and his family? Or should he yield to the threat of the gangsters and stay away from court? Well, he yielded to the gangsters and dismissed his lawsuit..."

"That butcher was not so stupid," someone muttered.

As usual, the faces at the bar came and went like birds at a feeder. Some placed racetrack bets, others paused to peck at the slots by the men's room or sat in for a few hands of blackjack.

The little black-and-white TV screen looked like a watery porthole view of the hearing room in Cleveland. Governor Lausch was wrapping up.

"...a plague, it is an evil that will require the joint attack of the local government, the state government and the federal government...

"John Smith today, the worker with the family, is gambling his money away at one of these joints.... Today he is an honest man, working, and tomorrow he is in jail because of embezzlement. His children, his family, happy today, but tomorrow the home broken because of the poison spread by these men."

"John Smith?" a wise guy joked. "I think I saw him sign in with a hooker at the Glenn Hotel."

As laughter rippled along the bar, Knuckles thought: They're talking about us.

"...a final word. The fact is that the Ohio men are now in Nevada with that large-scale casino."

"The Desert Inn," Sen. Estes Kefauver replied. *"Yes, sir."*

"...that shows the extent..."

The hearing continued. The mayor of Cleveland testified. Then the owner of a betting wire service, flanked by two slick Washington lawyers. Sheriffs, police chiefs, prosecutors. Bookies, nightclub owners, crime bosses. The U.S. Senate Select Committee on Organized Crime in Interstate Commerce, aka the Kefauver Hearings, was just starting its eighth month. It would continue with hearings in 14 cities over two years. Six-hundred witnesses would testify as millions watched on TV or in movie theaters, where the day's hearings were replayed as a public service at no charge.

The tall, lanky Tennessee senator who launched the investigation only by the paper-thin margin of the Vice President's tie-breaking Senate vote, would appear on the cover of *Time Magazine* and other national publications, wearing round glasses and a toothy, aw-shucks grin.

Cultivating the image of Davy Crockett played by Jimmy Stewart in *Mr. Smith Goes to Washington*, he posed for pictures in the coonskin cap that had made him famous during his first run for the Senate. When his opponent had accused him of being a troublemaking communist "racoon," Kefauver embraced the insult, put on the coonskin cap and declared he was nobody's pet racoon.

His organized crime hearings proved it. Before they were over, he would be hated by some in his own Democratic Party for exposing corruption that ruined an ambassador and at least two Democratic governors, spreading an epidemic of heartburn in courthouses and statehouses all the way to the White House.

He also won the admiration of most Americans who watched him grill a colorful parade of underworld thugs, murderers, gamblers, crime bosses and money handlers, always with grace and courtesy. He nearly won his party's nomination for the presidency, but ran instead as Vice President on the ticket with Adlai Stevenson in 1956. They lost to Dwight Eisenhower and Richard Nixon.

But in early 1951, Kefauver was lifting rock after slippery rock to see what slimy things crawled out and squirmed in the glaring light of flashbulbs, newsreels and coast-to-coast broadcasts on television.

One of those wriggling witnesses was Alvin E. Giesey, a former U.S. Treasury official, accompanied by his lawyer. While working for the IRS, Giesey had testified against Cleveland mobster Morris Kleinman to help convict the underworld boss of income tax evasion in 1933. Two years later, Kleinman got out of prison and hired Giesey to work for the mob, keeping books at their nightclubs and casinos and preparing personal tax returns for Kleinman and the other Cleveland crime bosses.

The senators waved papers and held up stacks of tax returns from Giesey's accounting firm. They showed Giesey's business partnerships with Kleinman, Dalitz, Tucker and Rothkopf—the Cleveland Four—that earned him a fortune in stocks and fees for keeping the books of numerous businesses, including the Beverly Hills Country Club and the Lookout Club. Asked why he did it, Giesey replied with galling candor, "The almighty dollar."

The witnesses, like regulars at the Alibi Club in Newport, came and went, removing coats and hats, adjusting ties, taking a seat, huddling in whispered conferences with their lawyers. The gangsters looked stiff, uncomfortable, cutting nervous sidelong glances at the herds of reporters and photographers lugging cameras as big as shoeboxes, with tall, blinding flash attachments that popped and sizzled.

As they entered marble-floored courtrooms with towering ceilings and stone pillars in the grand pharaonic scale of omnipotent government, they looked lost, confused, out of their element, like predators suddenly caught in the open, night creatures blinking in glaring sunlight.

Some sat silent, like Kleinman, who uttered not a word until the senators and their staff gave up and threw up their hands in disgust.

Some answered like push-button recordings: "I refuse to answer on the grounds it may incriminate me."

"What is your name?"

"I refuse to answer on the grounds it may incriminate me."

"What day is this?"

"I refuse to answer on the grounds it may incriminate me."

"How old are you?"

"I refuse to answer..."

Some seemed as surprised by their own answers as the TV audience was. "What was your experience before becoming sheriff?" the committee asked Kenton County Sheriff John Diebold, whose law enforcement jurisdiction included Covington, Kentucky.

"I was a goodwill man for the Hudepohl Brewing Company in Cincinnati," he replied.

"Did you have any law-enforcement experience?"

"No."

Maybe that's why he congenially denied that he had ever raided or even set foot in any of the dozens of casinos in his county. The former beer delivery man who had serviced most of the clubs in Northern Kentucky claimed he was unaware of any laws against gambling.

Audiences held their breath as they listened to Ohio Liquor Control officer Anthony Rutkowski describe a raid at the Jungle Inn in

Youngstown, a nightclub and casino owned by the Cleveland Four.

Rutkowski's squad arrived in a chorus of squealing tires and brakes and pushed through the doors, as nightclub owner John Farrah came running and shouting, "Kill him, goon, kill him, shoot him!"

Rutkowski looked up to see who the gangster was shouting at and was stunned to see a gun turret high on the wall of the nightclub.

As Rutkowski stood there, frozen, waiting to be shot at any second, one of his men busted through a door into the turret and wrestled a 12-gauge shotgun away from Farrah's "goon," then blocked the door when Farrah tried to push his way in and shoot the raiders himself.

Inside the turret they found shotguns, rifles, pistols and an assortment of blackjacks to deal with difficult guests.

"...Out of the Prohibition period came the same kind of city-wide and regional and even interstate gang organizations that plagued other major cities..."

"Who's this guy?" a newcomer asked as he leaned on the bar and ordered a beer.

"Cleveland's police chief, or something," the bartender said. "It's right there on the screen, 'Alvin Sutton, public safety director.'"

"...highjacked each other's liquor loads. Murder became a standard tool for all the illegal gangs as they fought for territories, for sources of supply, trucks, boats that ran the liquor blockade on the lakes..."

"Hey, Gus, didn't you run some Canadian whisky on Lake Erie?" someone asked.

"Yeah," Gus replied. "Coldest I ever been. Brass monkey cold. I thought if it got any colder we could get out and walk home across the lake."

"...top of Cleveland's bootleggers were Morris Kleinman, Lou Rothkopf, Moe Dalitz, Sam Tucker..."

"Hey, that's our board of directors," said Gus.

"...ruthless beatings, unsolved murders and shakedowns, threats and bribery..."

The Cleveland Safety Director testified that former boxer Morris Kleinman, known in the ring as "One Punch," was also the "King of the Bootleggers" in northern Ohio, making nearly $1 million a year as he left a wake of murder, shakedowns, extortion and beatings.

Then the mob's "green eyeshade guy" and taxman Giesey was called back. He dodged, wiggled and curled up in knots like a worm on a hook. He was told that records of the Beverly Hills Country Club had been seized in the raid of a mob-owned Cleveland nightclub. Giesey said that did not surprise him. He was finally forced to identify the partners in the Beverly Hills Club that grossed nearly $530,000 in 1949.

They were a Who's Who of organized crime, including Moe Dalitz, Lou Rothkopf, Morris Kleinman, Sam "Sambo" Tucker, Sam Schrader, Thomas McGinty, John Croft, "Big Al" Polizzi and Jimmy Brink.

The crime networks were traced from Cleveland to Covington and Newport, from Miami to Los Angeles, from Phoenix to Detroit, from Havana to New Jersey.

Rent-a-cops for the mob

America was stunned to find out how organized this hidden crime network was. Pieces of casinos and businesses were passed around like dishes of baked beans and Jell-O salad at a potluck church dinner. Everyone seemed to get a taste. Mobsters in Miami had a piece of Newport; Phoenix was connected to Cleveland and Detroit; New York gangsters migrated back and forth to Los Angeles; and they all flocked to the new wide-open Shangri-Las Vegas.

In Vegas, the fix did not need to be installed. It was wired into every casino from the ground up, part of the blueprints. And it went all the way to the top.

Nevada Lieutenant Governor Clifford Jones told the Kefauver Committee that he owned an interest in the Golden Nugget that paid him $12,000 a year; a share of the Pioneer Club that paid $14,000 a year; and part of the new Thunderbird Hotel where Myer Lansky had taken up residence.

Asked about Lansky, Jones said, "I never met him."

At hearings in Cleveland on Friday, January 19, 1951, Newport City Manager Malcolm Reet Rhoads, a lawyer and former country schoolteacher, testified that gambling was "practically eliminated" in Newport's 126 saloons, 43 nightclubs and numerous small groceries that offered convenient backroom slots and handbook betting.

"I think, Senator, that it is one of the best examples of what an aroused citizenry can do to eliminate a blight on the community that has been there a long time, when they are properly informed and when they have officials who are fearless and willing to do their duty."

He was followed by one of Newport's not-so-fearless officials: Newport Police Chief George Gugel, who had recently been reinstated after a 28-day suspension for refusing to enforce gambling laws.

"Is the Yorkshire Club open, Mr. Gugel?" he was asked.

"To my knowledge, no."

"The committee had some very definite information, Mr. Chairman, that the Yorkshire Club was opened just recently, just a few days ago," the committee's counsel said. "Have you any idea on that Mr. Gugel?"

The chief shifted, looked around and finally insisted that his men checked it regularly and it was closed. But he couldn't offer any records to back it up. He admitted he had known Red Masterson for 25 years.

As Gugel recited the gambling places in Newport—Yorkshire Club, Glen Rendezvous, Merchants Club, Flamingo Club—Senator Kefauver interrupted, looking directly at the man seated next to the chief: "Excuse me, sir, what is your name?"

"Charles E. Lester, lawyer."

"You are an attorney, from Newport?"

"Of Newport."

"Representing Chief Gugel?"

"Yes sir."

The questioning turned back to Gugel: "You were chief of police there for five years?"

"Yes, sir."

"And you didn't know that there was gambling going on in these places?"

"I told you I had never visited them."

"Are you going to sit here and say you were too busy to find out if there was gambling in these places?"

"Objection," Lester shouted. He was overruled.

Kefauver said, "The question was whether he knows that the Cincinnati papers ran advertisements as to the gambling places open for business in Newport, which is a fair question, and the witness will be called to answer."

Gugel replied, "I never read them."

Finally, Chief Counsel Rudolph Halley asked, "Are you the only man in that entire vicinity who didn't know that any taxi driver could take you to a selection of five or six gambling joints?"

"We object," Lester shouted again.

As Lester and Halley argued back and forth, Kefauver cut in: "Well, Mr. Lester, I think this is such a flagrant situation. The chief may have a number of explanations why these places weren't closed, which might be reasonable, but I think it is utterly flagrant and contemptuous for him to sit there and say he didn't know."

"Contemptuous of whom?" Lester fired back.

"Of this committee."

"He is not accountable to this committee."

"He certainly is."

"For what?"

"For telling the truth," Halley said.

Halley turned back to Gugel and asked if he would be surprised to discover gambling in Newport. The chief said yes, he would be.

From there it devolved to comedy. "Do you think anybody with that little knowledge of conditions in his own area is competent to be chief of police?"

"Yes, that is possible," Gugel nodded.

Lester interjected, "The answer is that *he is* the chief."

Asked about Newport's new reform council, Gugel said, "Well, their slogan was 'Clean up but not close up."

"Clean up what?"

"Well, I didn't know. That was their slogan... It wasn't mine, sir."

Kefauver said, "Let the record show that he has 1,733 arrests in 1950 and that 41 of them were for gambling and 518 for violation of road and driving laws."

That devastating arithmetic was only part of the story. The crime statistics for 1950 in Newport showed six homicides in a city of 32,000, which was nearly four times the national rate of five per 100,000. Although holdups and beatings were routine, only 12 aggravated assaults and 11 robberies were recorded by police. In a wide-open town where conventioneers came to soak up the wild side of Newport's high-octane nightlife, there were no arrests for drunkenness, only one liquor violation and a mere 44 arrests for prostitution. The biggest category of arrests was disorderly conduct, at 762.

The numbers described a lawless town where bust-out dives outnumbered gambling arrests and there were a dozen hookers for every prostitute who went to court; where beat cops ignored assaults, beatings and an alarming murder rate, choosing instead to book gangsters and their hapless victims on the misdemeanor charge of disorderly conduct.

Rent-a-cops for the mob.

Halley said he had personally found plenty of wide-open gambling on a visit to Newport, and had then sent a letter to Gugel listing dozens of names and addresses involved in an elaborate illegal bookmaking operation in Newport. Gugel claimed he knew nothing about it.

"You got this letter and never replied to it?" Kefauver asked.

"I turned it over to Detective Chief Donnelly."

"What did you do about this?"

"I say I don't know whether it was answered or not."

As the Senators leaned in, hands cupping chins, eyebrows raised in disbelief, Lester and Gugel produced a memo of a meeting. It claimed that the city manager had told Gugel and his chief detective that they should leave the mob clubs alone and only raid the ones run by "local talent," as Lester put it.

But when asked to hand over a copy of the memo, Gugel balked and said he would send a copy when he got back to Newport. It wound up like the reply to Halley's letter—unsent, "misplaced" in the papers that littered the chief's office.

Rhoads was called back to the stand, still under oath, and said, "The statement made in the (chief's) memorandum is absolutely untrue."

The senators and the crowd of reporters in the back of the room shook their heads and rolled their eyes. The Newport police chief had just accused his own city manager of lying under oath about protecting the syndicate. And the city manager replied by calling his own police chief a liar.

The senators' capacity for surprise had already been stretched to the limit by weeks remarkably weak memories and missing records concerning men called "Chinkie," "Little Augie," "Cappy," "The Waiter," "Big Owl" and "Cutcher Headoff."

They had been asked to believe doctor's notes about sudden gallbladder surgery, ulcerative colitis and that old gangland subpoena side-effect, angina, all sent by mobsters with stage fright.

In this case, there was no doubt who the five senators believed. And it was not the Newport police chief. They would have sooner believed it if Detroit's police chief told them he had never seen or heard about automobiles.

'I never got no letter'

City Manager Rhoads submitted exhibits showing repeated letters ordering Gugel to enforce the law, reprimanding him for refusing to do his job, and finally suspending him. He got the last word: "Chief Gugel knows quite well that every order that has been given to him has been to enforce the law, period."

The committee moved on to hear underworld and law-enforcement witnesses from Toledo, then adjourned and moved their road show to New Orleans and then Detroit.

The following summer, after returning to Washington, they circled back to take another look at Kentucky and brought Chief Gugel in for another entertaining session of creative ignorance and selective myopia.

But first they interviewed Lookout Club owner Jimmy Brink, who was accompanied by three lawyers, including Daniel Davies and an attorney who was there to represent the Beverly Hills Country Club.

Brink dodged and weaved and stalled and evaded but was finally forced to admit that he and several partners had paid the Cleveland Syndicate almost $35,000 to buy back the Lookout House because the mobsters said "they were washed out of it" and "no longer needed to be there."

The same crime bosses who muscled Brink out just a few years before were losing interest in Northern Kentucky.

Business was "very poor" since gambling was shut down early in 1950, Brink explained. Like nearly all other Newport witnesses, he insisted there was no gambling in Newport in 1951.

Then Senate staffer Lawrence Goddard testified about his visit to Newport on June 1, 1951. He found wide-open gambling at several clubs in Newport:

"I observed at least two men whom we shall describe as heavies, that is what they are commonly known as, big, burly men, who stand at a door that would be more or less the first entrance, and then the gambling casino itself, which is usually off to one side from the bar, there would be at least one man standing immediately outside the door there."

He saw 250 gamblers in one club, a mix of men and women crowded around the tables.

Chief Gugel said he had men stationed outside all of the leading clubs to report gambling. And then, suddenly, he remembered he *had* seen gambling in Newport, but only before 1950.

After Gugel's comic testimony the previous year, Kefauver sent the chief a letter urging him to resign.

"Did you ever make public a letter sent to you by (Senator Kefauver) suggesting that you resign?" he was asked.

"I never got no letter."

"Didn't you receive a letter?" the committee counsel pressed.

"No sir."

"Are you sure about that?"

"I would have to go through my papers down there to look, because if I did, I didn't pay much attention to it."

"You did not *pay attention* to it?"

"Well, I am saying, I did not resign."

The committee then asked City Manager Rhoads what had been done about Gugel since they testified the first time: "What has happened in your community since the middle of January?"

The answer was "not much." Rhoads said he had no confidence in Gugel, and had to work around him through subordinates, but was unable to remove him because of civil service rules.

Then Rhoads was confronted and forced to admit that his law office was in the Newport Finance Building, mob headquarters for betting wires. But like Gugel, he insisted there was no gambling in the building.

Thiem song

Newport Police Detective Sergeant Jack Thiem disagreed: "First of all, there is gambling in the Newport Finance Building, and there always has been and there is right now."

Thiem described an attempted raid there. "It was May of 1950. I had the city police judge and prosecutor's office with me, as I was swearing out the warrant, and the prosecutor excused himself and went into Mr. Rhoads' office, and within a few minutes Mr. Benton, the owner of that building, came to the prosecutor's office and grabbed me by the arm and pulled me outside and asked me what I was trying to do to him. I told him I was attempting to raid them, the (gambling front) Bobben Realty Co.

"He said for me to stall and I says, 'I don't have to stall, the prosecutor is doing that.' With that he ran into the manager's office and after some time I got my warrant and I went to the Finance Building and the place was closed down."

"Who told you to stall?"

"Mr. Benton, owner of the building."

"Who is he?"

"He is the senior member of Benton, Benton & Ludeki, the firm that Mr. Rhoads is a member of."

The Senators took a surprised second look at the "admirable" Mr. Rhoads whom they had lavished with praise for his valiant attempt to tame Newport.

Sergeant Thiem was taking no prisoners.

"Sir," he told the senators, "all you have to do is call the Bobben Realty Co. by its telephone number advertised in the telephone book, and they will answer it. You hear the results over the phone."

"You have reason to believe that it's in operation and that a person can place bets and get results over the phone from there?"

"Yes sir."

On another attempted raid, Thiem said, the city manager's secretary called ahead to alert the gamblers that Thiem and his squad were on their way.

After Thiem's explosive testimony, various Newport city officials scrambled to change the subject. Rhoads demanded the right to reply. He said Thiem's testimony was "absurd," and accused Thiem of trying to cut deals with gangsters. "Sergeant Thiem—I am going to make this blunt—is not sincere, he has never been sincere in his efforts."

As Rhoads and his lawyers continued to bluster and demand time for statements, the chairman gaveled the hearing closed. They had heard enough about Newport and its lying, finger-pointing, crooked politicians, lawyers and police.

On the following July 23, the Kefauver Committee met again to discuss its concerns about Kentucky. To clear the air, they brought in as their first witness W. Sharon Florer, the Covington insurance and real estate salesman who was leader of the Kenton County Protestant Association.

"We began our campaign to get law enforcement as far back as 1946," he testified. "For years and years this thing just mushroomed without much being said about it, and it was at this time that we began to call attention of the people to see just what was taking place in the community."

He described their first victory: The disbarment of the county attorney, Ulie Howard, who had refused to enforce gambling laws for 20 years.

Florer told the committee that a local judge had estimated that 80 percent of cases involving family breakdown were caused by gambling and related drinking. Florer said the judge had been shocked by "the number of cases to come before him for nonsupport and domestic trouble that can be attributed to the gambling situation, where husbands lose their paychecks in slot machines or racehorses or something like that."

He described repeated efforts to get cooperation from police, prosecutors and judges. They would nod and agree to help, then do nothing. The gambling, prostitution, crime and corruption continued.

After his organization subpoenaed various underworld bosses, things got scary, he testified. "A lot of heat and tension was aroused and I was receiving many threats over the telephone to the point where it got so bad that they would call me up at night. They would sound like crackpots around saloons. It sounded to me like they might have been drinking a little bit and they thought they should do something about it ... I had these calls where they were going to get me. They were going to run me over. I was being trailed. They were going to get my youngster. Our house was going to be burned down, and all these things.

"Then it was not too long ago that a very nasty incident happened where five whisky bottles full of bad stuff and also a lot of—I don't know how to call—were thrown up on my porch, thrown into my door and just missed coming into my living room."

Florer said local talent and the syndicate "are evidently so entwined and so cooperative with each other."

"It's our No. 1 industry," he said. "We hope that the day will soon come when we can get somebody to enforce the law. We are at our rope's end in Northern Kentucky with the present officials. There is no doubt about that." He added, "I don't know how far the (mob) control goes in Kenton County, but it is certainly well enough that we can get nowhere."

As Florer finished, Kefauver offered a compliment: "He certainly deserves to be highly commended as a good citizen who, in the face of terrific odds, is trying to do something about a bad situation."

2.

Gambling: Refuge of Thugs

Just "how far" organized crime influence extended was vividly underscored later the same day when Leonard Connor, sergeant at arms for the Kentucky Senate, was forced to admit under oath that he was the owner of the Turf Club in Latonia, where he had been operating slots and taking bets for illegal gambling since 1936. His "wire" that delivered race results cost $28 a week. It was delivered through Cincinnati by Cleveland gangster "Mushy" Wexler, a brother-in-law of Sam "Game Boy" Miller. Miller was a frequent visitor to Newport and the Beverly Hills Country Club as a lieutenant of Cleveland Four principal Lou Rothkopf, aka "Lou Rhody."

"Your operation was against the law, was it not?" the committee asked.

"It probably is, in some people's mind—according to the law it is," said Connor, who also served on the state's election board.

"According to the law it is?"

"Yes, but you have to get caught first."

William Wise, the commonwealth attorney for Campbell County, was brought in. He was informed that the Beverly Hills Country Club annual report showed "the money wheels took in $70,000; chuck(a-luck), $7,000; blackjack, $51,000; craps and others, $244,000... and the slot machines took in $69,000."

Would that merit a grand jury investigation of the owners? "Do you have anything to say about that?"

Wise replied, "The only thing I can say is that the figures are to me fabulous and the names of the (owners) you have mentioned I have never heard before."

After six years as prosecutor for Campbell County, Wise had never heard of Sam Tucker, Moe Dalitz, Morris Kleinman, Lou Rothkopf,

Jimmy Brink, John Croft... all well known in Newport.

Newport City Manager Malcolm Rhoads made a third appearance to clear his name. He claimed great progress—which mainly consisted of the arrests of two men he called "Big Porky" and "Little Porky." He was asked about the "profit sharing plan" offered by the Cleveland syndicate to a Newport city commissioner.

Rhoads said, "I have had suggestions made that there could be a lot of money to be made."

He was asked to describe it.

"It probably wasn't more than a week or two after becoming city manager, I received a call, and this particular person went ahead to say that if I would let things alone that they would be willing to pay a thousand dollars a week for letting them operate."

In today's dollars that would be $10,000 a week.

"I turned it down," he said. "Except, then began the second phase of their attempts. The first phase of it is an attempt to buy what they want. Failing to do that, the next step is to harass and to bluff and try to push you around."

"How do they do that?"

"They do that by calling your home and threatening your family," he said.

When he tried to fire the police chief for dereliction of duty, he said, corrupt lawyers, court officials and city leaders retaliated. "They put me on trial. They tried to do everything they could to embarrass me in a public hearing... Personal matters were brought into the hearing, things that were so obviously attempts to intimidate."

He said he got phone calls, such as, "If you don't lay off gambling, one of your children will be run over in the street." He said his family was torn up, his wife was harassed by anonymous calls, sometimes in the middle of the night. "I have gone through, I guess, about as much as any man could have in the last two years."

"I remember on one occasion, Senator, when Gugel's (suspension) trial was in progress, they brought a woman in and stood her up in front of where I was testifying and asked if I knew her. Now, she never opened her mouth at any time. But the insinuation was there. I have tried to find out where she is and who she is. I have even had detectives trying to locate her... but she never showed up and, of course, they never intended for her to show up... That is the type of things they will stoop to."

"Who brought the woman in?" Kefauver asked.

"The attorney for Chief Gugel... Lester, Charles Lester."

"He is the same attorney that represents the gamblers?"

"Oh, yes. Yes."

Rhoads was a man caught in a sticky spider web, whose struggles only made it worse. He was working for a law firm linked to the mob. But when he threatened the crooked police chief, the mob tangled him up in threats and accusations, spun by Charles Lester.

Bodies that bobbed to the surface of the Ohio River, or never were found, were all the warning he needed of what could happen if he went too far. Meanwhile, whatever pride, integrity and faith he had in justice was being sucked dry.

Once again, the senators had to reevaluate the Newport city manager. Kefauver was sympathetic. "Now, Mr. Rhoads, I am going to risk taking a shot at sizing a man up. In my opinion, there have been some things brought against you here, but you look like an honest, forthright man, and I believe you are conscientiously and correspondingly trying to do a good job. I hope I am never proven wrong."

"Thank you, Senator. I am sure you won't be," Rhoads said.

"I wish I could say that about Chief Gugel," Kefauver added, "but I cannot."

3.
Mistress to the Mob

Virginia Hill lived a glamorous life as the party girl for Moe Dalitz, Bugsy Siegel and other gangsters. Her appearance at the Kefauver hearings was a national sensation. As she left she told the press, "I hope the atom bomb falls on every one of you."

Senator Charles Tobey could have played a politician in a Marx Brothers movie. He was balding and overweight, buttoned up as tight as a parson's collar in his three-piece suit, with rimless eyeglasses that made him look like a stern high school principal or an ill-tempered church deacon.

But when he preached to mobsters, calling down the wrath of God and almighty justice, he spoke for many Americans.

"Lucky Luciano is a moral pervert, scum of the earth," he railed against Luciano's gangster friend Moe Sedway during a hearing in Los Angeles. "A farmer in my state of New Hampshire who makes $2,000 a year is richer than you because he has peace of mind and can look everybody in the eye."

Sedway took umbrage. Being a gangster "is harder work than you think," he said.

The press laughed, but Senator Tobey was not amused. He demanded that Sedway show some gesture of shame, a token of regret or remorse.

"I would not do it over again," Sedway finally conceded. "Look at what I got out of it. Ulcers and heart problems. I would not want my children to do it over again."

Tobey had the last word. Sedway and his underworld thugs were "a cancer spot on the body politic," he said.

The scolding was almost enough to make viewers feel sorry for Sedway. But then the rest of the story came out. He was vice president of the Flamingo Hotel in Las Vegas. And he did not get to the top of that casino ladder by accident. He was "promoted" by being the first to seize control from the cooling corpse of Bugsy Siegel on the night Siegel was killed. It was survival of the quickest. Siegel was plotting to kill Sedway when he was "removed" instead.

Siegel was shot through the head on June 20, 1947, with a .30 caliber M-1 rifle fired through an open window at his girlfriend's swank Los Angeles home in Beverly Hills.

The hit had apparently been arranged with help from his girlfriend, Virginia Hill, who was conveniently out of the country when Siegel was murdered. Or perhaps she had only been warned to stay away.

Siegel had been the mob's Cortez in Vegas, opening the El Dorado of legal casino gambling, where the streets were paved in gold. He started with the Flamingo Hotel, which staked the claim for an organized crime empire in Nevada. Siegel was handsome, a sharp-dressed man with movieland charisma. Bugsy glamorized gangsters as he socialized in Hollywood with Clark Gable, George Raft and other stars, who enjoyed being seen with a genuine mobster they only played on the screen.

Benjamin Siegel got his nickname "Bugsy" by being more volatile than nitro glycerin on a bumpy road. As part of New York City's Meyer Lansky gang, he was violent and famously unpredictable. That made him a natural choice as a founder for Lansky's hit squad that became known as Murder Incorporated, which took credit for more than 400 killings by 1940.

As the Kefauver hearings followed the trail from the Flamingo to Seigel and his girlfriend in Beverly Hills, public anticipation pushed the Nielsen television ratings off the charts for the live testimony of Virginia Hill. It was the "sensation of the country."

She came in wearing a mink stole and a saucy black hat as big as a Cadillac hubcap, pulled down coyly with one hand to shield her face from a throng of bug-eyed photographers. She could have been a Hollywood extra or a Vegas showgirl. But she was "Mistress to the mob," the newsreels said. The "Brunette Beauty."

In grainy black-and-white Movietone News film, she is introduced as the "fabulous sweetheart of the notorious underworld figure" as she takes a seat almost within arm's reach of the gathered Kefauver Committee. She seems to have great fun sassing the stuffy senators, barely able to suppress a smile. Before the first question is asked, she interrupts to show them who's in charge.

"Make them quit doing that," she says as photographers huddle around her like Peeping Toms outside a stag show, cameras popping and flashing like Fourth of July fireworks.

"All right, let's not flash any more bulbs," Senator Kefauver nods.

"I'll throw something at them in a minute. I hate those things," she pouts.

The flashbulbs continue for several more minutes until Kefauver says, "Now boys, let's get the picture-making over with." The witness, he says, "is right nervous."

She looks about as nervous as a fifth of bourbon.

As the questioning resumed, she told the gathered crowd that she ran away from home in Alabama at age 17 and went to work in Chicago, where "the men I was around that gave me things were not gangsters or racketeers or whatever you call these other people. The only time I ever got anything from them was going out and having fun, and maybe a few presents. But I happened to go with other fellows. And for years I have been going to Mexico. I went with fellows down there. And like a lot of girls that they got, (they were) giving me things and bought me everything I want. And then when I was with Ben, he bought me everything."

She seemed surprised that anyone would be interested in her dull story of an ordinary gangster girl. In her world, she was just another party girl who was passed around by mob "fellows" that included Moe Dalitz and Joe Adonis before Siegel. She had houses in Florida and Beverly Hills, furs, diamonds, expensive cars, a bottomless bankroll to bet at racetracks, gambling in glamorous nightclubs, a penthouse at the Flamingo Hotel in Las Vegas...

"I was just going out and having fun, and maybe they gave me a few presents. The men I was around would give me anything I wanted. He gave me a house in Florida and some money, I guess," she said of Siegel.

When Siegel found out she was going to Paris, he told her she couldn't go because, "He didn't like this boy that I knew in France," she said. "So then, later on, I had a big fight with him because I hit a girl in the Flamingo and he told me I wasn't a lady. We got in a big fight. I had been drinking and I left, and I went to Paris when I was mad."

What about rumors that he was in trouble with his gangster friends?

"All I know, he was worried about the hotel. I hated the place, and I told him why didn't he leave it and get away from it because it was making him a nervous wreck."

She described Siegel waiting for the ax to fall, pacing the floor at night, muttering that he had "lost," that everything was upside down.

Asked where all the furs, houses, diamonds and cash came from, she insisted, "I don't know anything about anybody."

She added: "Those people who are supposed to be racketeers (said) the worst possible thing I could do (was) that people talk too much."

She was sharp-tongued and flirty with a hint of a Southern Belle—just what was needed to add the missing spark to the Kefauver Hearings high-octane mix of money and violence: sex.

Asked if she had been given anything by New York crime boss Frank Costello, she snapped, "No!" She made it sound like a curse.

Perhaps she had heard like many others that the New York mob had ordered the hit on Siegel during a summit in Havana, because Siegel had "borrowed" too much of their money and he was threatening to murder Lansky's man in Vegas, Moe Sedway.

On her way out of the courthouse, as she fought her way through the scrum of reporters and photographers, she slapped a female reporter in the face and cursed the press. "I hope the atom bomb falls on every one of you," she barked as she climbed into a big black car.

"She is absolutely a screwball," said Barney Ruditsky, a former detective from the New York City Police Gangster Squad who had moved to Los Angeles to become a private detective and collect debts for Siegel and others. "I have met her and I have known her," he testified. "I think she is psychopathic."

Ruditsky said Hill called him one night and told him to come over immediately. When he arrived he found mobsters Al Smiley and Swifty Morgan having dinner. "She was there in a bathing suit and had a gun in her hand. She said, 'I am going to kill everybody in the house, the maid, and the Chinese butler, and everybody.' She said, 'They have been stealing and robbing me.' Well, looking at the woman, when you see her, you know she is definite—definitely a mental case. That was my opinion of her."

4.
Law of the Jungle

Something like alchemy happened when the hot lights were turned on and the Kefauver Committee went live on television, coast to coast. The alloy of politics, crime and entertainment was stronger than any of the elements alone. Outside of staged, jumpy newsreel clips, Americans had never seen their highest elected leaders actually working. And it was pure gold to the networks and the senators.

Tobey's angry-old-man rants sound in retrospect like scandalized parents shaking their fingers at Elvis Presley for causing the "moral decline of our youth." He was a Republican running for reelection, after all, and most of America was worried about all those young "rebels without a cause." But connecting the dots between brazen organized crime "hoods" and juvenile delinquency, alcoholism, broken families, dropouts, poverty and disrespect for authority was not such a reach.

Tobey was onto something that many Americans sensed.

It was time to reconsider: Maybe the rebellion against oppressive government during Prohibition had gone too far. In their haste to chase Uncle Sam's temperance police out of their homes, restaurants and nightclubs, good people might have overreacted. Their tolerance for bootlegging also laid out the welcome mat for gambling, prostitution, protection rackets, beatings, political corruption, bribery and murder.

Corruption had spread like a social gangrene that made parts of the public body rot and stink. Amputation would be painful. Americans might lose their adult playgrounds in Hot Springs and Newport, but the alternative looked much worse.

Even the mobsters unconsciously revealed their own shame by creating aliases for themselves, sometimes in the dozens, as if they hoped to protect the "honor" of their family names by hiding from the ugly things they did.

In city after city, people began to see just how far that "cancer spot" described by Senator Tobey had spread. Cincinnati's Chamber of Commerce might wink and boast about Newport's attractions to lure conventions; after all, it was safely contained across the river in Newport and Covington, like porn under the mattress or that hidden bottle in the garage. But lawlessness was like dye in the water. It tainted everything with the dark stain of cynicism.

Cops were crooked. Judges were bought. Politicians took bribes. Everybody knew it and there was nothing anyone could do about it. The Kefauver hearings showed that the tentacles of corruption reached to governors and ambassadors and probably into the White House.

The "wise guys" were in the syndicate. Only chumps played it straight and honest. Why not cheat the customer? Why not lift a few dollars out of the till when the boss wasn't looking? Why not shoplift a magazine or a pair of stockings? Why not skim off the top, put a thumb on the scale and cut corners? Wasn't everyone doing that? Look at those gangsters in their tailored suits and polished Cadillacs, with pretty dancers and cute bargirls on their arms, hanging out in those carpet joints with stars like Frank Sinatra and Dean Martin and Jean Harlow. Why not just take it if you want it?

Radio personality Walter Winchell watched gangsters smirk and laugh at "square" America and said, "When the chic Virginia Hill unfolded her amazing life story, many a young girl must have wondered: Who really knows best? Mother or Virginia Hill? After doing all the things called wrong, there she was on top of the world."

The "Mob Mistress" would kill herself with an overdose of pills a few years later, but in 1951 she seemed to have the world on a string.

So as it turned out, it was not such a reach from hip-thrusting Elvis to Mick Jagger's *Sympathy for the Devil*. It was only a few blocks from the *Asphalt Jungle* to burning draft cards, riots and burning cities. As late as the early 1960s, pervasive criminal corruption was no exaggeration. As America would find out in 1963, it was far more dangerous than anyone thought.

The Detroit race riots of 1967 were triggered by a police raid on a "blind pig"—the local version of a "bust-out joint." Narcotics, numbers rackets and prostitution in black neighborhoods were supplied and managed by the mob, usually with help from crooked cops on the take. When Detroit's inner-city blacks rioted against the police, how much of their anger was an effort to shake off the unseen hand of organized crime that held them down in poverty and hopelessness? Connecting the dots, from the distance of 50 years later, is not so hard after all.

The Kefauver Committee huddles before a hearing. Senator Charles Tobey is at left; Kefauver is second from right. Their tenacious chief counsel, Rudolph Halley is at the rear. Kenton County Library archive

But in 1951, the backlash on Kefauver was vicious. The committee members and their staff were threatened, slandered, mocked and stonewalled. When hearings traced bookmaking to Florida Governor Fuller Warren, the governor attacked Kefauver as "an ambition-crazed Caesar who is trying desperately and futilely" to run for president.

His own party turned on Kefauver because so many of the corrupt urban politicians he exposed were Democrats, who were quickly attacked by Republicans. The Senate Majority Leader, Illinois Democrat Scott Lucas, lost re-election because of the underworld corruption exposed in Chicago. On his way out, Lucas tried to yank the plug on the Kefauver hearings. He failed.

Hearst Newspapers Editor Jack Lait, a leading national columnist who had covered Al Capone's Chicago, wrote that Kefauver was "shattered" when he discovered how deep the mob had reached into his Democratic Party.

"He was called on the carpet. He was let in on the tie-ups between the big mobsters in New York, Chicago, Kansas City, Miami, Cleveland, St. Louis and other Democratic centers ... the traffickers in gambling, dope, vice, labor, dry-state bootlegging and commercial monopolies..."

"Every effort has been made to keep Kefauver concentrated on gambling."

But it did not exactly work out that way. Soon mob connections were followed to the governor of New York and to AT&T, which was paid a fortune to service betting wires. The lanky senator from Tennessee would not flinch in his promise to leave "no stone unturned, no holds barred, right down the middle of the road, let the chips fall where they may."

He often had to explain to angry citizens that local enforcement was beyond his authority in the Senate. The FBI at the time, what there was of it, struggled with its own corruption hangover from bribery during Prohibition. FBI Director J. Edgar Hoover brushed off the Kefauver hearings and insisted organized crime was a myth. He insisted there was no such thing.

So it was up to local leaders to "struggle out from under the rule of the law of the jungle," Kefauver said.

His goal was to create "a national crusade, a great debating forum, an arouser of public opinion on the state of the nation's morals."

He did that by opening up a vein in what he called "the lifeblood of organized crime," illegal gambling.

Kefauver and his team of four senators forged on. Senators Herbert O'Conner from Maryland, Lester Hunt of Wyoming, Alexander Wiley from Wisconsin and Charles Tobey of New Hampshire followed Kefauver and his staff of lawyers and investigators from town to town, city to city. They crossed the country on trains, stopping to unpack their bags in yet another hotel room, then bang the gavel to start another hearing in another federal courthouse with tall windows that let the light shine in on the darkest corners of the underworld.

When their one-year authorization for the investigation expired, casinos in Northern Kentucky celebrated with advertisements and handbills that announced they would throw a party to re-open for business the same day the Kefauver Committee turned off the TV lights.

It was premature. Senator Tobey persuaded the Senate to extend the investigation into 1952. The casinos had to call off the party.

The senators had discovered that they had an almost magical Excalibur to wield: Their "sword in the stone" was a gavel, enchanted by Merlyn's mesmerizing spell: Television.

5.

The Prime Minister of Crime

**New York underworld boss Frank Costello demanded that
TV cameras could not show his face, but his nervous hands were the
"tell" that he lied extravagantly during the Kefauver hearings. He
finally walked out in contempt but his gravelly whisper left behind an
indelible impression that became a model for *The Godfather*.**

Charles Lester sat in his quiet, comfortable office on a Tuesday
afternoon, March 13, 1951. He stared at the new television installed
on a chrome stand across from his desk, then turned the knob and
watched a little dot of light glow, expand and blossom across the screen
like a tiny atom bomb. The black-and-white picture showed gray men
in dark suits looking down from a judge's bench in a federal courtroom
in New York City.

"Everybody's sweating," he said to himself as the cameras zoomed in to show Frank Costello's hands clutch and release a damp, crumpled white handkerchief. Now and then one hand would flutter away to wipe his brow, then it would settle back on the desk again like a nervous pigeon, twitching, moving, restless... guilty.

"... Not to my recollection," Costello answered.

The Kefauver Committee's chief counsel Rudy Halley asked another question, something about selling or buying liquor.

"Not that I remember," Costello replied in that reedy voice that always sounded like he had laryngitis.

The man described in melodramatic headlines as "The Prime Minister of Organized Crime" and the "King of the Underworld" wiped his face again. Then the hands returned to the desk and made involuntary jerking movements, like they wanted to get away from the lights and the questions and light up a smoke, tip up a tall glass of scotch or ball up in a fist and punch one of the senators in the face.

Lester thought: You shouldn't have complained about the cameras. That lawyer Wolf may be a big deal in New York, but he played the wrong cards, going on and on about how "I strenuously object on the grounds that Mr. Costello doesn't care to submit himself as a spectacle," and "it would interfere with Mr. Costello testifying properly."

If you don't want them to call you the King of the Underworld, stop acting like one, he thought. You should have known they would figure out a way to get even. They control all those TV cameras with the big Micky Mouse ears. And they're showing full shots of your face in the evening replays anyway. This thing with the hands just makes you look worse. It makes us all look worse.

"I am here to deny under oath and forever silence the false stories and rumors that I was connected with any crime syndicate," Costello said.

Lester laughed out loud.

Everyone was talking about these hearings, everywhere you went. You couldn't get away from it. It was even more awkwardly obvious when the conversations suddenly died whenever Lester entered a room.

And they would all be talking about how Costello had complained that the microphones and the cameras were unfair and bothered him. So someone at NBC got the clever idea to zoom in on the small porch of a desktop, where his hands fiddled with a pair of glasses and squeezed a handkerchief. If Italians talk with their hands, Lester thought, Costello was singing like a mockingbird.

Halley asked him about his various aliases: Castiglia. Hoffman. Severio. Stello. Venti...

"Not that I remember."

"Are you sure you were not in the liquor business at that time?"

"I'm almost positive I wasn't."

Halley was able to pry loose the sensational detail that this completely innocent, blameless businessman kept $50,000 in cash in a strongbox in his house. Now *that* would make the papers, Lester thought. Newsmen never passed up a chance to incite some envy. With what they were paid, no wonder. They thought everybody made more money than newsmen. And they were right.

Next, Halley asked about his net worth, but Costello slammed the door.

"I refuse to answer, it may tend to incriminate me," he replied.

Lester glanced at the newspapers on his desk. They called the broadcasts "the sensation of the nation," "the greatest TV show ever aired." It was bigger than the World Series. There were even block parties to get the whole neighborhood together, mix some drinks and watch "Kefauver Fever."

What was it that some newsreel said about Costello the other night, Lester tried to remember. That's it: "Defiance and categorical contempt."

I hope Moe and the rest of the Cleveland boys are watching this, he thought. They were smart to take a vacation in Mexico and dodge subpoenas for the hearings in Cleveland. Leave it to Dalitz to see the big picture. He had to know they can't dodge the senators forever. But now they had time to watch and learn. If they asked me, I'd tell them not to make the same mistakes of "defiance and categorical contempt."

But they won't listen to me, he thought. They will get a better team of attorneys than Charles E. Lester, Esquire. A Newport gang lawyer was good enough for small-timers, but not for mob royalty such as Dalitz, Kleinman, Tucker and Rothkopf.

A new voice was talking, that angry old coot from New Hampshire.

"It has come to my mind in a flash," Senator Tobey said, that Costello's lies about his criminal record made him eligible to be deported for "naturalization under false statements."

He urged Costello to just come clean. "No man, whether it is Frank Costello or anybody else, need fear God, man or the devil if he tells the truth," said the senator.

Yes, Lester nodded, but Frank Costello fears something worse than God and the devil. His friends.

Tobey continued. "You must have in your mind some things you've done to speak of to your credit as an American citizen. What are they?" he demanded.

There was a pause. Costello seemed to think about it. Then he croaked, "Paid my taxes."

The hearing room broke out in laughter. Costello looked around at the room as if he couldn't decide if he wanted to laugh too, or maybe shoot someone for laughing at him. Score one for our side, Lester thought.

But then it was back to the questions, and Lester could tell by the hands and the voice that Frank was losing his patience. Nobody talked that way to Costello. He was a boss of bosses, in the same crowd with Meyer Lansky, Lucky Luciano, Joe Adonis and Murder Incorporated. Maybe not exactly King of the Underworld. But definitely a Duke of Darkness.

And now here they all were, right on television like an episode of *Dragnet* or *Texaco Star Theater*. Adonis and Costello, testifying almost back to back.

Lester had met Costello at the Beverly Hills Country Club, during one of the Prime Minister's visits to keep an eye on things as the nightclub's "goodwill ambassador." He was soft-spoken, quiet. He mainly listened. But when he spoke in that gravelly voice, almost a whisper, you listened very carefully, because that was usually the last word.

As Lester watched Rudy Halley grilling Costello, he was reminded of how he traded punches with Halley in Cleveland while representing the bumbling Newport Police Chief George Gugel. Next time I will bring a better client, he thought. I hope we get a rematch.

The senate's prosecutor was like a mosquito in your bedroom, buzzing around in your ear. You never knew where he was coming from or where he would land until he stung you. No wonder Frank's hands were itchy. Lester's attention was drawn back to the hearings on TV.

Someone had mentioned the Beverly Hills Country Club.

"Is there gambling attached to it?" Halley asked.

"I refuse to answer the question. It might tend to incriminate me."

The back and forth continued. Halley buzzed and stung, Costello twitched and swatted.

"Do you expect this committee to believe that story, Mr. Costello?" Halley asked.

"I am not expecting you to believe anything. I knew you weren't going to believe anything when I first come here. I have been prejudged."

Halley buzzed away and landed again on the money question.

"What is your net worth today?"

"I refuse to answer that question."

"On what ground."

"I am going to exercise my rights that it might incriminate me."

Lester turned off the TV. Nothing to see here, folks.

Categorical contempt

The next day, Lester shook hands with Dan Davies as they settled in to watch Frank Costello return for a fourth day.

"I think they came back so his New York lawyer could try to repair the damage," Lester said, making "New York lawyer" sound like a sarcastic insult.

"Too late," Davies nodded. "Hey, nice picture on your new set. Where'd you get it?"

"Johnny TV Peluso's shop. He owed me for some legal work."

"What does it go for retail?"

"Shhh," Lester said, holding up a finger. "I want to hear this."

They fell silent as George Wolf, Costello's lawyer, made a statement for the record to the Kefauver Committee.

"... they did not televise his face but they did televise the hands and the *movement of the hands..."*

"Sounds like Frank is unhappy," said Davies.

"...during the entire proceeding, powerful, blinding klieg lights were focused on the witness and counsel. During all of this time, numerous cameras were audibly grinding, hordes of photographers were constantly roving about the room, standing on chairs and other elevated portions of the room, as they are just at this moment, placing themselves directly in front of the witness, as they are at this moment, dashing about the room, brushing by the witness, taking close-up pictures by flashbulbs, at various angles. Numerous reporters crowded into the room, in such close proximity to the witness that they actually frequently brushed against him. The room was intensely hot, and without proper ventilation..."

"Imagine that," Davies said, shaking his head with a smile. "Some common peasant of the press actually brushed the hem of the King of the Underworld. Doesn't this moron know how that sounds to Jane Potroast and Jimmy Janitor?"

"Yeah, he's just making it worse," Lester agreed. "That horse's ass is out of the barn. I've never seen Frank Costello sweat. I don't think anyone has until this. And now everyone saw it."

"The blinding lights, the heat and the incessant interruptions made it impossible for this witness to properly concentrate on the questions..."

The phone rang and Lester picked it up, "Charles Lester, Esquire."

Davies watched Lester smile.

"Not guilty?" he spoke into the phone. "You're one-hundred percent certain that it will go that way? Nothing to worry about? No last-minute seizures of conscience?"

He nodded as he got the answer he wanted and smiled again, throwing a wink at Davies as he spoke into the phone. "All right, I'll send someone by with your consulting fees. Look, I gotta go, I'm watching the circus in New York... Yeah, not good for Frank. Or his lawyer, I think. But Virginia was hotter than a floorshow at the Tropicana."

As he hung up the phone, Davies asked, "Our Wilder Marshal is in the clear?"

"Big Jim is back in business," Lester said with a wink.

They went back to the hearings. Kefauver was talking.

"If the lights bother Mr. Costello, I hope you will say so and we will turn them off him. And if he does not want to have his hands televised—well, I will leave that to you, sir."

"Senator, they do bother me. I am in no condition to testify."

"You refuse to testify further?"

"Absolutely."

"You ask questions, Mr. Halley and we will see. Now just a moment, let us not have the television now on any part of Mr. Costello..."

"Here we go," Davies said. "It looks like Frank's had enough."

"Mr. Halley, am I a defendant in this courtroom?"

"No."

"Am I under arrest?"

"No."

"Then I am walking out."

"I think he's going to do it," Lester agreed.

Davies chuckled and slapped his fat knee.

On the little TV screen, Costello abruptly stood up as if his train was boarding, picked up his coat, turned his back on the crowd and the cameras and the senators and all the spectators who crowded into the courtroom... and walked out.

The room erupted in a clamor of raised voices and popping flashbulbs. Halley shouted for order and Kefauver banged his gavel. The Chairman's words came in snatches.

"...but to have anybody attempt to defy the committee... Mr. Costello is trying... will use every recourse in our command to see that he is brought to contempt and he is arrested ... Is that understood?"

Costello was not listening. He had already left the courtroom, exiting the back way through the judges' chambers, trailed by his lawyer who followed in his wake the way a remora swims after a shark.

"Do you think they can make a contempt charge stick?" Davies asked.

"Probably not," Lester said. "He voluntarily came to the hearing, told them he had laryngitis and showed them a doctor's note to back it up.

No court will enforce contempt for that."

Lester was right. Costello spent less time in jail than George Gugel spent visiting casinos. The New York mafioso won the battle at the federal courthouse that day. But in the court of public opinion, the verdict was "guilty."

The *New York Post* said his "illness" was all in his head: It was "mental anguish ... in the cards for Costello from the moment that he began his faceless act. For the first time since his rise to power he was caught in a corner. He was apparently unable to put in a 'fix.' He was being trapped in his own evasions and nobody was coming to his rescue. The bigshot was in trouble. So he ran."

6.
'I've Never Had Any Publicity'

Cleveland Four boss and former Purple Gang leader Moe Dalitz waits his turn for testimony at the hearings that spread 'Kefauver Fever' in TV Land. He was charming, smooth and as honest as loaded dice.
Kenton County Library archive

"Hard times make hard people," Moe Dalitz liked to say.

Like nearly everything else the public knew about him—which was not much—it was cleverly misleading.

Hollywood gangsters were bad guys in the movies, but they nearly always had the same motivation delivered by Scarlett O'Hara in *Gone with the Wind*. Silhouetted against a dramatic orange sky she swore, "As God is my witness, I will never be hungry again."

And that was the script for gangsters. They were dirty-faced street orphans of the Depression, stealing apples to feed their kid sister who had polio, picking the pockets of drunks and "swells," all the time gradually, step-by-step, drifting into more serious trouble until they got killed, thrown in prison or were smart enough to work their way up to become junior syndicate executives and mob bosses in organized crime.

Moe Dalitz was none of that. He grew up in a comfortable family. His father and uncles, Jewish immigrants from Russia, owned and ran a large laundry business in Detroit, then expanded with the Varsity Laundry in Ann Arbor that catered to students, faculty and staff at the University of Michigan.

Moe always kept one hand in the laundry business. "I have been in that business all my life, practically," he told the Kefauver Committee.

But that was only the part he wanted them to see—the quarter inch of shirt-cuff showing at the end of a tailored sleeve. There was a lot more to Moe than what he allowed to be visible. And he never *needed* to resort to crime when he was growing up. It was just in his DNA.

He dropped out of high school and got involved with Detroit's Purple Gang, started by a few of his friends, all teen thugs, dropouts and juvenile delinquents from his Jewish neighborhood. When Michigan voted to go "dry" in 1917, three years before the rest of the nation adopted Prohibition of alcohol, they saw their main chance.

Soon Moe and his pals, including the Levinson Brothers—Ed, Mike and Sleepout Louis—were running booze across the state line in laundry trucks. When Ohio went dry a year later, Moe Dalitz already had a head-start on the bootlegging business, and the Purple Gang soon had a reputation for ruthlessness that even exceeded Al Capone's murdering knuckle-draggers in Chicago. They got into rackets, gambling, bootlegging, extortion, leg-breaking, head-busting and murder.

If a businessman, factory owner, union or newspaper needed to eliminate or intimidate the competition, the Purple Gang was for hire. They launched what became known as the Little Jewish Navy, a fleet of fast boats to run booze from Canada to Detroit. They also built hidden stills on a massive scale.

In 1929 Dalitz moved south into Ohio and soon became the boss of Cleveland, where he was the CEO of a syndicate that rivaled mobs in New York, Chicago, Miami, Kansas City, Boston and Philadelphia.

Senator Kefauver asked him, "You fellows got your start in rum running, didn't you? ... Is that how you got the money to make your original investments?"

"Well, not all of those investments, no," Dalitz replied.

"You did get yourself a pretty good little nest egg out of rum running, didn't you?"

"Well, I didn't inherit any money, Senator."

As the crowd of reporters and spectators laughed at the senator's expense, most probably missed what that remark revealed about Dalitz. He may not have inherited any money, but he could have made a very comfortable living in his family's laundry business. His remark was typically dishonest, but it was also charming and strategic. It contrasted the School of Hard Knocks gangster to the Yale-educated, Ivy League senator—following the Hollywood script.

He was Jimmy Cagney in *Angels with Dirty Faces*, a bad guy with a good heart.

To twist the knife, his lawyer was Yale-educated Charles Carr, a classmate of Kefauver.

It was the kind of thing that set Moe Dalitz apart from the rest of the underworld bosses. He was smart. And not just street smart. He was, in his own way, smarter than the Yale crowd. While others crowded close to see the little TV screens, he saw a bigger picture that would fill a movie screen.

'Fabulous and fantastic'

Moe Dalitz had a big-featured, rubbery face that could change in an instant. In his younger years, pictures show a smile that was engaging and disarmingly innocent. In his final years he had the face he deserved: features so ravaged and bloated they could be a Halloween mask to frighten children.

It's easy to imagine the younger Moe laughing in 1951 as he read a *Miami News* editorial about the Costello testimony.

> "The show is fascinating because it hauls out into the public view a lot of shady and semi-shady characters who are much discussed but seldom seen.

> "Most of them are extremely modest guys and dolls when it comes to personal publicity, and they don't like to have their faces imprinted in the memories of many people.

> "To have these folks come before television cameras and expose their mannerisms and speech to the onlookers is a first-class thrill. The excitement mounts several degrees when you reflect that here before your eyes are the moving images of persons who live dangerously, mingle with other fabulous and fantastic inhabitants of the underworld, and may be bumped off in very picturesque fashion at any minute."

But as Dalitz laughed, he probably learned from that, too. By the time he was brought in to testify under oath in Los Angeles in 1952, the most sensational hearings were over. By watching Frank Costello and the others, he avoided their mistakes. He was friendly and cooperative, up to a point. If it didn't matter, he told the truth. If the truth could get him in trouble, he lied or refused to answer.

And by evading subpoenas to appear in Cleveland the year before, he was now lost in the wash of more colorful mob characters from Los Angeles and Las Vegas.

His low profile paid off. Compared to Bugsy Siegel, Dalitz was a nobody, even though he was probably one of the bosses who ordered the hit on Bugsy.

"Why did you deliberately dodge the committee?" he was asked.

"Well, senator, I, frankly, was just alarmed at the whole thing and all the publicity; I have never had any publicity in the past," he replied.

As their questions explored his ownership of steel companies, laundry companies and casinos including "one of the biggest in the nation," the Beverly Hills Country Club in Northern Kentucky, Dalitz often refused to answer, but the senators were nonetheless impressed. They must have realized they were only brushing snow off the top of the submerged iceberg that was the Moe Dalitz empire.

Kefauver asked, "How do you get by with these operations down in Kentucky, especially, Mr. Dalitz? Gambling is illegal down there, isn't it, and also in Cincinnati? How do you get by with that?"

"Well, I don't know, senator," said Moe, acting just as perplexed. "I don't know if I can answer that intelligently, senator."

"Who do you see for protection?"

"I don't see anybody."

Of course not. Moe Dalitz was the man *other people* came to see for protection. He was the boss of the Midwest, already diversifying into Havana, Miami and the West, where he would soon be known as the "Godfather of Las Vegas."

The record of his interview includes a statement from Virgil Peterson of the Chicago Crime Commission:

"(Dalitz) became the power in Cleveland, Ohio, and anyone who would question it would have to deal with Lucky (Luciano) and (Meyer) Lansky and Bugsy (Siegel)."

The statement accused Dalitz of sending a Pittsburgh hitman to murder Cleveland City Councilman William Potter in 1931, and listed his casinos and nightclubs in Cleveland, Youngstown and Northern Kentucky.

Asked about it, Dalitz closed the door. He invoked his Fifth Amendment rights and refused to answer. He had good reasons to avoid publicity.

Based on testimony from mobster Dixie Davis, the report said Moe's Cleveland Four partner Morris Kleinman was credited with at least 13 murders, and the Purple Gang was responsible for the grisly Miraflores Apartment Massacre in 1927, in which three victims were so riddled with bullets from a Thompson submachine gun that the autopsies could not determine how many times they were shot.

Kleinman went to prison briefly for tax evasion. But over the years, the lawmen never laid a fingerprint on Dalitz. Not even Elliot Ness and his Untouchables. Dalitz was indicted twice early in his career for bootlegging but the charges were dismissed and the records disappeared. He never spent a day or even a night in jail.

And as of 1950, he was the treasurer of the new Desert Inn Hotel in Las Vegas, after investing more than $1 million to finish construction when the project started by Wilbur Clark had stalled.

Again, Moe Dalitz was ahead of everyone.

While mobsters such as Siegel enjoyed press attention, Dalitz stayed deep in the shadows. When Dutch Shultz decided to murder reporters who "knew too much," he was killed to protect the rest of the mob from the backlash. Dalitz was among the first to see how such reckless stupidity would draw more heat.

Moe Dalitz was not as foolish as mobsters in Phoenix who car-bombed *Arizona Republic* Reporter Don Bolles with six sticks of dynamite in 1976 because his stories on organized crime were getting too close. That shocking murder drew a swarm of 38 investigative reporters, who exposed widespread organized crime corruption in the Southwest that pointed to mob boss Kemper Marley. (Marley hired and mentored Jim Hensley, whose liquor distributing business made him one of Arizona's wealthiest men; Hensley's daughter Cindy married U.S. Senator John McCain.)

While other mobsters went to war over ancient tribal and ethnic vendettas, Dalitz united the Italians and the Irish with the Jewish mob. His inner circle included Jews (Kleinman, Lou Rothkopf and the Levinsons); Lithuanian Sam Tucker; the Irishman Thomas McGinty, who got his start busting heads in the Cleveland newspaper wars as circulation manager for the *Plain Dealer*; Italians (Costello, Luciano, Adonis); and various gangsters who flew no ethic flag, such as Red Masterson and "Game Boy" Miller.

While other mobsters transitioned from bootlegging to gambling to prostitution and drugs, following the path popular demand, Dalitz evolved from Purple Gang leader to Cleveland Four kingpin to... revered philanthropist and founding father of Las Vegas.

His final act in Vegas may have been his most amazing performance. It would have made Senator Kefauver's eyes roll like dice in a chuck-a-luck tumbler.

In Las Vegas, Dalitz teamed up with Teamsters Union President Jimmy Hoffa to tap the union's pension fund for loans to finance casinos and luxury hotels. Dalitz sold the Desert Inn to Howard Hughes, then built the Stardust. Along the way he used his wealth, power, connections and influence to start the PGA Tournament of Champions, while he built golf courses, hospitals, shopping malls and... a brand new Moe Dalitz.

He was named Humanitarian of the Year in 1976 by the American Cancer Research Center and Hospital in Las Vegas. He was presented with the Torch of Liberty Award by the Anti-Defamation League of B'nai B'rith by Joan Rivers in 1982.

"Las Vegas used to be just a gambling town. Now we are a resort destination. The Convention Center complements our purpose," he said in 1983 after leading the fundraising campaign.

In 1999, the *Las Vegas Review Journal* published a story that called him one of the city's "priceless" pioneers. Among the quotes:

"I was in awe of meeting him. As far as I'm concerned he was a great man ... Moe's charity is legendary around this town. There has never been a greater influence on this city."

"Moe was always such a gentleman... He gave back to the community."

"Moe almost never complained, but he was feeling down. He said, 'I'll bet your grandpa drank whiskey,' and I said that he did. 'I'm the guy who made the whiskey, and I'm considered the bad guy. When does the time ever come that you're forgiven?' "

But some who knew the dark side of Dalitz were not so forgiving. Ed Reid and Ovid Demaris, authors of *Green Felt Jungle*, were surprised when Dalitz burst into tears during an interview for their book.

From *Green Felt Jungle*:

> "Why, why," he implored, his arms rising in supplication, the tears streaming from his hard little eyes, "why are they persecuting me?"
>
> "Who?" Reid asked.
>
> "Them. All of them! I've fought hoodlums all my life. What are they trying to do to me?"
>
> He was a sanctimonious little mobster from Cleveland. He is still a hoodlum in conscience and mind, but his heart has weakened.

Nonetheless, the story concluded, "His contributions to the growth of Las Vegas are priceless."

Money can't buy everything. But it bought sainthood for Moe Dalitz.

"When I left home it was during Prohibition in Ann Arbor, Michigan, and I went into the liquor business while it was illegal," he told a reporter. "Then when the repeal came along, we went into the casino business in Kentucky and Ohio where it was illegal. I learned everything I know there."

By the time he charmed the cameras at the Kefauver hearings, he had learned everything he needed to know from his sentimental favorite nationally renowned, diamond-studded carpet joint in Northern Kentucky, the Beverly Hills Country Club.

As he moved to Vegas, the Sin City underworld squid followed, slowly disengaging its tentacles and floating away to a better feeding ground.

By the mid-1950s, as dealers and showgirls migrated to jobs at flashier new clubs in Las Vegas, there were so many who boarded flights leaving Cincinnati that they joked about flying "Syndicate Airlines."

Kefauver show cancelled

America's first "reality TV" show came to an end late in the summer of 1952. It was followed a couple of years later by a sequel that was nearly as riveting: the dramatic McCarthy hearings, when Senator Joseph P. McCarthy's anti-communist crusade was finally derailed in a televised Senate showdown.

The Kefauver crew had covered thousands of miles and produced enough testimony give a hernia to an encyclopedia salesman. The hearings had been watched by 30 million viewers, about a third of all voting-age adults.

Some Northern Kentucky gangsters ducked the hearings altogether. Red Masterson dodged a subpoena by having surgery. Beverly Hills Country Club partner John Croft was a no-show, and got away with a contempt charge that was not enforced. So did Sam Schrader, who had been the Cleveland mob's manager of the Arrowhead Club casino in Loveland, Ohio, then was rewarded with ownership shares in the Beverly Hills.

When Cleveland mob bosses Morris Kleinman and Lou Rothkopf were finally forced to testify under threat of arrest warrants for contempt, they defied the committee and refused to answer questions unless all the cameras were turned off.

Senator Tobey shook his finger at Kleinman: "The people of this country are outraged. You will come to justice. This is only the beginning."

Kleinman and 45 other gangsters were held in contempt and threatened with prison and fines. But only three spent any time in jail. Kleinman was not one of them.

In fact, Senator Tobey was wrong: It was not "only the beginning," it was the beginning of the end. Although some states enacted tougher laws and launched local "little Kefauver" committees to investigate corruption, no meaningful federal legislation was passed.

Two dozen gangsters who were in the U.S. illegally were deported. And when the final Kefauver report concluded that, "The Treasury of the United States has been defrauded of huge sums of money in tax revenues by racketeers and gangsters engaged in organized criminal activities," the ever-alert IRS smelled money and went after nearly 900 mobsters for unpaid taxes during the next decade. Many Americans nodded and thought, "I knew it. Uncle Sam just wanted his cut."

Senator Kefauver's report said, "Beyond any question a noteworthy effect of the committee's work has been the tremendous response in the nature of public awakening and its constructive reaction to enlightenment. There has been a far-reaching chain reaction, the extent of which can only be assayed broadly because in many cases the translation of this awakening into action is only in a formulative phase at the time of this writing."

In English: We did what we could to wake people up. What comes of it is anyone's guess.

If only he had still been alive, Judge Northcutt certainly would have been elated to watch the hearings plow the same hard and rocky ground that he wore himself out on in 1936. He might have been reminded of the wisdom of the Roman Emperor Trajan: "Being right too soon is the same as being wrong."

The "far-reaching chain reaction" hoped for by Senator Kefauver fizzled. It all quietly evaporated, tangled in bureaucracy, lost in a swamp of finger-pointing, inertia and sabotage by mob-owned politicians and the time-honored Capitol Hill custom of talking a topic to death. The formula never changes: Hold a hearing, appoint a committee, declare victory and run for re-election.

Northern Kentucky Judge Joseph Goodenough captured the spirit in his testimony to the committee in 1951. "I don't know why court orders are not enforced," he shrugged. "Gambling is a tradition."

7.
Gambling High, Morals Low

In late spring, when the Ohio River Valley can get as humid as the inside of a tight shoe, the Reverend Leland Jerome Powell was just warming up.

His message that Sunday morning in 1936 at the Norwood Baptist Church: "The Sin of Gambling."

"In earlier days, gambling was mostly confined to the back alleys and low dives," he said, pausing to gaze out on the church-scrubbed faces of his hard-working, blue-collar congregation. "But now it has climbed out and taken its stand on the public square."

A few members of the flock, who had spent Saturday night dancing in the gaudy lights and honky-tonk heaven of Newport, wiped their damp brows, dropped their chins and shifted uneasily.

"It has entered high society and claims to be indispensable..."

A few sighed quietly with relief. It looked like the reverend was going to cast another stone at church bingo.

"Since we must pronounce this as the age of the highest record in gambling, we must follow the implication and confess with alarm that this is the age of the lowest morals," he said, raising his arm dramatically, then sweeping it down to illustrate the swift fall of mankind.

"The gambler," he said, "is a *parasite* on human society."

It was just two months after the fatal Beverly Hills Country Club fire. Gambling and its underworld of liquor and prostitution was in the news. The congregation of factory workers, who punched time cards at General Motors, U.S. Playing Card, Le Blond Machine Tool Company and Norwood Sash & Door Company, had no sympathy for gangsters. But the choking-tight collar of Prohibition was a fresh memory, and most of them had made quick "rum runs" across the river to pick up some holiday cheer in Newport or Covington.

Two years later, Methodist District Superintendent Dr. James P. Simmonds picked up the baton and delivered a similar sermon:

"The widespread and increasing sin of gambling is a great menace to business integrity, and it permeates all society," he preached.

He called on all Methodists in the Cincinnati region to "rise in spiritual might to create a social conscience that will end this growing evil."

Like an old man charging out the door to yell "Get off my lawn!" local churches would occasionally stir themselves in righteous anger and threaten dire retaliation. "Or else!" But like kids on the lawn, the gamblers never took it seriously. That old man couldn't catch anyone.

And gambling flourished.

By 1948, the leaders of Protestant churches were beginning to organize for reform. The Rev. Albert Conley of Madison Avenue Presbyterian Church in Covington preached that, "When gambling exists, corrupt politics exists," and "the gambler corrupts all that he touches."

By 1950, the Kenton County Protestants Association was beginning to cause a twinge of worry among the mobsters who ran Newport and Covington. But every year seemed to usher in a new highwater mark for gambling and a new rock bottom for lowest morals.

Newspapers reported in 1950 that more than 50 million people in the U.S. were spending $13 billion each year on gambling. At the time, the population of the United States was 150 million, meaning one out of every three men, women and children was betting on horses, cars, dice, dogs, numbers, ballgames, slots or anything else that could win, place or show.

Still, most Catholics stayed on the curb and did not join the parade for reform. The Diocese of Covington took an agnostic position on gambling and even condemned the Protestant crusades. "Graft and prostitution, unlike gambling, are evil acts in themselves," a Diocese statement said. "The paying or accepting of bribes and the operation of houses of ill fame are always wrong."

Then came the loophole. "But it isn't always wrong to gamble."

Never mind that graft and corruption were paid for with gambling profits. Catholics insisted the Bible contained no doctrine against gambling, or God would not have created bingo. And didn't the apostles cast lots to choose a new disciple in Acts 1:26?

While the Kefauver Committee was still turning over rocks in 1951, an editorial published by the *Cincinnati Enquirer* captured the average citizen's determined ambivalence.

'Now is the time'

"We have gone a long while in America without a sincere, fundamental, true public conscience. Graft, corruption, illegal connivance, moral turpitude and plain rottenness have been excused, overlooked or ignored with a shrug of the shoulders by the man in the street and the woman in the home.

"So, clever politicians (and even some not so clever) have taken over ... with their retinues of men who make crime a business; the hordes of gamblers, chiselers and grafters, the percentage-hungry influence peddlers, the mink coat traffickers and big city bosses and whatnot!"

But the editorial did not blame the crooked politicians and mobsters. It blamed *the voters who elected them.* Some readers must have wondered if the April 1 editorial was some kind of an April Fool's joke.

The editorial asked: What did the Kefauver hearings reveal "that the general public *and local law enforcement authorities didn't or should not have known already?"*

Its answer, in bold type and capital letters, was "that the conscience of the nation is reviving and may again become effective ... but general morality and public conscience cannot be achieved by legislative fiat or Washington decree. If EVER they are to be attained, they must be grown from grass roots of American communities. **And now, if we may say so, now is the time."**

The mobsters could not have said it better themselves. The hot potato was tossed right back in the laps of the people who had the least influence and ability to enforce the laws.

As Kefauver himself put it, America had turned the bright lights of TV on "the sordid face of the underworld." The next move was up to the voters.

They passed.

8.
Big Jim's Hi-De-Ho Club

Town Marshal of Wilder Is Indicted as Panderer

Charge Stems From Grand-Jury Probe
Of Alleged Prostitution at Campbell Club

Newport, Ky., May 14 (AP)—The Town marshal of neighboring Wilder was indicted today on a charge of pandering.

The indictment was returned against 41-year-old James Harris after a Campbell County grand-jury investigation of alleged prostitution at the Hi-Dee-Ho Club.

Under Kentucky law, pandering is defined generally as the procurement of women for purposes of prostitution or taking the earnings of prostitutes.

The indictment arises out of a 2-year-old case that started with a State police raid on the establishment. Harris was in the club at the time.

Four other persons who were arrested at that time—one woman and three men—were given jail sentences for keeping a house of ill fame. All four appeared before the grand jury yesterday.

JAMES HARRIS
Called the 'boss man'

Complaint Was Cited

Harris, often called the "boss man" of Wilder, said he was in the club because of a complaint that a drunken man was creating a disturbance.

The marshal was once convicted and sentenced to a year in jail and fined $200 after a bank cashier told officers he had been

"I picked up a sucker at the Cincinnatian Hotel last night and ya know what he asked me?"

Myron the Cabbie always had good stories. Like the time he picked up that hired gun from Chicago, who tried to get Myron to run someone off the road. Myron refused, which took guts because the Chicago gangster was waving around his gun like he was bidding at an auction for a free pass to shoot somebody. When Red killed the guy the next day as he sat in someone else's cab, Myron swaggered into the Alibi and announced, "The worm's on the other shoe now." The rest of the gang still quoted Myron when someone got what was coming.

"I'll bite," said Knuckles, "what?"

"He comes out in a tuxedo lookin' like Huey Dewey, that guy Truman beat, and he leans in the window with 80-proof breath smellin' like Jim Beam's spitoon and he says, 'Where do you find the wilder women?'"

Everyone laughed, even Bill the bartender, who did not laugh at much since he had acquired a foot-dragging limp after a beating behind the Merchants Club. Bill wouldn't talk about it, but Knuckles had heard it involved one of the bargirls and a bad night at the blackjack table. Fat Danny, one of "Trigger Mike" Coppola's boys, also liked the girl, and he enjoyed hurting people. But he wouldn't hurt anyone for a while now, if ever. Knuckles had waited for him in the same alley. Danny was big but slow, and threw punches like a drowning man in deep water. Knuckles ducked inside the windmill arms, bounced Fat Danny's head off a brick wall, broke his nose and then, as the bouncer flopped on the ground like a speared walrus, he straightened each of his arms, one at a time, and stomped the back of his elbows, shattering the joints. He'd be lucky to swat a fly for the rest of his life. Trigger Mike had made some noises on the grapevine, but Knuckles knew he didn't like Danny much either, which was sort of surprising given that they shared a favorite sport of slapping women around. No matter, Knuckles thought. If Mike wants to settle something, he knows where to find me.

Bill limped came over and put down a fresh draft. Nothing needed to be said. It was on the house.

"So what did you tell him?" Gus the Bookie asked Myron.

"I told him, 'As you might expect, sir, the wilder women are in Wilder.'"

They laughed again.

"Yeah, and Big Jim just got a blank check to keep his whorehouse doors open. So much for Senator Do-Right and his army of citizen saints," Gus said.

"None are so blind as those who cannot see," Myron added.

Knuckles smiled and started to correct him, then shook his head. Now *that* was funny. Myron was a regular Yogi Berra. And he had a point. The voters in Wilder must be legally blind.

"Big Jim" Harris, the marshal of Wilder, had defeated a clean-up slate of candidates, even forcing one town council member to quit in frustration. Harris had been re-elected last year, in 1952, on the comical promise to clean up gambling and prostitution on the Licking Pike "sin strip." And that was *after* he had been arrested at his own club on Licking Pike in 1951, along with 42 others. The raid was part of a series ordered by the governor to respond to the Kefauver hearings. That raid rounded up 11 women, eight gamblers and 15 managers and dealers, including Big Jim's brother.

Everyone knew the town marshal ran one of the biggest bust-out joints in Campbell County, right there in Wilder, the Hi-De-Ho Club. He had a dozen prostitutes who worked in upstairs rooms where hidden microphones were wired to tape recorders. One secret room could only be found through a drop-down panel in the ceiling.

Big Jim's game was to have his prostitutes ask scripted questions to pry loose a few key details from their customers—address, phone number, domestic details. Then he used those to extort payments from John Familyman after he went back home to Cincinnati, Lexington, Toledo or wherever. After a few days, Harris would call the guy up, play the tape with bedsprings background music and offer to sell it to him for a very "reasonable" price. For a guy in that situation, any price sounded reasonable.

Harris was paid $100 a month as marshal. But he took in $700 a night by splitting the take with his "girls," and made a lot more by selling tapes.

He had found the sweet spot. Just small enough and far enough from Newport to be overlooked by the mob, yet still big enough to live the Hi-De-Ho life on a modest marshal's salary. He had nothing to fear from the law because he *was* the local law.

"Ya gotta love that guy," Gus said. "Remember the raid last year where the state troopers came in and arrested all them people, including Big Jim? He said, 'I just happened to walk in at that time.' He claimed he knew nothing about prostitution or gambling in his own joint, and got the charge dismissed with help from our good friend the fixer, Charles Lester."

"Thick as thieves on the cross. They don't call Big Jim the 'Boss of Licking Pike' for nothin'... Hey, Bill, draw me another Wiederman," Myron said, mangling the name of his favorite beer as usual.

Esquire comes to 'Sin Town'

In 1957 a reporter for *Esquire Magazine* visited Northern Kentucky and reported: "Every cab driver I met was most happy to take me on a guided tour of what is now reputed to be America's most wicked city."

Newport.

"You ain't been here before," one of the cabbies told him. "Just don't let 'em steer you to a bust-out joint. Brother, if you get into one of them places they'll turn you upside down and shake you good to be sure you got nothing left before they let you out."

What the *Esquire* reporter found was the same scenery that a team of Louisville reporters described on their safari into Northern Kentucky in 1939—just more colorful, more wild and more glitzy nearly 20 years later.

And Big Jim Harris was still King of the Jungle, at least in Wilder.

"Probably the most notorious bust-out ... was run by a marshal, the sole law in his community until recently. He offered wickedness on a department-store level. Downstairs was the bar and crooked gambling. Upstairs was the whorehouse section, with every bed wired to a recording machine."

That was Marshal Harris in his prime. In 1957 he was finally put out of business and sent to prison for three years on pandering charges that stemmed from a raid in 1954. Harris had escaped that raid, too, but his madam and a manager did not. After they were given plenty of time to think about it in jail, they cut a deal for reduced sentences by testifying to a grand jury.

The madam, Ruth Jarvis, explained how Harris had profited from prostitution. The manager, William Elam, testified that Harris said, "I have $167,000 at home and I will spend it all to beat this case."

Apparently, even that eye-popping roll of mattress cash was not enough for Wilder City Attorney Charles Lester to beat or bury the charges. Lester, who had represented Harris in the past, ignored a subpoena to show up in court as a witness for the defense and said, "Harris is badly in need of a good lawyer."

Lester was fired from his $35 a week job as Wilder City Attorney. Harris was convicted and sent to prison.

The *Esquire* reporter also described how Cincinnati's local economy was hooked on gambling: "Hotels, bars, gas stations and stores get considerable business from the 365-day flow of visitors on luck or pleasure bent, for Newport has no hotels for them."

Even "some churches and charitable organizations ... do not inquire too deeply into the identities of their generous contributors."

The reporter estimated that Newport drew more than a million visitors and pulled in $30 million each year. As the 1950s drew to a close, the whole nation could see that "Little Mexico" was more lawless than ever.

The latest name for Cincinnati's wide-open adult theme park was lit in neon on the front of Pete Schmidt's new nightclub on Fifth Street in Newport: The Playtorium.

It had a bowling alley, a bar, a restaurant and, of course, a casino stocked with gaming tables and slots. By then Schmidt had built and "sold" so many casinos to the mob, he was practically their unofficial developer. His business motto could have been: "If you build it, they will come—and muscle you out or burn it down."

It must have been eating him up inside to see what was happening at the Beverly Hills Country Club he used to own. Crowds poured in to see future Las Vegas headliners such as Eydie Gorme, Shecky Green, Buddy Hackett, Pearl Bailey, Liberace, Frank Sinatra, Marilyn Monroe, Dean Martin and even Ozzie and Harriet.

What could possibly be wrong with a nightclub that featured Eagle Scout Ozzie Nelson and his lovely "Mrs. America" wife Harriet?

"Sin City" was not ready for salvation just yet.

Pete Schmidt's Glenn Hotel Rendezvous, above, would become the Tropicana and the scene of the failed frame-up that changed Newport. His new club a few blocks away had the perfect name for Cincinnati's adult playground: Glenn Schmidt's Playtorium. **Both were named after his son.** Northern Kentucky Views

Part IV — 1960s

1.
Disorganized Crime

LOUISVILLE, SUNDAY

Car Bombed At Antivice Residence

Newport Abuzz After Woman Seriously Hurt

By HANK MESSICK
Courier-Journal Staff Writer

Newport, Ky., April 29.—A bomb . . . a change in ownership . . . the price of eggs . . . a British accent . . . the grand jury.

Those are the things people in Newport were taking about Saturday.

The bomb went off about 12:30 p.m. at 30 Riverview

It was a peaceful springtime Saturday in 1961 when suddenly the wealthy Fort Thomas suburb in Northern Kentucky was rocked by an ear-splitting explosion. Dogs howled and sirens wailed as a column of dark smoke rose into the blue sky like an exclamation point, dotted at the bottom by a heap of twisted, burning wreckage that had once been a car.

Virginia Menefee had just left the home of friends she was visiting in the fashionable neighborhood on the outskirts of Newport. She got into her station wagon that was parked at the curb, put her purse on the passenger seat, turned the key in the ignition... and 12 volts of electricity surged through wires that ignited a bundle of dynamite strapped under her car.

The blast shook the neighborhood, shattered windows and blew Mrs. Menefee to pieces.

Hank Messick, the fearless reporter for the *Louisville Courier Journal* who covered the mob in Northern

131

Kentucky like a termite on a rotten log, informed readers the following day that Mrs. Menefee had been visiting a leader of the Committee of 500, "which has been seeking to rid Newport and Campbell County of organized gambling and other vice."

The bomb seemed to have all the fingerprints of a mob hit—which was hardly unusual except that it happened in safe, quiet Fort Thomas where the wealthy "cake eaters" lived, including Cleveland Four mob boss Sam Tucker. Those things were supposed to happen in Newport or Bellevue or Southgate.

But this time, Messick's underworld connections had dialed a wrong number. A couple of days later, Mrs. Menefee's husband broke down and confessed to detectives that he had rigged the deadly car bomb to "bring her to her senses" because they were having marriage difficulties. He pleaded insanity.

"It was just a crazy husband who was having domestical problems," Myron the Cabbie said during the regular afternoon gathering at the Alibi Club. "I can sympathize. I been in the doghouse ever since I told the wife her heartthrob Wayne Newton musta declared a war on puberty. But I never thought about blowin' her up with dynamite." He paused. "Well, maybe once I did."

Gus the Bookie said, "I was sorta almost hoping it *was* one of Red's guys. That mob of reformers is getting out of control. Before ya know it we will be as clean as the Pope's confessions."

"I wonder what that would sound like," Knuckles said, seeing an opportunity. "What do you think, Myron?"

Myron held up one finger to show he was thinking about it, paused, sipped his beer and said in a squeaky falsetto, "The papal nose, I a-pick it on-a Wednesday."

He paused, thinking. "Then on-a Thursday, I pass-a the gas in-a mass. Cardinal Linguini, he-a suffer so much his eyes they a-water. They were not the tears of-a joy, I'm-a sure."

As the laughter died down, he held up his finger again.

"And this-a morning, I wake up with-a the impure thoughts of the most-a lovely thick ankles of Sister Inuendo, which I-a see when she clean-a the Papal commode."

"Is that all?" Knuckles asked in a stern voice, playing the father confessor.

Myron smiled. "I know it's not-a much, but next time I try-a harder."

When Gus stopped laughing and wiped his eyes, he called out, "Bring a beer for Myron on me. That's the best laugh I've had in a month. And I'm-a the Catholic. 'Sister *Inuendo*.' Where do you get that stuff?"

"Divine exasperation," Myron said, raising his glass. "But you know, Gus, you were starting to make sense for a change about those reformers. First that *Esquire* story, then the *Saturday Evening Post* last year with that big spread on Newport the 'Open City.' We're getting entirely too knowntorius.

"I had a fare in town from Kansas City the other day who said, 'Take me to the open city.' From *Kansas*. I shoulda told him 'The Open City is next door to Oz, but I think I can find you a hooker who looks a lot like that scarecrow.'"

"What was it that they said in the *Post*?" Knuckles said, rubbing the bridge of his nose to remember the quote. "They said their reporter was 'approached by the local Jezebels'. You guys know any Jezebels?"

As Gus laughed, Myron made a washboard of his forehead, searching his mental inventory. He shook his head. "For 40 percent commission I can take you to Judy, Janet, Josephine, even a Jasmine. But I never heard of no Jezebel. Geez, that would be like namin' your kid Judas."

"Speaking of names," Gus said, "the one we should be worried about is that Christian guy."

"These reformers are all Christians, ain't they?" Myron said. "That's their problem."

"No, that's his real name," Gus said. "Christian-something..."

"Siefried," Knuckles offered. "It's right here in the paper. Another letter to the editor. They've been sending out church ladies and deacons to collect evidence. They walk right in on the casinos, buy drinks, roll the dice—even in the bust-outs. He says here in his letter that he will never give up on cleaning up Newport because of what it's doing to the children."

"What is he, some kinda Boy Scout?" Gus complained.

"Worse than that, he's a Boy Scout leader and Sunday school teacher. And a mailman." Knuckles shook out the paper and moved it into the light coming from a neon Wiedemann's Beer sign behind the bar that flashed "Fresh From the Barrel."

"Says here he promised God himself he would clean up Newport after all that he saw while he was delivering the mail."

"Well, why doesn't somebody do somethin' about him, maybe give him a package to deliver to Mr. Tarzan of the Apes in Africa?" Myron asked.

"Who?" said Knuckles.

"Yaknow, the guy with the pet monkey that swings on ropes in the trees, Tarz—"

"I know who Tarzan is," Knuckles said. "I mean who's left around here to do something about the reformers and back it up when the Keystone Kops come around? Not Dalitz, he's in Vegas. So is Kleinman. Lou Rothkopf killed himself in 1956. And Sam Tucker is busy in Havana, I hear. The only guys left are Joe Palookas like us. The big bosses are small-timers now, like Screw Andrews, a numbers runner who thinks he's Al Capone. They couldn't bomb a mailman if you gave 'em a B-52 and a map to the Post Office."

"Yeah," Myron had to admit. "They'd probably leave it to Tito. I heard he put sugar in that Louisville reporter's gas tank. Sugar. So then this 'Jimmy Olsen' writes about it in the paper the next day and tells a judge he's afraid to walk the streets of Newport without a bodyguard supplied by the Committee of 500."

Gus shook his head. "You'd never catch Red putting sugar in a gas tank. A match maybe. Once upon a time around here if a couple of gorillas in suits asked if you wanted one lump or two, they was not talking about sugar."

"The good old, bad old days are gone, boys," Knuckles said. "These new guys like Tito will just get us all in trouble." .

2.
A New Sheriff in Town

Another bomb exploded that spring in 1961, and it "rocked Newport's vice empire," Hank Messick reported on May 20. This time he was right on target.

It happened in police court when a surprise witness exposed a mob conspiracy to frame former NFL quarterback George Ratterman, who was running for sheriff as a reformer.

More than 100 members of the Committee of 500 packed the courtroom to cheer, hoot and applaud as charges of breaching the peace, disorderly conduct and resisting arrest were dismissed and Ratterman raised his arms in victory. The case made international headlines and became the first major battle in America's new war on organized crime.

"I think this should be presented to the grand jury," the flustered and embarrassed judge stammered.

"Grandma Blows Case Sky High" was the headline the next morning in the *Kentucky Edition of The Cincinnati Enquirer.*

Banner headlines dominated the front-pages for weeks all over the nation. The story had everything: a glamorous football player; a sexpot stripper called April Flowers; a shadowy mobster who ran the Tropicana Club, with a name from the Mafia phonebook, Tito Carinci; Newport mob lawyer Charles Lester; crooked cops, knockout drops and a dramatic sudden reversal victory for reformers against the "liberal ticket" gangsters, crooked politicians and voters who wanted Newport to stay dirty.

Born to reform

George Ratterman grew up in Cincinnati's wealthy Hyde Park neighborhood and graduated from elite St. Xavier High School. His classmates would have voted him most likely to succeed at anything he chose to do.

He was a straight-A student and a gifted athlete who played basketball, pitched for the baseball team and starred as quarterback of the St. X Bombers football team.

Ratterman at Notre Dame

He excelled at any sport, but football was his favorite. On a scholarship at the University of Notre Dame from 1944 to 1946, he joined the exclusive club of "four-letter men," by playing varsity tennis, basketball, baseball and football. But it was Fighting Irish football that drew the spotlights. He was such a talented quarterback, he played alternate possessions with Heisman Trophy winner Johnny Lujack. Coach Frank Leahy called Ratterman "the greatest all-around athlete in the history of Notre Dame."

At six-foot-two and 175 pounds, he was tall and lanky, with blond hair and a winning smile that was often lit by a sparkle of mischief in his blue eyes.

He worked summers in college as a counselor at a Boy Scout camp, but those who knew him in his NFL days would probably agree that his summer job was about as close as Ratterman ever came to *being* a Boy Scout himself.

They liked to tell the story of the time he threw an interception during a big game at Notre Dame and was scalded by his irate coach, who demanded to know why in the name of Mary and Joseph and all the saints with four-letter names had he thrown the ball directly to a player wearing the wrong jersey.

"He was the only one on the field who was open," Ratterman replied.

In fact, the people who knew and loved George Ratterman would probably have voted him *least* likely to succeed in a crusade to clean up Sin City, USA. He enjoyed having fun far too much to throw a wet blanket over party-town Newport.

Drafted by the Buffalo Bills in 1947, he set a rookie record for touchdown passes, 22, that stood until it was broken by Peyton Manning in 1998. He played for several teams and led the NFL in touchdown passes in 1950. While playing for the Browns he went back to school and earned a law degree. After he was injured in 1956, he worked as a radio announcer on ABC and NBC. He once lost a major sponsor by "accidentally" promoting their competitor on the air. Pro football hall-of-fame quarterback Otto Graham called Ratterman "the best natural clown and comic I ever saw in professional football."

He returned to Cincinnati in the late 1950s to work as an investment advisor. He was doing very well. His NFL salary had been paltry by today's standards, but $170,000 a year was lots of money in 1960, when some of the nicest new homes could be purchased for less than $20,000. He and his wife, Anne, had one of those beautiful homes across the river in Fort Thomas, where they raised their eight children.

His brother was a priest and dean of men at Xavier University in Cincinnati. The Ratterman family was well known and well respected, and George Ratterman was the kind of All-American success story that little boys and young men dreamed about.

Then one night a neighbor invited him to come over for a meeting of the Committee of 500.

As the neighbors described the maddening frustration of trying to clean up a town that was saturated with corruption, Ratterman listened and learned and began to get interested.

The most recent outrage was a Campbell County grand jury that had investigated gambling and found nothing. Nothing at all. The report was written by County Attorney William Wise, who knew the vice epidemic in Newport as well as anyone. But Wise played dumb, and insisted the city was squeaky clean.

Time Magazine had no problem finding an encyclopedia of vice in Newport, Ratterman's neighbors pointed out. And plenty of newspapers and magazines had come to town and painted a scene of brazen gambling and prostitution more colorful and wide open than a Saturday night midway at the county fair.

The *Louisville Courier-Journal*'s Hank Mesick had reported that he counted three hundred prostitutes per mile in Newport, working at

"Day Houses" and "Night Houses" named Kitty's, Mabel's and the Stork Club.

Just the previous spring, *The Saturday Evening Post* had told the whole nation, "The brothels of Newport did everything but put up electric signs and take space in the newspapers to advertise their presence. Gambling was not restricted to casinos and saloons. Almost every drugstore, candy shop, grocery and dry-cleaning establishment had slot machines on display."

The headquarters for the Committee of 500 reform group was at the corner of Monmouth and Third Street, directly across the street from a gambling club and a brothel.
Northern Kentucky Views

And then the most painful cut, as the *Post* described the lovely view of Newport from Cincinnati: "Newport is viewed as a disreputable relative, too close to be disavowed, but certainly not to be invited to a family dinner."

One of the women got the attention of the crowd and waved a copy of the *Kentucky Post*. "How many of you saw what our distinguished underworld lawyer Dan Davies told everyone in the paper?" she asked. "According to Mr. Davies, we all *like* it this way."

She held up the paper and read: "I quote: 'The reformers don't stay around here. They catch too much hell from the merchants. Everybody expects a little gambling, a little vice. Everybody's liberal around here.'"

As the neighbors fumed, Ratterman began to get steamed too. Before the evening was over, he said later, his mind was made up: "Somebody has to run for office if this situation is going to be cleaned up."

A couple of years later, when the smoke of battle had finally cleared a bit, he told well-known columnist Jimmy Breslin: "Since I had the background of making my living with the public, as a pro football player and an announcer for games and the like, I felt it was my duty."

So the quarterback called his own number, took the ball and ran for Campbell County Sheriff.

The Committee of 500 must have felt the way Coach Leahy did when he landed Ratterman as a recruit: With this guy, you couldn't lose.

And when it was over, the underworld crowd must have felt like so many opposing football teams that had made the fatal mistake of underestimating Ratterman's determination, grit and toughness.

"The minute these people tried that business on me, all they were doing was making sure I'd be in this thing to the end," he told Breslin for a story in Saga, a pulp men's magazine that ran stories about fighter pilots, lion tamers—and fearless town-taming sheriffs.

"That business" they tried on Ratterman made headlines as far away as Thailand and was called "the story of the century" by local newspapers. It lit a spark in Ratterman that kindled the biggest brushfire of reform Newport had ever seen.

It began when mob lawyer and crime mastermind Charles Lester decided the reformers were getting too uppity. Lester could feel the wiggles and tugs of power in his web as the big bosses from Cleveland and New York began to migrate to Havana and Las Vegas.

Finally, he had a chance to become the Godfather of Little Mexico. And now here was this Ratterman rat giving hope to the church ladies and do-gooders. He knew just the man to go after the upstart reformer: A former All-American linebacker at Xavier University who had nearly made the cut to play in the NFL.

Who better to tackle Ratterman than Tito Carinci? The Steubenville, Ohio classmate of crooner Dean Martin had tried out for the Green Bay Packers, but was cut and chose another career: organized crime. It required measured violence, like pro football, but without the annoying referees and rules. And now Tito might have a chance to hit Ratterman hard enough to knock him out of the game, Lester figured.

Carinci had taken over the Glenn Hotel, where he was now running a low-rent casino called the Tropicana. He was dark, stocky and lethal, still tough enough to bring 210 pounds of menace to an argument.

Lester came up with a game plan and Carinci called the first play: He phoned a friend he knew from football, Tom Paisley of Medina, Ohio, who was also an acquaintance of Ratterman.

Carinci told Paisley a fable: That he wanted to go straight and open a restaurant in New York to get away from the underworld, but he needed help from Ratterman. He asked Paisley to set up a meeting, and Paisley obliged.

Meanwhile, Lester called a local photographer, Tommy Withrow, and told him he had a job for him at the Tropicana, "taking pictures of a man and a woman." Lester assured the photographer that it would be safe and would pay well. He told Withrow that he got his name and number from the county attorney, William Wise.

Withrow agreed, "Just to be nice," he explained later. But he had no intention of doing it. "I mean, these pictures of a guy and a girl, that's not my pitch."

Ratterman and Paisley met Carinci at the Terrace Plaza Hotel bar in downtown Cincinnati the afternoon of May 8. Ratterman was suspicious that it might be a set-up or a bribe—but not suspicious enough to decline a scotch on the rocks that was placed in front of him.

"Snatches," he told Breslin, "after the drink I only recall snatches of what happened. I remember I was in a car. And I remember being in a room and feeling terrible and lying down on a bed. And I remember a girl in a red dress, and then I remember I was being knocked down on the floor and I kept getting up and whoever it was kept knocking me down again. But that's about all."

Ratterman was too groggy to remember how two Newport detectives kicked the door open, dragged him out of bed and knocked him around before they wrapped him in a bedspread and hauled him off to jail along with Tito and a woman he had never met.

'Ratterman Victim of Knockout Drops'

The next morning, the police report said detectives had received an anonymous tip to find Ratterman in bed with a naked strip-tease dancer, April Flowers, with his clothes strewn about the room at Carinci's Tropicana.

Flowers, whose real name was Juanita Hodges, was booked for prostitution, along with Carinci. They were both bailed out by Lester, who showed up in 15 minutes. But Ratterman was locked up in a jail cell, where he sat dazed, trying to clear the thick fog in his head and figure out what was happening.

He was released the next morning on $500 bail paid by his lawyer, who showed up at Ratterman's cell and told him to zip up his pants. He tried, and discovered the zipper had been ripped apart. Fortunately for Ratterman, the lawyer was not Charles Lester or his underworld colleague Dan Davies. It was former U.S. Attorney for Eastern Kentucky Henry Cook, a wiry but tough, honest prosecutor who had battled corruption and crime in Eastern Kentucky's hardscrabble coal towns. He knew Newport the way Charles Lester knew loopholes.

Cook peered into Ratterman's clouded eyes, noted his confusion and told Anne Ratterman to send him to a doctor that morning for blood and urine tests. Dr. Frank Cleveland, a pathologist who became the county coroner across the river in Cincinnati, conducted tests and found a dangerously heavy dose of chloral hydrate "knockout drops."

Ratterman slept off the drugs, cleared his head and went to the press with his story: He had been drugged and framed.

"We were in Tito's suite" at 2 a.m., he told local WCPO-TV Reporter Al Schottelkotte. "I remember suddenly becoming very groggy. I walked over to one of the beds in his bedroom and laid down ... I remember I was about powerless. I just had to lay down. And I guess that's when the knockout drug took its effect.

"The next thing I remember is a tremendous commotion in the room. Several men were in there yanking on my clothes, tearing my pants and my underwear off. There was a woman in the room, too, and that was the first time I had seen her."

He said he was too weak to have resisted arrest. He showed the reporter his torn pants. "When I take off my own pants, I normally don't tear the zipper off."

The May 10 *Enquirer* headline said, "Anti-Vice Leader Ratterman Victim of 'Knock-Out' Drops." Photos showed Carinci and Flowers, both wearing dark glasses, near the top of Page One. They seemed to glare across the page at Ratterman as he held up his torn trousers.

Public reaction was swift and devastating. It was not what the gangsters expected.

THE CINCINNATI ENQUIRER

Kentucky Edition

121st YEAR NO. 31—DAILY   WEDNESDAY MORNING, MAY 10, 1961   PRICE 7 CENTS

ANTI-VICE LEADER RATTERMAN VICTIM OF 'KNOCK-OUT' DROPS

Chloral Hydrate Found In Kentuckian's Blood

Charity Study Shows

Cost Of Giving
Is Soaring Here

Doctors Get
Fees Guide

General Speaks:

"We're sure it was an attempt to defame his reputation and also to discredit the movement which he represents," said Committee of 500 leader Christian Siefried.

Ratterman's brother, the Reverend P. H. Ratterman, said, "I thank God that my brother George is alive. Threats of violence have been communicated to George through others and through me. We did not know exactly what form of foul play was to be expected. We are not surprised by what has been done. I just thank God he is alive."

Detective Pat Ciafardini, who was off duty but happened to be at the police station when the anonymous tip came in, said, "I just don't like a pimp and a whore."

A week later, in a Newport police court that was packed like a Kentucky Derby infield with more than 300 people scrambling for 75 seats, the trial began. Mayor Ralph Mussman made it clear where he stood by sitting at the prosecutors' table. He called it "a ten-dollar police court case blown up out of proportion."

The "ten-dollar" case went on for four days, spilling over into an unusual final session on Saturday. One man fainted in the cloying heat. There were outbursts of jeers and cheers by the underworld crowd and the reformers. Carinci chewed bubblegum and blew bubbles that he popped like cap guns. At one point, a bomb scare cleared the courthouse.

Ratterman and Cook wanted to go first, but the judge put April Flowers on trial instead. That was Lester's strategy: Let the stripper and the mobster run the clock, smear Ratterman and crush the hopes of reformers with salacious perjury.

'Stuffy Courtroom Rocks With Sin and Shame'

Carinci testified that Ratterman and Paisley nagged him to find them women, asking, "Where are the dancing girls? When do we get the broads?" So he finally took them to his apartment on the second floor at his Tropicana Club in Newport, he said.

Ratterman begged him to meet April Flowers, he said, so he introduced the quarterback to the stripper and left them alone. When the police arrived, Tito said, he ran into the room and saw Ratterman holding the naked woman "in a sort-of Valentino grip, and kissing her."

April Flowers was next on the stand. She told the judge that she followed Ratterman into a bedroom at Tito's place and "took off the underparts of my clothing." Her strip-tease costume was covered in "mirrors," she explained, and the sharp-edged sequins hurt.

She put on a leopard "slave robe" instead. "I'm a strip-teaser," she said when asked about taking off her clothes in front of a man she had just met. "That's just like sitting down and typing out a letter to me."

When the police burst in, "I ran out and grabbed my G-string," she said. "I was going to take off." It was hard to imagine anything that could shock Sin City, but police chasing a topless stripper in a sequined G-string through the streets might have done it. Newport never found out. April Flowers was grabbed by the detectives before she could run.

Then Ciafardini and Detective Joseph Quitter told their version, making Ratterman look like just another guilty, wife-cheating "John" who got caught in bed with a hooker.

It looked bad for Ratterman. As he sat and listened day after day, unable to defend himself, the prosecution painted a lurid picture that looked worse than any grainy "love tryst" photos that could have been taken.

"A city is on trial in a stuffy little courtroom rocking with sin and shame," Margaret Josten reported for the *Enquirer*.

But then Cook finally got his turn and dropped the bomb.

He called a surprise witness: Nancy Hay, 68, the grandma who blew the case sky high. She was asked to describe a phone call she answered on the night Ratterman was arrested. She said a man on the line asked for her granddaughter's husband, freelance photographer Thomas Withrow. The man wanted him to come to the Tropicana immediately to take those "pictures of a man and a woman" for Charles Lester. The phone kept ringing and ringing with the same urgent message until nearly 3:00 a.m.

The detectives winced, the stripper blushed and Carinci squirmed as Cook calmly called his next witness: Tom Withrow.

Withrow testified that Charles Lester had asked him to go to the Glenn Hotel to get instructions from "Marty" on how to shoot the pictures. When he met Marty, he was told: "They'll be in a room. We'll open the door, you take the picture and we'll jump out."

He said Marty reassured him that he would not get hurt because there would be plenty of "our guys" there to protect him. "Marty" was Edward "Marty" Buccieri, Carinci's partner at the Tropicana.

Withrow wrinkled his forehead and asked the judge what it meant when they used words such as "indignation" and "remonstrated." But he knew right from wrong, and insisted he wanted no part of the Tropicana plot.

His wife took the stand to testify that he told her that night that if Lester or Marty called, "Tell them I'm not home." And that's what she did.

**Soon to be Sheriff George Ratterman leaves the courtroom
after his victory over Charles Lester and Tito Carinci.
He was given knockout drops and framed in bed with stripper
April Flowers. The mob's plot to kill the reform movement backfired.**
Kenton County Library archive

"The backbone of the case against Ratterman had been broken," Josten wrote. "Some people could not believe what they had just witnessed in the courtroom. The end came so suddenly, so dramatically after four days of what seemed to be never-ending testimony against Ratterman."

The Police Court prosecutor, Thomas Hirschfeld, was stunned. He suddenly had to switch from prosecuting Ratterman to defending him. He met with Lester in the hallway during a break and asked him if he had indeed tried to hire Withrow to take pictures.

"I'll see you in several days," Lester brushed him off. "Don't do anything. We'll come up with something."

Hirschfeld returned to court and told the judge the case should not even be in court; it should be investigated by a grand jury. The judge agreed, slammed his gavel and the charges were immediately dismissed.

Pandemonium broke out. "The courtroom became a seething mass of humanity trying to shake Ratterman's hand," Messick reported. "Women members of the Committee of 500, who had won their own 'Battle of the Courtroom Seats' with the underworld, cried happy tears."

Cook and Ratterman received a standing ovation as they left the courtroom. Anne Ratterman walked out with them, at her husband's side, as she had been throughout the ordeal.

"It's been particularly difficult for us because we knew the photographer's testimony would eventually come out," Ratterman told a TV reporter. "And it's extremely difficult to sit there and hear the things that are said that are perhaps damaging to one's reputation, and not be able to get up and shout, 'I can prove this is all a frame-up! This is all false!'"

A grand jury indicted Lester, both detectives, Newport Police Chief Upshire White, Carinci and Tropicana owner Ed "Marty" Buccieri on federal charges of violating Ratterman's civil rights.

It looked like that angry old man Senator Tobey, who had died shortly after the Kefauver hearings ended 10 years earlier, might finally be right: The people were outraged. And it was finally "just the beginning."

Ratterman rallies suddenly began to draw traffic-jam crowds. "Committee of 500 Expects 15,000 at Meeting," said a headline on May 21.

Ratterman wisely reassured voters that his clean-up of gambling would make exceptions for bingo, and that was enough to get Catholics to rejoin the reform movement. He also promised he would not interfere with Sunday liquor sales that were so profitable to Northern Kentucky, as parched Cincinnatians fled Sunday liquor bans north of the Ohio River.

In June, the underworld tried a new scheme, probably hatched by Lester. They let it be known that they were now in favor of "reform" to clean up dishonest bust-out joints and keep the "honest" carpet joints in business.

Messick reported that the gangsters also wanted voters to know that, "The Syndicate did not frame George Ratterman because Ratterman 'hasn't a chance' to win his race for sheriff."

Besides, the underworld source said, "If the Syndicate did try to frame someone, it would do so far more efficiently than was done in the

Ratterman case."

The mobsters even generously offered to shut down the Tropicana, which was known as one of the most crooked clubs. They promised that Newport would be more like Las Vegas, with clean, glamorous, trustworthy illegal gambling.

It was the same "reform" scam that had worked so well when they used crooked cops to raid bust-out joints that competed with their classier casinos; or when they launched reform crusades secretly backed by Red Masterson. "Leave it to us, we will clean it up."

Ratterman responded by reminding voters that the mobsters would kill anyone who got in their way. There were plenty of examples who had been found floating in the Ohio River.

Backing him up, honest investigators scoffed at the denials of mob participation in the Ratterman frame-up. They said it was a mistake, alright. What Lester really intended was quiet blackmail, not a front-page scandal. He wanted pictures of Ratterman in bed with Flowers before he woke up. Then he could be persuaded to drop out of the race or join the mob team. The reform movement would have been snuffed again.

"The picture was intended as insurance," Messick speculated.

In September, the aftershocks of the Ratterman blow-up continued.

A Campbell County grand jury investigating vice and gambling heard from a mystery witness: Big Jim Harris, the former Wilder marshal who had been paroled in 1958.

'Sensational Testimony Expected'

Harris took the stand and poured out the sordid details like he was narrating a bedsprings tape for one of the suckers he blackmailed.

He told of payoffs to "Mr. Big," a kingpin from the Cleveland "outfit" that controlled gambling in Newport. The names of Mr. Big and his partners were too dangerous to speak aloud, he said, and the newspapers didn't print them. But he gave them to the grand jury. Big Jim "talked as tough as he looked," a reporter wrote.

By then the feds already knew that "Mr. Big" was Moe Dalitz.

"There's no place like Newport in the country," Big Jim said. Not even Las Vegas could take bets as big as the action that went through the national betting-wire hub in Newport. He said his own Hi-De-Ho club and brothel was just another typical operation, including the wiretaps.

"We have to know what they were being paid," he explained.

His club had been left alone by the mob until it got too big, he said, but then the raids came, orchestrated by Mr. Big.

Another headline witness was Commonwealth Attorney William Wise, who earlier that year had written the grand jury report that found no gambling in Newport. But he was not there to say "I see *nothing*" like Chief Gugel. He was one of the *targets* of the grand jury, accused of taking payoffs. Hattie Jackson, the "madam" at a Newport brothel on Fourth Street called the Haidi Club, had testified in a separate case in Frankfort that she had made payoffs to Wise and other police and politicians, including Campbell County Judge Ray Murphy.

She told the grand jury that she had offered to name names earlier, but backed down when she saw the prosecutor walk into court and recognized him as one of the men on her list for payoffs: Wise.

Then the grand jury heard another amazing story from former Newport Police Sergeant Jack Thiem.

Pete Schmidt leaves police headquarters with Detective Chief Leroy Fredericks after his arrest in a raid at the Playtorium. Kentucky Views

In 1953, Thiem raided Pete Schmidt's new Playtorium with 16 private detectives he had secretly recruited from Louisville to prevent leaks and sabotage by dirty cops and politicians in Newport. But his leakproof plan failed. As he arrived to make the bust he walked into an ambush staged by Newport Police Chief George Gugel and Chief of Detectives LeRoy Fredericks.

"We went to the Playtorium and ran into our own police department. Gugel, Fredericks and others were there," Thiem said.

Asked by the grand jury if

the Newport police brass interfered with the raid, Thiem replied, "That's what they were there for. They did. I was manhandled by members of my own police department. They took my gun and disarmed the other men."

Also there to block the raid was Charles Lester, "the brains" of the ambush, according to Thiem.

The Newport police charged Thiem with attacking Lester, then framed him as the operator of a brothel and fired him from the police department. He said, "All of a sudden I became a procurer and I was charged with owning a hotel filled with prostitutes. I was thrown out of the police department as an unclean person."

Thiem said he was told by rackets gangster Frank "Screw" Andrews that the charges would be dropped if he sold his home and moved away from Newport.

Thiem also testified that former Mayor Robert Sidell, the nightclub bandleader who was elected in 1952 with backing from Lester and Schmidt, told him to join the crooked team and take bribes from Schmidt. He said Sidell told him, "Take his money and get along with him and do what he says."

The grand jury indicted 13 politicians and policemen for conspiracy to "pervert, corrupt or obstruct public justice."

Working with a Lexington judge who was not a member of the Newport "profit-sharing" plan, the grand jury said it was "convinced that many public officials have conspired, combined, confederated and agreed together to pervert, corrupt and obstruct justice by permitting these sordid conditions to exist."

Almost the entire Newport government was indicted: Mayor Ralph Mussman; City Manager Oscar Hensch; and three of the city's four commissioners, Roland Vories, Clarence Lehkamp and Joseph Schaber. The unindicted fourth member was new to the profit-sharing game, a widow who had replaced her recently deceased husband as commissioner.

The indicted police were Detective Ciafardini, retired police chief George Gugel, former chief of detectives Leroy Fredericks and five cops, including Gugel's son, Edward "Buzz" Gugel.

Governor Bert Combs applauded the grand jury. Former Governor A.B. "Happy" Chandler deplored it.

Campbell County agreed with Governor Combs. By November, there was a new sheriff in town. Ratterman was elected in a landslide, winning twice as many votes as his nearest opponent, Johnny "TV" Peluso, an anti-reform Democrat who ran a TV store and placed wiretaps for the mob in nightclubs and city hall offices. (After losing his race for sheriff, Peluso ran for mayor and was elected twice, in 1964 and 1976.)

But while the county chose Ratterman and reform, Newport was still firmly undecided about its future. The city elected four pro-mob commissioners who were vocal opponents of reform, including two of the incumbents who had been indicted for corruption that summer.

Meanwhile, the federal civil rights indictments against Carinci, Lester and the police detectives continued. Their cases became the most costly court battle over misdemeanors in Kentucky history. The defendants faced fines of only $100 and up to a year in jail. But they fought on relentlessly through two local trials, then all the way to the U.S. Supreme Court. The lawyer for Police Chief Upshire White and Detective Quitter was smooth-talking Dan Davies.

The prosecution had a secret weapon: the enthusiastic backing of U.S. Attorney General Robert Kennedy. It was his first big case against the underworld.

During the first trial, Ciafardini sobbed in court about his family and swore on his wife and children that *he* was the victim of a frame-up. But prosecutors were sure he was lying, and not just to protect his girlfriend who worked at the Glenn Hotel.

Another witness testified that when he mentioned Ratterman to Lester, "I've never heard such filthy language from a man." He was unable to forget the "unnatural sex acts" that Lester described as part of his plot to accuse Ratterman of deviancy.

The first trial lasted 16 days and ended with a hung jury. The second went 17 days. Federal Prosecutor Ronald Goldfarb urged the jurors to finally "close this Pandora's Box of slime" and find them guilty.

But what happened between those two trials was a mob drama of its own, as Goldfarb would later reveal in his excellent 1995 book, *Perfect Villains, Imperfect Heroes: Robert F. Kennedy's War Against Organized Crime.*

Newport finally delivered its own strange brand of justice in 1963. Tito Carinci, Police Chief White and the detectives who perpetrated the frame-up and made the false arrest were all acquitted. But the prosecutors' main target, slippery mob lawyer Charles Lester, was found guilty, along with Buccieri, who had by then moved to Las Vegas. Both were convicted of conspiracy and sentenced to one year in prison.

The verdict was so bewildering that the Sixth Circuit Court of Appeals in Cincinnati called it "almost impossible to understand."

As soon as the trial was over, Carinci announced that he was running for mayor—then dropped out, saying he was too stressed by all the legal "harassment."

Buccieri and Lester appealed. In 1967 they lost again when the U.S. Supreme Court refused to hear their appeals. Charles Lester, the brains and briefcase behind local organized crime for 30 years, was sent to prison. By then, Buccieri was already paroled. He had dropped his appeals to go directly to a "club fed" prison while Lester fought on.

By 1968 Lester was paroled and back at work, representing a woman who accused Newport Detective Kenneth "Moose" Jones of beating her in the Jai-Alai Club. The city dismissed the charges and described the case as the kind of tangled mess only Newport (or Charles Lester) could invent: it was a frame up by a former prostitute who was married to the club manager, in retaliation for a gambling raid of the Jai-Alai Club by Detective Moose Jones.

Lester also represented owners of the Yorkshire Club and the Flamingo Club when they were raided that year for skimming from "bingo" gambling. Dan Davies represented owners of the Latin Quarter, the Merchants Club and the Playtorium in the same case.

At the end of 1968, Charles Lester ran out of strings to pull. State court officials finally noticed his prison record and he was disbarred. He appealed, claiming disbarment was "tantamount to economic death" at his age, 65. His appeal was rejected.

'I must have them terrified'

After his election victory, George Ratterman went to work immediately... without a salary. The previous sheriff had spent the entire budget to give raises to friends in the department before Ratterman moved in. The budget was paltry to begin with. Why pay the sheriff and his deputies adequately when the underworld was subsidizing their payroll with bribes?

Looking back on the stormy year they had endured, George and Anne Ratterman told *Cincinnati Enquirer* Reporter Dan Pinger that the ordeal had brought them closer to God. Anne said, "I'm sure God helped me to remain calm."

George said he was often amazed at how God worked miracles through the darkest times. For example, they only heard about Tom Withrow's key testimony because he was at the hospital taking pictures of newborns when Ratterman was brought in for blood tests after the arrest. Someone overheard Withrow remark that he knew something about it, and passed that on to the Rattermans. Later, Withrow confessed his role in the frame-up to his pastor, who encouraged him to contact Ratterman's lawyer, Henry Cook.

"I don't want to bring God into it," Anne agreed, "but it's true."

Years later, "barbershop history" would tell the story of Newport's cleanup as if Ratterman didn't do all that much because the mob was leaving town anyway. Not true. Sheriff Ratterman fought the mob to clean up Newport.

POP040601-4/6/62-NEWPORT,KY.: In the continuing uneasy situation at times since reform sheriff George Ratterman took office there have been events to punctuate the actions of the former pro gridder who has turned to politics. Yesterday for example while Ratterman was in a now closed night spot bent on seizing equipment to satisfy a $121 delinquent tax bill, a city policeman issued a parking ticket to the sheriff's auto. Here Ratterman claims the ticket as a deputy aide muses over the situation. UPI TELEPHOTO   jak

Sheriff George Ratterman raided mobsters such as Screw Andrews but had to battle crooked Newport Police, who ticketed his car while he was serving a warrant on Andrews. The sheriff got even by towing and impounding Screw's new white Cadillac. Northern Kentucky Views

Almost as soon as he took office, he hired ten "clean" deputies and began planning raids. Headlines show that his "Untouchables" stayed busy:

- Early in 1962 he raided the Turf Club and arrested a bookie, seizing phones and betting slips.

- Next he raided the Flamingo Club to collect back taxes. A Cincinnati photographer was slugged and slammed against a car by Screw Andrews, who was charged with assault, but Ratterman's raid came up empty. While the sheriff tried to serve papers that had been filled out naming the wrong owner, his patrol car was ticketed by a Newport cop. But he learned fast. A few weeks later he towed and confiscated Screw Andrews' white Cadillac for unpaid taxes.

- He raided Tito Carinci's new Riviera Club on Monmouth Street and arrested a stripper for prostitution. Tito protested that Ratterman was getting even. He was probably right.

- In 1963 the sheriff raided two clubs and arrested a dozen gamblers.

- In 1964 he raided a Newport bookstore three times for obscenity.

- In 1965 he raided 13 bars and issued 63 liquor violations, then raided five gambling parlors and arrested four gamblers and mobsters.

What he was doing was not spectacular. But for Newport it was like watching a circus dog dance on its hind legs. It was not how well it was done that mattered. The amazing thing was that it was done at all.

"If they get only a ten-dollar fine we'll arrest them again, maybe 50 times till they stop," the new sheriff vowed.

Ratterman also tangled with grand juries as the gangsters struck back. He was gradually worn down by the corruption around him, which had roots like a rotten tooth, deep and decayed, painful to extract. But he kept the pressure on, hitting prostitution, gambling, liquor violations, obscenity... whatever it took to make the underworld dance on its hind legs.

"The thing that must have everybody worried is the gun," he told Jimmy Breslin as they met in a Cincinnati hotel bar. As sheriff he had to carry a sidearm, he said. "I've never had one in my life and I don't intend to learn what to do with one of them, either. If something happens, that means anybody can get hurt. I'm liable to shoot anybody. Some big mobster who shouldn't be shot at under any circumstances is likely to get hit.

"The trouble is, ole Sheriff George will be blazing away at somebody down the block. I'll be shooting one way, aiming the other. I must have them terrified."

It was a humorous, smart and subtle warning to anyone paying attention. Ole Sheriff George was no fool. He was a loaded gun that could go off and shoot anybody, even big mobsters such as Screw Andrews and Tito Carinci.

Breslin and his *Saga* magazine readers were saddened to learn that Newport's new lion tamer was closing bust-out joints and boarding up brothels. National attractions like the Beverly Hills Country Club were now padlocked, dim and empty, with nothing to gamble on in Newport but the soup of the day.

When Ratterman left office in 1966, Newport was no longer Las Vegas on the Ohio River. Years later, from his home in Centennial, Colorado, Ratterman looked back and said, "We didn't have to bust down doors— oh, we did something like that with one or two places. But once we did, the other side knew what was coming, and they left quietly, on their own. We knew who was in charge of the corruption, and they knew we knew. In four years I got rid of the gambling and the prostitution, and I didn't get killed."

Who killed the constable?

Not getting killed may have been a closer call than he realized. In 1980, a skull washed up on the banks of the Ohio River south of Newport. It had been crushed on top by a long, deep depression that showed a fatal headwound, as if walloped with a heavy pipe or a tire-iron. Detectives believed it was the last remains of Constable George Hawkins, who vanished in 1961.

Hawkins was "the egg man," a well-liked, rotund city constable who lived with his family above his general store in tiny Persimmon Grove, south of Newport. His nickname did not come from the store. It came from the fresh eggs he sold for $100 apiece to the bosses of gambling joints and strip clubs. Buy some eggs... or get busted.

When he went missing, Constable Hawkins was facing an IRS tax audit and had raised his price to $500 per egg.

He was last seen the day before a big campaign rally for George Ratterman, April 3, 1961. Hawkins called home to say he was on his way to meet with his attorney, Charles Lester, to discuss the audit. Then he disappeared. Four days later, his tan 1959 Plymouth Fury station wagon was found downriver in Dayton, Kentucky, parked near the riverbank. The keys were in the ignition. The car had been wiped clean with river water.

There was no doubt that it was a mob hit. Maybe the egg prices were too high. Maybe he told Lester he would give names to the IRS if he could get a break on the audit. Or maybe it was his black book.

In 1944, the wife of gangster Pete Schmidt had sideswiped the constable's car in downtown Newport. Hawkins chased her, forced her to pull over and found thousands of numbers slips, $3,000 in cash and a little black book on her car seat. The book contained betting information and the names of various prominent citizens and policemen on both sides of the river.

"Black Book Is Veiled in Mystery," said the *Enquirer* headline. "Detectives Unable to Recognize Names in Memo Found in Woman's Automobile."

They certainly *did* recognize the names, but also recognized that it would be better for everyone if the black book was quickly lost.

"It could not be learned yesterday who now has the book," the story concluded. So the little black book of IOUs and blackmail names went missing. But Constable Hawkins knew who was in it, and may have kept it when the detectives decided they wanted no part of it.

Maybe the IRS agents breathing down his neck made Hawkins desperate enough to use it as a bargaining chip. Maybe his lawyer, Lester, tipped off the mob that Hawkins could name important names. Or perhaps one of the names in the book was Charles Lester.

Whatever the reason, Hawkins was never seen again.

In 1980, forensic reconstruction of the skull showed a face remarkably similar to that of the constable. But when his mother's remains were exhumed to get DNA samples, they did not match the DNA of the skull.

It was not Constable Hawkins, but the discovery rekindled memories of the case, including a forgotten footnote: A few years after Constable Hawkins disappeared, a sheriff's deputy stopped by one day to give

Mrs. Hawkins the red-stone Masonic ring and gold watch that her husband had worn every day. The deputy told her they were given to him by Charles Lester.

3.
Two Kennedys, Two Newports

President Kennedy liked to escape the pressure of the White House by sailing his yacht _Manitou_ off Newport, Rhode Island in 1962. His brother was busy battling the mob in another Newport in Kentucky.
John F. Kennedy Presidential Library archive

The morning after George Ratterman was hauled out of a dingy hotel room by Newport detectives, wrapped in a bedspread and trailed by a mobster and a stripper in handcuffs, Ronald Goldfarb read about it in the *Washington Post* on his way to work at the Justice Department in Washington, D.C.

His boss was waiting for him that morning with new orders: "There's a case breaking in Kentucky. You can go there and use it to start a broadscale grand jury investigation into payoffs to public officials in Newport. Newport's a notorious sin city the attorney general would like to see cleaned up."

Goldfarb groaned. As an assistant to Attorney General Robert Kennedy, he had hoped for something more heroic: Al Capone's Chicago, sun and guns in Miami, the New York kingdom of Lansky and Costello.... But no, he was stuck with the crime capital of Kentucky, Newport.

As Goldfarb describes it in his book, *Perfect Villains, Imperfect Heroes: Robert F. Kennedy's War Against Organized Crime,* the Ratterman headlines were almost irresistible for the young, crusading brother of President John F. Kennedy.

"Newport was an interesting sociological case history, and I could see why Robert Kennedy would target it," Goldfarb wrote. "Of all the wide-open, corrupt cities in the country, Newport competed to be the worst."

Bobby had the full backing of his brother. In the spring of 1961, the new president, John Fitzgerald "Jack" Kennedy, had hardly been in office long enough to unpack photos for his Oval Office desktop. JFK had visited Newport, Kentucky while campaigning in 1960, leading a motorcade parade like a celebrity grand marshal, perched on the back of a new Ford convertible, waving to the excited crowds.

But when he was not at the White House he was likely to be found in another Newport, the one in Rhode Island, where he could escape to his vacation estate for peaceful sailing weekends. The "Kennedy mystique" was captured on Kodachrome there in 1962. The young president looks almost impossibly cool, handsome, smiling, squinting off over the deep blue Atlantic into a never-setting summer sun. He wears a periwinkle polo shirt, Annapolis-white slacks and an aura of happy, confident command as he casually grips the wheel of a yacht with one hand, seated next to a pretty woman in a lavender mohair sweater. The woman was not his wife, Jackie. Most newspapers discretely cropped her out of the picture and showed only the fair-haired, youthful president, firmly at the helm of the free world.

It was the kind of image that symbolized everything glamorous and magical about the Kennedys—an image that was shorthand for their Gatsby wealth and "Camelot" lifestyle of American royalty. And like nearly all of the Kennedy mythology, it had to be carefully cropped to hide the truth.

While Jack was sailing in the sunshine, his brother Bobby was on a collision course with another Newport that represented the shadow side of Camelot: the one in Kentucky that symbolized all the grimy, grubby, seedy, blood-stained darkness of the underworld. Like a yacht in thick fog, the Kennedys were foreordained for a tragic wreck.

It was their father who put them on that course. Joe Kennedy, bootlegger and ambassador, friend of Nazis and mobsters, pulled strings to get Bobby a job as an assistant U.S. attorney in New York. From there Bobby went to work with another of his father's friends, Senator Joseph McCarthy, whose anti-communist crusade captivated TV Land and finally led to McCarthy's censure, downfall and early death from drinking. Ironically, Bobby reported to McCarthy's hatchet-man Roy Cohn—a fact airbrushed from history by progressives who still idolize the Kennedys.

During the McCarthy era in the early 1950s, mob informants were often helpful to the anti-communist crusade. And FBI Director J. Edgar Hoover was not just agnostic about the mob, he was an underworld atheist. He stubbornly insisted that there was no such thing as organized crime, despite overwhelming evidence from the Kefauver hearings. Hoover preferred to chase communists, and the mob was glad to help. Mobsters also openly said Hoover was in their pocket, compromised by his trips to racetracks, where he had an uncanny ability to pick winners—as long as he got tips from his race-fixing mob hosts. His secret life as a homosexual also made him an easy target for blackmail.

When McCarthy's crusade collapsed, Bobby Kennedy stayed on as chief counsel to the Senate Permanent Subcommittee on Investigations and began a new crusade against corruption in labor unions that inevitably led to the mob.

Bobby's target was curious, given his father's entanglement in organized crime. But Bobby was politically driven. Jack Kennedy had hoped to be Adlai Stevenson's running mate in the presidential election of 1956, but Stevenson chose Senator Estes Kefauver. Bobby, who was Jack's campaign manager, noted the national acclaim Kefauver had earned by investigating the underworld. He would not let Jack be upstaged again.

He started by going after corrupt labor unions. His No. 1 target was the most high-profile, bare-knuckles leader: Jimmy Hoffa of the Teamsters Union. According to files at The Mob Museum in Las Vegas, compiled by Jeff Burbank, author of *Las Vegas Babylon: True Tales of Glitter, Glamor and Greed:*

"Old Joe became furious when he learned about his son's intent to investigate organized crime influence within labor unions. ... Joe blasted his son for being ignorant and putting his brother Jack in danger of losing the important backing of labor unions for Jack's intended run for president in 1960."

Joe also knew that losing union votes was not the biggest hazard Bobby was risking. Joe Kennedy had only survived being killed by the mob himself thanks to the intervention of his friend Meyer Lansky.

Bobby ignored Joe's warning and led the 1957 Senate McClellan Committee investigation of labor unions as chief counsel, with his brother, Senator Jack Kennedy, on the committee. Building on the work of the Kefauver Hearings, it produced thousands of pages of testimony and reports that linked dozens of top mobsters to the Teamsters.

A bitter personal feud that would smolder for years was ignited between Bobby Kennedy and Jimmy Hoffa, who called Kennedy "a damned spoiled jerk" and poked a fat finger at his chest in one of their volatile physical confrontations.

Bobby swore he would get Hoffa, sometimes shouting at witnesses, his face red with rage and frustration. But Hoffa would slip free and be re-elected as Teamsters president by landslides. Bobby and the McClellan Committee were getting nowhere.

Then late in 1957, some alert state troopers patrolling in Apalachin, New York, a tiny village near the Pennsylvania border, spotted something unusual: A convoy of Cadillacs with out-of-state plates was streaming into the 53-acre farm owned by gangster "Joe the Barber" Barbara. The police set up roadblocks and brought cameras. They surrounded the farmhouse and captured more than 60 crime bosses as they scattered and ran into the woods in their wingtips, silk socks and custom-tailored suits. Another or more mobsters escaped.

The 'parking lot' at the mob's Apalachin Summit.

More than a hundred bodyguards, soldiers, caporegimes, consiglieres, bosses, underbosses and Mafia "bosses of bosses" had gathered for a summit to carve up territory and discuss marketing and distribution of narcotics, gambling, casinos, extortion and rackets, just as they had convened in Atlantic City in 1929. It became known as the Apalachin Meeting of 1957, a milestone in Mafia history.

The gangsters had names such as "Don Peppino," "Fat Joe," "The Cheeseman" and "Big Nose Sam." They were rooted in the crime-family tree, with branches spreading to Chicago, New York, Miami, New Orleans, Kansas City and Phoenix: Trafficante, Bonanno, Bufalino, Gambino, Genovese...

None of the so-called Jewish Mafia led by Moe Dalitz was present, and they probably were not invited. But the Italian Cosa Nostra was exposed in national headlines. Even J. Edgar Hoover finally had to admit that it existed.

'J. Edna Hoover'

In an interview with a *New York Times* columnist, Bobby made Hoover sound like blind Mr. Magoo. Bobby said that when he asked for files, he discovered that the FBI didn't have "the slightest piece of information" on any of the mobsters netted at the Apalachin meeting. "The FBI didn't know anything, really, about these people who were the major gangsters in the United States. That was rather a shock to me."

Reading that in headlines was rather a shock to Hoover and a lot of gangsters who thought that Joe Kennedy's boys were in their pocket.

Two years later Bobby Kennedy dragged Chicago mob boss Sam Giancana into a televised hearing to be grilled in front of the hot lights and whirring cameras, in a rerun of Frank Costello's performance in 1951.

When Giancana chuckled while invoking his Fifth Amendment rights, Kennedy humiliated him, hoping to trigger Giancana's famous temper: "I thought only little girls giggled, Mr. Giancana."

Giancana kept his cool and chuckled again. But he did not forget it.

Boston Herald columnist and Kennedy muckraker Howie Carr, in his book *Kennedy Babylon*, wrote: "There were two ruthless, powerful men who likewise assumed that they did have something coming to them from the Kennedys. They expected to be taken care of, or at least treated with kid gloves, by the new administration.

"One was a cop, FBI director J. Edgar Hoover. The other was a gangster from Chicago, Sam 'Momo' Giancana. Even if his sons didn't, Joe Kennedy understood what the Kennedys owed Hoover and Giancana."

Hoover had leverage over Jack and Bobby, with files and tapes of Jack's affairs, similar to the tapes sold by Big Jim Harris.

And Hoover knew that Giancana and President Kennedy had a lot in common besides power. They shared a mutual party pal in Frank Sinatra, who introduced both of them to a girlfriend they also shared, Judith Campbell. Later, Hoover collected similar files on the Kennedy brothers' affairs with Marilyn Monroe.

With his extensive secret FBI files, Hoover was accustomed to timid deference, even from presidents. But Bobby was different. They had battled before, but now Bobby was Hoover's boss, giving him direct orders, even mocking him in private as "J. Edna Hoover."

Giancana, meanwhile, answered to no boss. He figured he had the best insurance: He was *owed* by the Kennedys. As a favor to Joe Kennedy, and upon the recommendation of Sinatra, he had engineered the voter fraud in Chicago that gave Jack Kennedy his paper-thin victory margin of 188,000 votes out of 69 million.

Giancana told Judith Campbell, "If not for me, he would never have been president."

And Giancana was also helping the CIA plan assassination attempts on Fidel Castro, according to Judith Campbell's testimony to the Senate Church Committee in 1975. The CIA wanted Castro removed; the mob wanted its Havana casinos back.

The Kennedys *owed* Giancana.

But Bobby paid that IOU by continuing his ruthless attacks on the mob, using hundreds of illegal, unconstitutional, warrantless wiretaps.

When Jack appointed his brother as attorney general, he joked, "Bobby needs some solid legal experience, and this job should provide it." But even his allies were shocked at the nepotism.

Bobby immediately increased the Department of Justice task force on organized crime from three lawyers to more than 60. The mob, not communists, became the number-one priority. Hoover was checkmated and forced to create a "Most Wanted Gangster" list that was primarily a publicity stunt.

In 1961, Bobby launched raids in 22 states. In 1962 he targeted 700 mobsters. In 1963, he ordered the FBI to go after another 850 and indicted hundreds. He went after Hoffa and Giancana relentlessly. His "Get Hoffa Squad" finally did get Hoffa in 1963 with indictments for jury tampering and bribery.

But before all that, it started in Kentucky. When Bobby Kennedy read those *Washington Post* headlines in 1961 about a mob scandal in Newport, the national headquarters of organized crime wire betting, he sent Assistant U.S. Attorney Ron Goldfarb to investigate with a federal grand jury.

In his 1960 book about fighting the mob and unions, *The Enemy Within*, Bobby Kennedy warned, "If we do not on a national scale attack organized criminals with weapons and techniques as effective as their own, they will destroy us."

It proved to be a prophecy and an epitaph.

4.
A Prime Example of Corruption

If Ron Goldfarb groaned when he heard he was being sent to Newport, he must have wanted to weep when he got there.

After being informed that gambling was a $30 million business in a town of 30,000 people, he was disappointed to discover that Sin City was no posh Las Vegas. Not even a distant backwoods cousin.

"In the midst of such prosperity for the few, Newport, Kentucky, would never rival its sister city in Rhode Island," he wrote later. "There was no downtown shopping district, no newspaper; the streets were worn and dreary. In every respect except vice, the city of red brick buildings and old streets was stagnant."

For Newport, that description was like being caught from the worst possible angle in an unflattering snapshot; a crazy-hair, bloodshot-eyes mugshot; a glimpse in the mirror on the morning after, in the glare of harsh fluorescent lights.

Those glitzy casinos everyone was talking about? "The Tropicana Club, formerly known as Glenn Rendezvous, was on the first floor and the Sapphire Room for gambling was on the second floor ... the club's luster had tarnished and it had become a notorious bust-out gambling joint, a 'supermarket of vice' ... where second-rate exotic dancers stripped and B-girls vied with prostitutes for the suckers' dollar."

He continued: "A block from the police station, whorehouses ran day and night. For a southern state, life could get fast-paced. At Newport's biggest brothel, it was said, 11 girls averaged a new customer every seven minutes from noon Saturday until 6 a.m. Monday."

After taking in the squalor and lurid local color, he met first with Henry Cook, Ratterman's lawyer and the former U.S. Attorney who had contacted Bobby Kennedy to ask for help. Cook told Goldfarb that when he saw Charles Lester representing April Flowers and Tito

Carinci he was immediately suspicious of a mob frame-up.

At the time, the FBI was already watching Lester, who was suspected of carrying mob money to his Swiss bank account.

Goldfarb sat in for the first Ratterman trial in police court and reported to his boss, Bobby Kennedy. When it was over, they decided to prosecute the perpetrators of the frame-up for violating Ratterman's civil rights.

It was going to be a test case, the first salvo in the federal war on organized crime. Everything was riding on getting convictions to punish the mobsters and clean up Newport. It was Bobby's first chance to prove his brother had not made a mistake by appointing him attorney general—and it became a practice run for bigger challenges in Detroit, Chicago, Los Angeles and Miami. The young attorney general called it his "prime example" in national headlines and testimony to Congress. It all started in Newport.

5.
Make a Federal Case Out of It

"I suppose you heard that Red Masterson went to the Ratterman rally at the public library," Dan Davies said.

"I'm surprised he could find it," Charles Lester replied. "That had to be the first time he's ever been near a library."

Davies laughed. "He'd find it if we needed to burn it down. But maybe that should have been the headline: 'Read All About it: Red Masterson Seen in Public Library.'" He paused to take a bite of his Dover Sole that was probably something caught in the Ohio River. Catfish, most likely, he thought. But not bad as long as you didn't think about what kind of things bottom feeders ate in the Ohio River.

"I'm more interested in what he saw there," Lester said, sawing at his rare Delmonico and splashing dots of bloody juice on his pristine white shirt that was stretched taut over a thickening belly.

Charles has put on weight, Davies thought. If he's not careful, he'll get as fat as me. But he's either too vain or too stubborn to buy a larger shirt. Not as if he can't afford a whole closet full, custom made.

It was early summer, 1961. They were at a window table in the corner of a floating riverfront restaurant, on a barge that was tricked out to look like an 1870s riverboat, complete with dummy paddlewheels on the back. It was the latest thing for Covington.

The view across the river had the look of a postcard from the future: "Greetings From the Jet Age Decade of Prosperity." Gleaming cars, all chrome and primary-color reds, greens and blues, climbed Vine Street and Elm Street, their tail fins like the backs of salmon swimming upstream. The big canyons of Cincinnati's skyline were shadowed by the Carew Tower and the white obelisk of the Union Central Tower with its odd little ancient Greek mausoleum on top. It all was linked to Covington by the bright blue and gold Roebling Suspension Bridge in the foreground. It was the Blue Chip City in its prime, blessed by benevolent sunshine and cloudless skies while the quiet wheels of commerce turned quietly and wealth flowed unstoppable, majestic, like the mighty Ohio River, as if by magic. They didn't have to get their hands dirty over there. They were so clean they thought they invented soap. Yes, Cincinnati had all the success, all the wealth, all the headquarters towers. But Newport and Covington had the million-dollar views. Especially at night.

"Well," Davies paused and pointed his fork at Lester. "It was not good for our side. He said there were hundreds there, but the newspapers reported much larger crowds than that. This Ratterman and his Committee of 500 is starting to look like *The Life of Moses* with a cast of thousands. If we don't do something soon, they're liable to get the wild notion that they can actually elect the guy."

"Surely you don't believe that, not after all that came out when we dirtied him up in police court. We did everything but show a stag film of Golden Boy and the stripper doing--"

"Maybe because of it," Davies interrupted. "Red seems to think that whole Tito and April floor show did us no favors. Whatever you did to destroy Ratterman's reputation among our Newport voters just made him a martyr to the reformers and the rest of the county, not to mention how the press is playing it. Hell, even the *New York Times* sent someone to cover that trial. The *Enquirer* and *Post* are going after this story the way you're attacking that steak. Even our best friends across the river can't put a lid on this one."

Lester chuckled and took a sip of Old Forrester. "And in a few days they will think it smells like that mystery fish you ordered. You know they can't wait to drop the story before it hurts their convention business. Those newspaper guys have the attention span of a carp," he said, looking pointedly at Davies' plate. "Today, it's Kennedy and Kruschev. Tomorrow it will be the other Reds who play baseball. And don't forget, we can feed the reporters, too. Wait till the bartenders testify that 'Moses' Ratterman had enough drinks to float this barge. We've got three of them, from the Hilton, the Old South and the Caucus Room. We can still hang this thing on him, or at least stink him up enough to kill his chances in November. We can say he took the mickey when he got home, to cover his tracks with his wife. Who can prove he didn't?"

Davies lost his appetite after the "carp" remark and pushed his plate away.

"Have you heard what they're saying about him in the clubs?" Lester smiled. "George Ratterman went to bed in May and woke up in April."

Davies shook his head and laughed. "Perfect. Who came up with that?"

"I heard it from that gimpy bartender, Slow-foot Bill at the Alibi Club. He says he heard it from some cab driver who's a regular. He said the guy comes up with gems like that all the time. Says the guy looks like Ralph Kramden and sounds like Ed Norton."

As Lester continued to describe his brilliant legal strategy, holding forth as if he was making a closing argument for the Supreme Court, Davies eyed him and wondered if the great Charles Lester even knew or would admit to himself that he was in trouble. Deep trouble. His plot to frame Ratterman had been badly fumbled. Lester was kidding himself if he thought he could win. This one could leave scars, kill a career, maybe even send someone to prison.

That assistant attorney general in town, Goldfarb, was supposedly sent by the president's brother, according to Red Masterson's friend, who had been a secretary for Vice President Alvin Barkley and still had connections in D.C. And Red said she told him Bob Kennedy was declaring war on Newport, with Charles Lester at the top of his Most Wanted list.

Then again, you didn't need any hotline to Capitol Hill to understand that the Kennedys were on a crusade against organized crime. Anyone could see that Bobby was cutting corners with warrantless wiretaps and a vendetta against Hoffa. And nobody would stop him. If the president didn't like it and approve, he would've yanked on his brother's leash long ago.

The House had just passed the Federal Interstate Wire Act, outlawing bets across state lines by telephone. That alone could be lights out for Newport and Covington.

He half listened to Lester and thought, Charlie, the times have changed. Once upon a time someone like Ratterman would be no problem. We'd buy him out, burn him out or take him out. But now they were making a federal case out of it, and picking a fight with the federal government was like trying to stop a Sherman Tank with a slingshot. Suicidal. Just the other day there was a front-page story in the Louisville paper with a headline, "Robert Kennedy Calls Newport Gambling Big." He called us a "regional center for betting," Davies recalled, and "one of the largest gambling centers in the nation."

Lester doesn't even notice that I'm not listening, he thought. Or just doesn't care. As long as he's talking he doesn't have to listen to things he doesn't want to hear. Such as that for the feds, Newport was like one of Big Jim's clubs. Nobody cared when it was small-time. What was that old saying? "Pigs get fat, hogs get butchered." Newport is hog-fat, and the wrong people have started to notice.

Going after Ratterman had been a big mistake. The kind Lester did not usually make. It was like picking on some kid on the playground, then looking up to see his big brother standing behind him. And now somewhere in the Justice Department there was a stack of files on a desk, and the top one had Charles Lester's name typed on it.

Big Brother was coming for Charlie.

"Um-hmm," he mumbled as Lester droned on.

6.
Round Two: Kennedy vs. Lester

Assistant U.S. Attorney Ron Goldfarb, right, was sent by Attorney General Robert Kennedy to prosecute mobsters in Newport for violating George Ratterman's civil rights. It was a declaration of war on the mob by the Kennedys. Kenton County Library archive

After their first long trial ended in a stalemate with a deadlocked jury, the federal prosecutors began to have nagging doubts. Was it possible that Ratterman might not be telling the truth? Some of the evidence was troubling. What about the 11 scotch and sodas he had knocked back before arriving at the Tropicana, according to the bartenders? Was it possible that he had taken the knockout drops himself to concoct an alibi, as the defense lawyers claimed? And what about Tom Paisley, the owner of the Medina food-packing company where Ratterman was on the board of directors. Was Paisley part of the conspiracy, or was he innocent, as Ratterman claimed?

And then there was his statement on the day after his arrest. "Carinci suggested that we come to his place of business and be his guest for dinner," Ratterman explained. "I mentioned again that I did not believe his place of business was a proper one in which I should be seen. He said that he lived over his place and that we could get to his room unnoticed through a back door and eat in complete privacy. This was obviously the wrong place to go..."

Yes, as obvious as brass knuckles. But he went anyway. Eleven scotch and sodas.

And while Withrow's testimony was clear evidence of a plot, what if Ratterman and his buddy really had been looking for "broads" and were caught in one of the oldest snares for wandering husbands, the "honey trap."

They decided to give Ratterman a lie detector test, but the results were inconclusive. Goldfarb believed that was because Ratterman's genius IQ made him too talky.

They told him to just answer yes or no. The second time, he passed.

But prosecutors were still worried. Their case was circumstantial, with Ratterman's word contradicted by Carinci, Lester, the police and the stripper. Paisley was a wild card, so they had steered away from him in the first trial. By now, the defense had seen the prosecution's trial strategy and heard all their witnesses in round one. Lester was bragging about how easy it would be to win the second match.

Then came a miracle break. A Cincinnati reporter got a call from Port Huron, Michigan. It was April Flowers. She was dancing in a club there, billed as the "Red Hot from Newport." She wanted to talk to the FBI.

She explained that her mother was dying and her conscience was crushing her. She wanted to tell the truth and help George Ratterman.

Goldfarb described what came next: "Through a long night's meeting in a cramped room in the bowels of the Covington, Kentucky federal courthouse, April chain-smoked and talked."

The prosecutors were elated. "With April's new testimony, we had our case."

Just to be sure, they gave her a lie detector test. She passed.

She was ready to testify that everything she had said before in court was lies; she would tell the jury she joined a conspiracy to frame Ratterman, and got detailed instructions along with Tito Carinci at meetings in Charles Lester's office.

Marty Buccieri

Her new story confirmed reporter Hank Messick's theory: Ratterman passed out and was dragged up to Carinci's Tropicana apartment by Tito and Marty Buccieri, where they put him in bed with April. When the photographer didn't show up, they called Detective Ciarfardini, who was standing by. After that, the arrest took just 17 minutes.

The federal prosecutors now had the key witness they needed to win.

But it was not over yet.

Goldfarb flew back to Washington and got a green light from Bobby Kennedy to bring new indictments and risk everything on a second trial. If they failed this time, Kennedy would be humiliated and mocked, and his brother the President would be embarrassed. Bobby was ruthless and relentless—never known to retreat.

Goldfarb got back to Cincinnati charged up and eager to get back in court. As he got to his hotel, a message light was blinking on his room phone: April urgently needed to see him at her hotel.

"The room was a mess," he recalled later. "Liquor bottles were scattered everywhere, April was in an imitation leopard-skin kimono, her hair was up in curlers and cold cream was on her face. Her two poodles were yipping, scrambling over the bed. Her boyfriend, Charlie Polizzi, a gun strapped across his chest Pancho Villa-style, pulled us into the room. 'There's a contract out on April,' he reported. 'They want to get her before she testifies tomorrow. If they lay a hand on her, this town is going to have a bloodbath."

Polizzi was the brother of Al Polizzi, a friend and business partner of Moe Dalitz. Why he was ready to go to war over a stripper was anyone's guess. But FBI agents were immediately brought in to protect April Flowers.

After a sleepless night of high drama, April testified the next day as the second trial began on April 15, 1963.

This time, she was credible, sympathetic, even courageous. She described threats that were made against her and her son. She said she had been told to keep her mouth shut or she would wind up in the river, wearing a "Newport Nightgown" of cement.

When a defense lawyer mocked her for having a conscience, she sarcastically offered to spell the word for him, drawing laughter in the courtroom. This time, the crowd was on her side.

She said she recognized Ciafardini on the night of the arrest because he was often at the Tropicana to see his girlfriend who worked there. But she knew the arrest was not part of the script so she asked him what was going on. His reply, she said, was a broad wink, as if to say, "Relax, it's all planned."

She also said Tito seemed to know he was being arrested only as cover for the arrest of Ratterman. All the pieces fell into place, she said, when Lester showed up to bail them both out.

When Lester's lawyer overreached and described the mob lawyer as a respected, honorable member of the bar, the prosecutors pounced, offering evidence that he had been reprimanded for unprofessional conduct and had been arrested for attempted rape and assault. The judge overruled that evidence, but did allow testimony from a Kentucky State Bar official who left no doubt that Lester was seen as untruthful and untrustworthy in the local legal community.

Forensic pathologist Dr. Frank Cleveland testified that he was certain the knockout drops were ingested sometime between 11:00 p.m. and 2:45 a.m., based on his analysis of the amount remaining in Ratterman's blood when it was tested, and the time it would normally take for the drug to break down and pass through his system.

Then the federal prosecutors delivered their knockout punch: Another stripper who had backed up April Flowers during the first trial was called to testify. She reversed her testimony and described sitting in Lester's office as the frame-up was planned, listening as he gave instructions to Flowers and Carinci.

Lester and Buccieri were finally convicted. One FBI agent called Lester "the nucleus of a cancer that has existed in Northern Kentucky for many years."

The jury also indicted Newport: "The foul odors of vice, corruption and bribery cover Campbell County like a pall."

7.
Surprise Twist for
Screw Andrews

Even the most cynical crime reporters were startled when a federal agent told the press in 1961 that Newport's gambling income "makes even the Las Vegas handle look like peanuts." The Las Vegas gambling industry at that time was estimated at more than $3 billion. Which meant Newport's gambling take was bigger than the annual tax revenue for Ohio and Kentucky together.

It didn't really matter if the number was real or exaggerated. If Attorney General Robert Kennedy thought it was real, that meant Treasury officials thought so too—and drooled at the vast jackpot of unpaid taxes on that underground river of money.

While Sheriff George Ratterman began to raid bust-out joints and nightclubs, the feds assembled an army of 30 IRS agents from across the nation and raided the Sportsman's Club at 333 Central Avenue in Newport on August 23, 1961. The owner was Screw Andrews, aka Frank Andriola. The FBI named him as one of the top-40 racketeers in the nation. If there was a big boss of Newport after the Cleveland gang moved on, it was Screw.

The feds were in for a surprise. On the night of their raid, a spotlighted banner in the street said, "Welcome Shriners." The club was filled with red-fezzed members of the Ancient Arabic Order of the Nobles of the Mystic Shrine, who were having a well-oiled night on the town when the wet-blanket tax collectors arrived at 11:30 p.m.

The agents grabbed thousands in cash and charged Andrews and his team with 31 counts of tax evasion. The IRS turned on its adding machine and said taxes could amount to $4 million. Andrews was convicted in federal court of defrauding the government of $387,555 in taxes.

But when Sheriff Ratterman tried to get a Campbell County grand jury to follow up on the Andrews conviction, his efforts were dismissed with contempt. The grand jury said it found "nothing irregular" about the city buying urban renewal property "for a large amount of money" from Andrews, a convicted tax cheat, racketeer and mobster.

As Myron the Cabbie would say, "the worm was on the other shoe." The reformers were out, and dirty old Newport was back in.

Ratterman called it "The final act in the farce which our Circuit Court has been for over 20 years." He was just warming up. "Bill Wise (commonwealth attorney) blocks evidence, harasses witnesses, delays testimony and does just about everything imaginable in an effort to keep grand juries from indicting certain privileged members of our community."

And when rare indictments were occasionally delivered, "Judge Ray L. Murphy conveniently loses them in the shuffle indefinitely. We have had cases in the sheriff's office for over a year and a half that are still not on the docket. For Bill Wise not to present the overwhelming evidence which results in Frank Andrews' conviction in federal court is totally ridiculous."

But if the sheriff was hitting a brick wall of crooked prosecutors and judges, federal prosecutors and the FBI were standing by with a wrecking ball: They came after Andrews again in 1964 for tax evasion, and also indicted his lawyer.

The feds were immune to contagious "Newport eye," which blinded local cops, prosecutors and judges. Attorney General Bobby Kennedy's team was just getting started. Kentucky liquor control agents, the state attorney general and an alphabet-soup of federal and state agencies joined in to keep up the pressure.

Andrews finally was sent to prison in 1966 along with seven of his gang members, including his brother "Spider" Andrews. Each was sentenced to five years in prison and fined $10,000.

Bobby Kennedy and Sheriff Ratterman had made an example of Andrews and Newport. But Newport was stubborn. It was no longer the "wide open" Little Mexico of brazen casinos, bribes and 24-hour brothels, but it was not entirely clean yet, either. The underworld simply went underground. The raids continued for years.

As late as 1970, the New Plaza Lounge was raided by 26 FBI Agents, who padlocked the club for illegal gambling on horses.

In March of 1968, 90 FBI Agents launched a series of raids that hit the Yorkshire Club, the Flamingo, the Merchants Club, the Latin Quarter and the Playtorium. A few days later they raided five bookie operations and closed five bingo parlors. As usual, Dan Davies represented some of the gangsters.

A few months later, on June 5, 1968, Robert F. Kennedy was assassinated in Los Angeles while running for president.

By then he was long gone from the attorney general's office and had shifted away from attacking organized crime to focus on poverty and civil rights. His mob-busting crusade had been stopped in its tracks on November 22, 1963, when his brother, the President, was assassinated.

8.
'A Very Close Informant'

"Be careful what you say... I think this room is tapped."

"I don't know how they could get something in here. God, they must have got a lot of stuff out of here."

It was 1961. The FBI, with help of informants who were "very close" to Moe Dalitz, had placed wiretaps in his luxurious office at the Desert Inn in Las Vegas. They got a lot of stuff out of there.

The FBI recorded mobsters dividing the skim from casinos, bickering and dividing shares like a bridge club splitting the bill down to pennies at their weekly luncheon. The same tough guys and killers who hardly blinked at handing out $300,000 shares or paying a $75,000 bribe to a politician, quibbled and argued over a few hundred dollars.

During one of the bugged meetings in 1961, the monthly skim at the Desert Inn was more than $185,000. The FBI said it was "interesting to note that while Wilbur Clark is president and owner of record of 17.2 percent of the Desert Inn," he got a smaller cash share than a gangster from Miami and Cleveland "who has no ownership record."

Clark's share should have been the same as the $33,000 cut for Dalitz, but Clark was only a front man.

Doc Stacher, a Mafia casino manager and friend of Dalitz, helpfully explained in court: "The lawyers set it up so nobody could figure out who owned what."

In hundreds of classified FBI files and transcripts obtained for this book through the Freedom of Information Act, a portrait emerges of what might be called "1960s American Gangster, Las Vegas Species."

The glamorous life of a casino crime boss was not all showgirls, shotguns, sharkskin suits and Cadillacs. As the FBI agents listened for hours upon hours, the mobsters in Dalitz's plush office compared golf scores and gossip about Desi Arnaz as easily as they discussed getting various casinos to pitch in bribes to buy a Nevada governor.

In transcripts of the tapes they talk about how they can "neutralize" a troublesome lieutenant governor by blackmailing him over his secret spa vacations to "dry out." Dalitz is told by one of his underlings that a politician's secretary had recently quit after many years with him, and was fed up enough to dish the dirt about "bad books" she kept for him that would reveal graft and embezzlement.

The FBI wiretap summaries were sent to seven cities where Dalitz regularly visited and did mob business, including Detroit, Cleveland, Los Angeles and Cincinnati.

Under a routine FBI category of "Personal Habits and Peculiarities":

"Dalitz is an ardent golfer and when at the Desert Inn, usually plays golf daily," the FBI reported. "Subject is a moderate drinker and on occasion drinks to excess. He bets on all types of sporting events but rarely gambles at the gaming tables in Las Vegas."

"Mrs. Dalitz is extremely attractive and is considered to be an excellent hostess. Dalitz is extremely attentive and solicitous to his wife and affords her every luxury money can buy."

They also note: Dalitz is "armed and dangerous," the owner of seven pistols and a rifle; he was divorced from his first wife, Dorothy, in 1940 on grounds of personal neglect and extreme cruelty; and was believed to be born on December 24, 1899, but no birth certificate could be found.

"He is an ardent hunter and outdoorsman. He has purchased a lodge in Southern Utah and he frequently goes there for the purpose of relaxing and hunting lions."

The ranch was on 3,000 acres near Gunlock, Utah, with an airstrip, horses, a private hunting guide and 400 head of cattle.

"He enjoys living in the open and will take off for two or three days at a time," one of the FBI's close informants reported. "He indicated he is getting older and no longer has the personal interest in gambling that he had when he was younger. Every chance he gets now, he goes to his ranch without letting anyone other than his wife know where he is, and there he rests and relaxes."

In 1961, he may have been longing for a restful and relaxing mountain lion hunt to get away from dealing with more dangerous predators from Chicago, sent by mob boss Sam Giancana.

Chicago was trying to take over the Freemont Hotel and Casino in Las Vegas, and had sent mobsters Joe Pignatello and "Handsome Johnny" Roselli to stay at the Desert Inn.

Pignatello was Giancana's bodyguard and driver and a favorite chef for Giancana and Frank Sinatra. He owned restaurants in Las Vegas and was known in mob circles as "Joe the Cook."

Roselli was the Chicago gang's leading man in Hollywood and Vegas before he became the middleman in plots to kill Castro and the Kennedys. He was a wild card at the Desert Inn. As he looked over Dalitz's shoulder to make sure Chicago got its fair cut of the skim, he and Dalitz clashed and Roselli threatened Dalitz.

Roselli had "free run of the Desert Inn Hotel and he is given first-class treatment by the hotel executives," the FBI reported.

On the wiretaps, Dalitz and his crew talk about how some employees are terrified of Roselli, and say they suspect that the Chicago "strong-arm boy" is shaking down entertainers who perform at the Desert Inn, including Danny Kaye.

"To date, Dalitz has been able to keep them out of his local establishments," the FBI reported on the lineup of visiting Chicago gangsters. "He receives constant pressure from both the Chicago group and also from local gaming authorities ... who threaten to revoke his license if he does not keep hoodlums out of his hotels.

Charles Lester

"Many of the people with whom he has been associated in the past now accuse him of avoiding them and refusing to be seen in their company."

The FBI speculated that Dalitz was trying to stay "clean" to protect his license. The Nevada Gaming Commission published a "Black Book" listing names and photos of gangsters who were unwelcome at the casinos. Dalitz pulled strings and paid bribes to make sure he was not listed. Instead he found the Black Book useful. It gave him an excuse to throw out Chicago gangsters who showed up at his "respectable" hotels.

The Italian mafia "have their own code of ethics and have no use for Dalitz and his associates, most of whom are Jewish," the informant's reports said. "Dalitz and Roselli have an intense dislike for each other. ... Roselli never works and Dalitz does not know the source of his income."

"I catch it from both sides trying to keep the hoodlums out of the Desert Inn Hotel, and from the Nevada State Gambling authorities," Dalitz says in the FBI files. "I'm 61 years old and I'm getting too tired to fight them."

Dan Davies

Dalitz talked about getting out of the syndicates. Now that he was a big man in Vegas, he wanted nothing to do with the uncouth "hoodlum crowd" that made him powerful and wealthy.

But behind the flattering headlines and photos with Bing Crosby and Bob Hope, he was still a hoodlum, the boss of one of the most powerful and violent syndicates, the Cleveland Four. Respectability was just the shined-up skin on a rotten apple, buffed by philanthropic donations that came from casino-skimming.

He had ownership or a share of the skim in the biggest casinos in Vegas: the Desert Inn, Thunderbird, Riviera, Frontier, El Rancho, Stardust and Sundance.

He also owned nightclubs, oil wells and refineries, real estate, housing and golf-course developments, steel companies, laundry and cleaning companies and dozens of other "square" businesses—all made possible by his hidden life as a kingpin of organized crime.

But in 1961, FBI records show the new Moe Dalitz scorning those "hoodlums in the rackets" when they put his carefully cleaned and starched Las Vegas image at risk.

He had other nuisances to deal with besides Roselli.

In one wiretapped conversation Dalitz and his management team discuss how to handle "a group from Iowa that tried to come into the Desert Inn Country Club with shorts on."

At another meeting they bemoan the big hit they would take from a lucky gambler who won $50,000 in one night, playing blackjack at $500 a deal.

They study and argue over hotel remodeling plans for kitchens, dishwashing areas, bigger stages, lighting schemes and room updates by interior decorators. They talk about how to get showgirl jobs for "these two girls from Los Angeles (who) are real pretty and sing real nice."

They complain about tomato and strawberry prices for the hotel kitchens, then rant about how much they hate the Kennedys.

"Kennedy is in town," says an unknown voice. "I hope he gets poisoned." They all laugh, then talk about how hard some of their people worked to get him elected, and how "hurt" they were that, "Bobby did not even bother to call when he was in Las Vegas."

"The president and vice president owe a favor," someone says in a discussion of how to keep Moe's name off "the list" in the Black Book.

"You know what you ought to do with Kennedy," someone says at another meeting. Nobody had to spell it out. They could all finish that thought.

Dalitz was also busy organizing PGA golf tournaments that brought national publicity and thousands of tourists to Las Vegas, and gave him a chance to play and mingle with tour pros. The prizes for Arnold Palmer and other top pros at one tournament were dirt cheap. They were given appliances from General Electric worth "about six to eight dollars—coffee pots, toasters, etc."

"Most of the pros dislike Sam Snead and have made statements to the effect that some of them would not play in the tournament if Snead played," Dalitz says.

On other tapes, Dalitz talks about his good friend Jimmy Hoffa, whose generous loans from the Teamsters' pension fund helped to build new casinos and a Las Vegas hospital.

As the FBI listened, Dalitz complained about IRS problems and a lawsuit over a golf accident at the Desert Inn course. And he discussed his yachts, *Westward* and *Moby Dick*.

The names are interesting. *Westward* describes the big change in the life of Moe Dalitz when he left Cleveland and Newport for Las Vegas, where he discovered the really big jackpot at the end of the rainbow.

Moby Dick is the elusive white whale, Herman Melville's symbol of evil, pursued across vast oceans but never caught. So who played Captain Ahab, whose obsessive crusade to kill Moby Dick led to his own violent death? Was it the Kennedys?

While the FBI agents wore headphones, scribbling thousands of pages of notes, they must have been bored to the brink of insanity as the Dalitz gang discussed "chuckwagon" menus for hotel events and golf outings, hashed out hiring and personnel problems, griped about insurance premiums, then discussed national and local politics and the dark sides of various VIP guests such as Bing Crosby, Bob Hope, Eddie Fisher and Frank Sinatra.

"He's an immoral derelict and a person who has no respect for anyone or anybody, including women and children," Dalitz says of Sinatra.

He could have been describing another guy from the Detroit Purple Gang, the Cleveland Four mob, the Beverly Hills Country Club and Newport mob days: the old Moe Dalitz.

Las Vegas Moe was never very far from old Newport Moe.

In 1961, ten years after he claimed that he no longer had anything to do with the Beverly Hills Country Club or any of the casinos in Northern Kentucky, he and his team were caught on a wiretap talking about "Bobby Kennedy's most important case" and the fumbled "frame-up" of George Ratterman in Newport.

The FBI reported: "A check of appropriate real estate records at Newport, Kentucky failed to locate any holdings for Dalitz in Campbell County, Kentucky as of May 1958."

But, "It is the policy of these 'syndicated interests' not to own or control gambling enterprises in their entirety, but to see that the major portion of the ownership is centered in local people, and where local talent is available, they desire the establishments to be run and managed by local personnel."

As Doc Stacher said: Nobody could figure out who owned what.

In 1961, Dalitz flew to Cincinnati from Vegas for a meeting at the Beverly Hills Country Club with his Desert Inn partners Sam Tucker, Morris Kleinman, "Sleepout Louie" Levinson and local gangsters, including Red Masterson. The Beverly Hills club ownership was listed under several names, including Sam Schrader, who ran the Arrowhead Club for Dalitz near Loveland, Ohio in the 1930s.

In a 1962 meeting that was recorded, the Cleveland mob's longtime bookkeeper, Alvin Geisey, who had sworn that he was divorced from the mob years earlier, showed up in Las Vegas to report on activity in Kentucky. He updated Dalitz on the latest events in the Ratterman case and the gambling shutdown, and urged the Desert Inn boss to put up money to keep the Beverly Hills Country Club maintained at a cost of $100,000 a year.

Dalitz replied that he was worried that his Desert Inn could draw IRS scrutiny if his name showed up on Beverly Hills paperwork, because "all the wops in the world own the Desert Inn."

But whatever his concerns, visitors who went to the Beverly Hills Country Club to play bingo—the "near beer" of gambling—noticed that their bingo cards were labeled "Property of the Desert Inn."

The wiretap that backfired

The FBI agents who eavesdropped on mob meetings at the Desert Inn were not the first to wiretap hotel rooms in Las Vegas. The CIA had already bugged one of the luxury apartments at the Riviera Hotel in 1960—with less impressive results.

Fifteen years later, the Senate's Church Committee investigations of CIA abuses and assassination plots exposed the "Keystone Comedy act" that had been covered up to protect the government and the CIA from embarrassment.

Appropriately, the "spook" nightmare happened on Halloween, starring TV and Las Vegas comedian Dan Rowan, who later had a hit TV show from 1968 to 1973, called *Rowan & Martin's Laugh-In.*

It began while CIA operatives were negotiating with Sam Giancana in Chicago for help to kill Castro. Giancana told them he might have to postpone the meetings to fly to Las Vegas, because he suspected that his girlfriend was cheating on him with the funny guy, Rowan.

But the CIA persuaded Giancana to stay in Chicago by promising to bug Rowan's hotel apartment. "There is some evidence, however, that the CIA itself may have instituted the tap to determine whether Giancana was leaking information about his involvement in an assassination attempt against Castro," the Church Committee reported.

"Arthur J. Balletti (a private contractor) flew to Las Vegas and installed a tap on the phone. The (CIA) Support Chief characterized the ensuing events as a 'Keystone Comedy act.' ... Balletti, believing that the apartment would be vacant for the afternoon, left the wiretap equipment unattended. A maid discovered the equipment and notified the local sheriff, who arrested Balletti and brought him to the jail."

Balletti called his contact in Miami—who was CIA operative Robert Maheu, "tying Maheu into this thing up to his ears," the report said. Balletti's bail was paid by "Handsome Johnny" Roselli, adding the fingerprints of the mob's most notorious Las Vegas bully.

Maheu, who also worked for Howard Hughes, later used the incident as a "Get Out of Jail Free" card to avoid questioning and prosecution. The CIA vetoed investigations of Maheu to cover their tracks, and the FBI and Justice Department agreed that prosecution "would not serve the national interest." Meaning it would not serve the interest of government bureaucrats and politicians who could be embarrassed.

Rowan, not surprisingly, declined to press charges for the wiretap.

Roselli later said that when he told Giancana about the slapstick CIA foul-up, "I remember his expression, smoking a cigar, he almost swallowed it laughing about it." But Roselli didn't think it was so funny. "It was blowing everything, blowing every kind of cover that I had tried to arrange to keep quiet."

But the leak was plugged and the "Operation Mongoose" plots to kill Castro "which strain the imagination" continued, the Church report said. Castro himself kept a list of 24 assassination attempts by the mob and the CIA.

Top Secret files declassified in 2017 tell a story that reads like a rejected spy novel:

Before President Eisenhower left office, CIA Director Allen Dulles initiated a scheme to get rid of Fidel Castro by enlisting the mob, starting with Giancana in Chicago and Roselli in Los Angeles. With help from Maheu, who had worked for the FBI and CIA, they came up with plots that could have been lifted from *Mission Impossible* on TV— or maybe the *Spy vs. Spy* cartoons in *Mad Magazine*.

The plots to embarrass, humiliate or assassinate Castro continued through the Kennedy administration:

- Using aerosol LSD to crop dust a radio station where Castro gave weekly addresses.

- Cigars contaminated with a chemical "that causes temporary personality disorientation" (probably LSD), or treated with lethal botulinum toxin that would be fatal as soon as it touched his lips. ("The cigar does not have to be smoked," the top-secret report pointed out.) A box of deadly poisoned cigars in Fidel's favorite brand was carefully resealed as if new, but never delivered. (Ironically, botulinum toxin is now injected into the saggy faces of aging politicians and celebrities as a popular wrinkle remover.)

- Liquid bacteria in his tea, or in pills.

- A depilatory of thallium salt in his shoes to make his beard fall out. The plan was to abduct Castro's shoes when he put them out to be shined at a hotel, then return them loaded with beard-remover.

- And a poisoned skin-diving suit.

The Church Committee said: "The most ironic of these took place on November 22, 1963—the very day that President Kennedy was shot in Dallas—when a CIA official offered a poison pen to a Cuban for use against Castro, while at the same time an emissary from President Kennedy was meeting with Castro to explore the possibility of improved relations."

When Bobby Kennedy was briefed about the ongoing plots after becoming attorney general he asked, "Why can't you guys get things cooking the way 007 does?"

But James Bond was busy making movies. Castro laughed at the attempts and died of natural causes in 2016 at the ripe age 90, with his beard and his taste for cigars still intact.

9.
'Take the Stone Out of My Shoe'

U.S. Attorney General Robert F. Kennedy, appointed by his brother, the President, made a career of crusading against organized crime, especially in crooked unions. Confrontations with Teamsters President Jimmy Hoffa were profane, hostile and charged with hatred. Kennedy swore he would put Hoffa behind bars, and did; Hoffa vowed to "get" the Kennedys and celebrated when President Kennedy was killed in Dallas.

President Kennedy was shot at 12:30 p.m. on November 22, 1963, and was declared dead at 1:00 p.m. As his body was loaded aboard Air Force One at 2:38 p.m., Vice President Lyndon Johnson was sworn in as President, standing between his wife, Lady Bird, and Kennedy's shock-dazed and blood-stained widow, Jackie, in the front of the plane.

FBI Director J. Edgar Hoover seized the opportunity to bypass

Attorney General Bobby Kennedy and told the new President he would report directly to the Oval Office. LBJ agreed and appointed Hoover FBI director "for life"—or as long as Hoover kept his incriminating FBI files on Johnson hidden in a drawer.

Bobby resigned in September 1964.

Books about the JFK assassination could fill a small library, with several shelves listed as "Kennedy Assassination: Organized Crime."

Bobby Kennedy, with his brother's staunch support, had done more than even the Kefauver Committee to disrupt, harass, destroy and expose organized crime. As attorney general he formed a mob-squad of two dozen federal agencies to pursue and prosecute mobsters; he indicted hundreds of gangsters and sent them to prison.

More than that, he put a tourniquet on what he called the lifeblood of their business—illegal gambling that generated billions of dollars, laundered in hotels, casinos, real estate, restaurants and other "legit" businesses. He also shut off the spigot of loans that built lavish mob casinos in Vegas: union pension funds.

According to some accounts, when TV news bulletins announced that JFK had just died in Dallas Parkland Hospital, Teamsters Union leader Jimmy Hoffa climbed onto a chair in a restaurant and cheered.

All the big crime bosses in all the major cities had learned to fear Bobby's bloodhounds, or blinked in the spotlight of his root-canal interrogations and indictments. None had more reason to hate the Kennedys than Hoffa and mob bosses Sam Giancana and Santo Trafficante.

In 1976, an FBI informant testified that Trafficante, boss of the mob in Florida and Cuba, had told him in 1962 that JFK would not be re-elected in 1964 because "he is going to be hit."

Thirty years after the assassination, a lawyer for Jimmy Hoffa confessed that Hoffa had sent him to ask Trafficante to kill Kennedy.

Bobby was the most hated Kennedy. But killing the President made more sense. Without Jack, Bobby was harmless; but if Bobby was killed, his brother could come after the mob with all his power as President. Bobby could wait.

In 1979, the House Committee on Assassinations sifted through thousands of documents, witnesses and evidence from the original 1964 Warren Commission, and came to a new, starkly different conclusion that made the entire 888-page Warren Report look like an incompetent rush-job or a deliberate whitewash.

The Warren Commission had concluded that the assassination of President Kennedy in Dealey Plaza in Dallas was the work of a lone gunman, Lee Harvey Oswald.

The 1979 report said that a conspiracy was "likely." The chief counsel to the committee, Robert Blakey, went further: He said it was a "historical truth" that the mob killed JFK.

The 1979 report in the National Archives says, "The committee believes, on the basis of the evidence available to it, that President John F. Kennedy was probably assassinated as a result of a conspiracy. The committee was unable to identify the other gunmen or the extent of the conspiracy."

"The national syndicate" was probably not involved as a group, it said, but the evidence did not rule out "the possibility that individual members may have been involved."

The most likely suspects: Chicago's Sam Giancana, who was double-crossed by the Kennedys; Carlos Marcello of New Orleans, who was deported by Bobby Kennedy in 1961 and detested the Kennedys for "kidnapping" him; Hoffa, who was hounded by Bobby Kennedy; and Trafficante of Miami, who was involved in the failed CIA plots to kill Castro and invade Cuba to restore freedom—and reopen his casinos in Havana.

There was also a connection to Moe Dalitz. Sam Tucker, a boss in the Cleveland Four who supervised the Beverly Hills Country Club from his home in Fort Thomas, was a big player in pre-Castro Havana with Meyer Lansky and others. A confidential FBI report from 1958 reported he was there often, making millions from his interests in Havana's Hotel Nacional, as well as the Desert Inn and the Stardust in Las Vegas, with Dalitz.

The 1979 report includes a wiretapped conversation between bosses Marcello and Trafficante in early 1963:

Marcello: "Bobby Kennedy is making life miserable for me and my friends. Someone ought to kill all those Kennedys."

Trafficante: "You wait and see, somebody is going to kill those sons of bitches. It's just a matter of time."

The Warren Commission coverup

It may be 41 years old, but House Committee's "second opinion" in 1979 still packs the punch of a rifle shot and the smell of cordite in Dealey Plaza. As it says, what was found "demands a re-examination of all that we believed was true in the past." It exposed gaping holes in the "lone-gunman" theory of the Warren Commission, which was never accepted by most Americans. Nearly 60 years later, two thirds of Americans remain convinced the assassination was a conspiracy and the Warren Report was a whitewash.

Yet still today, thousands of pages of documents and evidence are kept secret, redacted or locked away.

As they trickle out, with the next release due on October 26, 2021, perhaps more dots will be connected. But this much is certain: One of those dots is Newport, Kentucky and the 1961 arrest of George Ratterman at the Tropicana.

That case was the first strike in Attorney General Bobby Kennedy's national crusade against organized crime. Mob bosses were already enraged by the Kennedys and their mob-busting work in the Senate. But they had been persuaded by Frank Sinatra and Joe Kennedy to help Jack get elected in 1960, assuming they would have a President in their pocket—until Newport.

The Kennedys attack on the mob empire in Newport was a betrayal that had only one response: *vendetta* (blood feud).

"An analysis by the committee revealed that the Kennedy administration brought about the strongest effort against organized crime that had ever been coordinated by the Federal Government," the 1979 report said.

Wiretaps showed that mob bosses were painfully aware of the "stepped-up effort against them and they placed responsibility for it directly upon President Kennedy and Attorney General Kennedy."

"Organized crime directly benefited substantially from the changes in Government policy that occurred after the assassination. That organized crime had the motive, opportunity and means to kill the President cannot be questioned."

Just weeks before his brother was killed, Bobby described how the mob could kill anyone and get away with it. "If they want to have somebody knocked off, for instance, the top man will speak to somebody who will speak to somebody else who will speak to somebody else and order it. ... To trace that back is virtually impossible."

The Warren Commission did not even try.

Their conclusion that Oswald acted alone leaned on his social isolation as a fringe "Fair Play for Cuba" protester. The notion that the mob would use someone so unstable was ridiculed.

But the 1979 investigation easily found connections from Oswald to organized crime. He had been raised by an uncle who was his "father figure," but also a "minor underworld gambling figure" in the Marcello crime family in New Orleans. His mother had "relationships" with at least two gangsters, including Marcello's personal driver. And Oswald's friend and mentor was Marcello's pilot, David Ferrie, who bailed Oswald out of jail when he was arrested for brawling at a protest.

The Warren Report also ignored obvious mob connections of Jack Ruby.

In 1947, the Dallas sheriff recorded conversations with mafiosos in Chicago, who offered him bribes to protect their move into Dallas, where they planned to open nightclub fronts for gambling, prostitution and narcotics.

Jack Ruby was affiliated with the Chicago mob, then moved to Dallas in 1947—to open a string of strip clubs, including the Silver Spur and the Carousel. Ruby's closest friend worked for Trafficante and Meyer Lansky.

"Jack Ruby was the mob's man in Dallas," the sheriff unequivocally said.

But rather than investigate that and other mob connections for the Warren Commission, FBI Director Hoover told his agents to discredit informants who incriminated the mob. In one memo, the FBI dismissed mob connections to Ruby—by quoting denials from one of Sam Giancana's hit men.

Also missing from the Warren Report:

- Hoover's FBI knew of but failed to report a 1959 trip to Cuba by Jack Ruby, where he may have met with Trafficante. The FBI also covered up Ruby's series of phone calls to Marcello-mob lieutenants, including a Mafia executioner, one month before the assassination.

- Although the FBI had wiretaps on most mob bosses (such as Dalitz in Las Vegas), FBI surveillance of Trafficante and Marcello was curiously "minimal or nonexistent."

- Marcello, as boss of a syndicate "first family," had authority to act without approval from the other bosses.

- At a 1962 meeting in New Orleans, Marcello "shouted an old Sicilian threat, 'Livarsi na petra di la scarpa!' ('Take the stone out of my shoe!') against the Kennedy brothers, stating that the President was going to be assassinated. He spoke of using a 'nut' to carry out the murder." The story came from a credible informant who was there, the 1979 report said. But the FBI deliberately left out the account after Hoover sent handwritten orders "that the Carlos Marcello incident would be deleted."

- The 1979 report said "the quality and scope of the investigation into the possibility of an organized crime conspiracy in the President's assassination, by the Warren Commission and the FBI, was not sufficient to uncover one had it existed."

- An informant said Trafficante told him that the hit on President Kennedy was being planned, and that Hoffa was principally involved.

- A mob conspiracy to scapegoat a flaky lone gunman was not at all improbable. The 1979 investigation listed similar mob hits. "In each case, the person suspected of inspiring the violence was a member of, or connected to, La Cosa Nostra. In each case, the person or persons hired were not professional killers, and they were not part of organized criminal groups. In each case, the persons recruited to carry out the acts could be characterized as dupes or tools who were being used in a conspiracy they were not fully aware of. In each case, the intent was to insulate the organized crime connection, with a particular requirement for disguising the true identity of the conspirators, and to place the blame on generally nondescript individuals."

- Such as: "The shooting of New York underworld leader Joseph Columbo before a crowd of 65,000 people in June 1971, was carried out by a young Black man with a petty criminal record, a nondescript loner who appeared to be alien to the organized crime group that had recruited him through various go-betweens. The gunman was shot to death immediately after the shooting of Columbo, a murder still designated as unsolved."

The 1979 report dug into FBI files to uncover the following quotes and evidence from mobsters recorded on wiretaps:

- "Bob Kennedy won't stop today until he puts us all in jail all over the country. Until the commission meets and puts its foot down, things will be at a standstill."

- "They should kill the whole family, the mother and father too. When he talks he talks like a mad dog; he says, 'my brother the attorney general.'"

- "During the course of Hoffa's discussion about assassinating Attorney General Kennedy, he did discuss the possible use of a lone gunman equipped with a rifle with a telescopic sight, the advisability of having the assassination committed somewhere in the South, as well as the potential desirability of having Robert Kennedy shot while riding in a convertible."

- Jose Aleman, an informant who listened as Trafficante talked to Hoffa by phone, heard him reassure Hoffa that the president would "get what's coming to him."

  "Trafficante had made clear to him (Aleman) that he was not guessing that the President was going to be killed. Rather he did in fact know that such a crime was being planned. In his committee interview, Aleman further stated that Trafficante had given him the distinct impression that Hoffa was to be principally involved in planning the Presidential murder."

Under the heading "Multiple Gunmen," the 1979 report said:

"In conclusion, the committee found that the scientific acoustical evidence established a high probability that two gunmen fired at President John F. Kennedy," and that, "The committee concluded, therefore, that the shot fired from the grassy knoll … missed President Kennedy."

Scientific evidence "compels acceptance" of the fact that Oswald did not act alone. "Further, the committee's investigation of Oswald and Ruby showed a variety of relationships that may have matured into an assassination conspiracy. Neither Oswald nor Ruby turned out to be 'loners,' as they had been painted in the 1964 investigation."

It took 15 years for the U.S. government to finally expose the Warren Commission as a cover-up and reveal the "historical truth" that President Kennedy was assassinated by the mob in a vendetta that began in Newport, Kentucky.

10.
Backrooms and Bingo Parlors

Used-up boxers and has-been celebrities sometimes stay in the saddle too long, flogging their spavined fame until its legs fold under in a sad, lathered death-rattle.

So it was with Newport. By the late 1960s, the speakeasies, bust-out joints and carpet joints were as old-fashioned as fedoras, pocket watches and high-waisted trousers. Anyone could hop a plane to Las Vegas where casinos were clean, modern, legal and relatively safe. Pot and psychedelics replaced bootleg booze as the new forbidden fruit. But the brothels clung to Monmouth Street and York Street like ticks on a dog, joined by strip clubs, porn movies and adult bookstores.

As baby boomers rejected their parents' vices along with their values, the end of the decade was shattered by protests, assassinations and wrenching generational rebellion, fulfilling the prophecy of poet W. B. Yeats in his 1919 masterpiece "The Second Coming."

> *Turning and turning in the widening gyre*
> *The falcon cannot hear the falconer;*
> *Things fall apart; the center cannot hold;*
> *Mere anarchy is loosed upon the world,*
> *The blood-dimmed tide is loosed, and everywhere*
> *The ceremony of innocence is drowned;*
> *The best lack all conviction, while the worst*
> *Are full of passionate intensity.*

Myron walked into the Alibi Club and stopped just inside the door to scan the faces at the bar. Gus the Bookie was gone, taken by lung cancer in 1965. Slowfoot Bill the bartender took off for Vegas in 1961, and was now working at the Stardust along with most of his dealer and bargirl friends from Newport. Even Myron's favorite pinup girls were gone from their place of honor behind the bar. He thought back to the first one, a nearly life-size reclining nude over the bar, with thighs like Civil War cannons. She was replaced by a classy Vargas girl pinup in a gauzy nightgown, drawn by the Peruvian painter and torn from an *Esquire Magazine*. Then it was Betty Page in her black fishnet stockings, followed by a Playboy centerfold, Miss June. Myron never failed to point to that one and remark, "June is bustin' out all over." Someone put up a *Hustler* pinup over the cigarette machine for a few weeks, until Knuckles threw it in the trash, saying, "Some things should be left to the imagination."

Now they were all gone. Nothing to look at over the bar but old beer signs. "Little Kings." "Hudy Delight." "Blatz." "Black Label." "Burger Beer," with the dots over the "U" that looked like eyeballs. There was even an old Quizz Beer sign from the dark days of the Depression and Prohibition, when the only legal beer was a watery "near beer" that tasted like it had been brewed in the men's room. No wonder we all turned to bootleg, he thought.

But there was Knuckles, standing at the bar, still in pretty good shape for a guy on the west side of his sixties. He had mostly given up his Lucky Strike "pimp sticks" in favor of cigars, and he had one lit, sitting in a tin ashtray as he read the *Post* and sipped on a draft.

The wooden bar top, varnished to a deep glow by coat-sleeves and elbows, scarred by 40 years of cigarette burns, chicken-scratched initials and phone numbers, was now replaced with impermeable prison-gray Formica, another jet-age product of Cincinnati, with little light gray squiggles that looked like bacteria under a microscope. The green-felt gaming tables were gone; so was the big Art Deco Wurlitzer jukebox that was shaped like a gaudy neon tombstone for Newport's dead nightlife.

"Hey, Myron the Cabbieman," said Steve, the new bartender, drawing out the "maaan" to make it sound almost cool. Steve had been there two years now, but he would always be the "new kid" to the old regulars.

"Get a haircut, ya bum," Myron growled, as always. Steve had blond hair to his shoulders like one of those shampoo girls on the magazine covers. Breck Girls. That's it. Turn him sideways to hide the mustache and Steve could sell Prell for the Proctoids across the river, Myron thought.

"One 'Wiederman's' coming up," Steve said, smiling that charming, likeable grin that always left Myron a little bit off balance, never sure if he was in on the joke or if he *was* the joke. You could never be sure with these kids. Like that tee-shirt he wore over his raggedy, faded jeans. Some half-finished sketch of a bearded guy in a headscarf, smoking a cigarette or something, with big letters that said "Zig-Zag."

Why doesn't anyone wear decent slacks and an ordinary clean shirt anymore, Myron wondered. They all had to display some kind of message: Make Love Not War. Tune in Drop Out. Ripple Cripples. Clapton is God. If it Feels Good Do It. Or pictures of marijuana leaves that practically begged, "Please arrest me." And the ones that looked like someone rolled a hand grenade into the paint department at Sears.

Most of the time the slogans made no sense at all, but the hippies all walked around wearing someone else's message and words like those winos who used to carry sandwich boards for the bust-out joints. At least the winos got paid to wear advertising. Pretty soon the kids would go all the way and get a tattoo that says, "This Space Available," Myron thought.

And what about the "Cabbiemaaan" thing? Those names were property of the regulars, not some boy-beatnik who was still pedaling a tricycle while Myron was driving Sinatra to the Beverly Hills Country Club.

Myron had retired and sold his 1953 Checker a year ago, with only 237,482 miles on the clock—still good as new. Those guys in Kalamazoo really knew how to build a cab. Sure, it looked like a Halloween version of Ike's staff car, a big yellow beetle on wheels, with a chrome beak, a humped back and pontoon fenders, but it rode like a princess on two peas.

"I keep tellin' ya Myron, you shoulda hired on at Weed-A-man's," said Frank Hanslovsky the beer-driver, pronouncing the name of his employer slowly and deliberately to make a point. As usual.

"I have to admit, I don't know how you guys at Weed-ER-man's do it," Myron replied, fracturing it just as deliberately. "They give you guys ninety minutes for lunch with all the free beer you can drink and then they send you back out on the road. It's a mystery how half the Boy Scouts and old ladies crossing the street in Newport is not flattened by beer trucks."

"Yeah, it's a tough job, but if it was easy, even cab jockeys could do it," Frank said, holding up his draft in a mock toast. "And things ain't so copacetical anymore since our shotgun wedding to the Heileman company last year. There are rumors that they might even make us work for a living."

It was still early, not even 3 p.m., but Steve was unwrapping a stuffed sandwich that looked like it was two feet long—as big as the rockets they put in bazookas to stop Panzer Tanks.

"Holy mother of pearl," Myron said, "where'd you get that thing, kid, at the psycho-deli?"

Steve laughed around a mouthful until it looked like he would choke. He put a fresh beer in front of Myron, the foam head dripping into one of the new cocktail napkins that matched the ashtrays and matchbooks with a red script: "We've Got Your Alibi... Club."

"Take it easy on the kid, he has the hungries," Knuckles said, rattling his paper. "It's that skunk cabbage he smokes when he thinks we're not looking."

"Farm out," Myron said. "Yaknow, kid, you'd be surprised what a cabbie can soak up from musicians in a ride to the casinos. There was nights when the smoke was so thick inside the cab I wished I had wipers on the backside of the windshield. If that old Checker could talk..."

"I'm still wondering if you can talk," Knuckles said, dry as a breadstick.

Steve started choking again on his submarine sandwich.

"And how does a nice Covington Catholic boy like you wind up in a dive like this," Knuckles asked, turning to Steve.

Steve cleared his throat, "Just lucky, I guess, Mr. Knuckles," he said. There was that blissful smile again. "I enjoy the ambiance."

"What did he say?" Frank asked. "Does he need someone to call an ambulance?"

"What I'd like to know is how the kid stays outta the Army," Myron said.

"He told us before, he's got a deferment," Knuckles said, "Right, kid?"

"Yeah, student deferment. As long as I take enough classes and keep my grades up."

Myron shook his head. "And if you're not a college boy and work for Trauth Dairy like my son Jimmy, off you go to Saigon or DaNang or Dang Me in Vietnam."

"I'm sorry about your son getting drafted and all," Steve said.

"Hell, you didn't make the rules," Knuckles said. "We mighta done the same in '42 if we had the chance. But that was different. We knew what we were fighting for. So how's Jimmy, Myron?"

The question was left hanging in the air long enough to make it clear that Myron didn't want to talk about it. Steve wandered off to find some glasses to wash. Frank studied the bubbles rising in his beer. Knuckles went back to the newspaper he had been reading before Myron walked in.

Knuckles sometimes felt like he was the punchline in a practical joke by God. Born with a body like the business end of an ax, with fists like Indian warclubs, he was made for violence, and he was good at it. Boxing. Brawling. The fine art of leg-breaking that separates two months in a cast from life on crutches. But he was also cursed with a conscience and a private love of reading. Books. Hell, most of the guys in the Alibi Club could read a street sign alright, but they wouldn't read a newspaper if their own name was in a headline on the obituaries page.

But he had been hooked ever since he did two-and-a-half in the Kentucky pen for "assault with intent" and met "Mr. Tolstoy" and his Russian friends in the prison library where he was assigned. "When you're killing time, go for the heavyweights," he was told by a lifer who knew a few things about killing. "Nobody beats the hell out of Old Man Time like the Russians. And if you don't read it you can always use it to knock someone's lights out."

The old con was right. He started reading and found out he couldn't leave it alone. It was like having a ticket to walk right through the thick stone walls and step into another world.

One day his new cellmate, Dave Whitfield, asked, "Y'all keep staring at that thang for hours. What all do you see in it?"

Knuckles sized up Dave. He thought he could take him without any help from *The Brothers Karamazov*. Or maybe the book in his hands, *Crime and Punishment*, might be more appropriate. He smiled.

"It's about a guy who wants to kill someone just to see what it feels like."

"You kiddin', raht? A dozen cons in this here cellblock kin tell you that. Why'nt y'all just ask me?"

"And?"

Whitfield was silent a while. "What's it say in the book?"

"I'm not that far yet."

Whitfield nodded as if he figured as much. No book could tell it. Not even one that thick. "It's lots of thangs," he finally said. "Sometimes it's like as if the whole world is leanin' over your shoulder, watchin' what y'all have done." He paused again. No hurry. Not in prison. Finally he said, "I reckon only one of 'em troubles me, and that was a flat mistake or I ain't in here. Weren't supposed to happen thataway. Place was supposed to be empty." He paused. "But I hear tell it gets easier."

"I'd like to know when," Knuckles said.

Whitfield took a second sideways look at him with raised eyebrows and new respect. "So you don't have to ask me nothin'. If you already knowed, why you waste time with a book?"

"I don't know everything," he answered. Whitfield nodded. Knuckles went back to Dostoevsky.

Long time ago, he thought, coming back from the dingy gray walls to the dark bar. He glanced up at Myron, took another sip on his beer and thought, now there's a name for Myron to mangle. Say "Dostoevsky" and he would say something like, "Gesundheit."

He wondered what Myron would think if he told him that the dead Russian was a hundred years ahead of his time, trying to warn us what happens when a whole generation is brainwashed by "Raskolnikovs" who think they can build Utopia without the mortar of morality. Steve might get it, he thought. But Myron and Frank and the others would stare at him like he had just walked in wearing his wife's church dress and high heels.

There was nobody he knew who read books. Only his son. Lucky for the kid, he had his mother's good looks. He was small like her. But maybe something rubbed off, because his son loved to read. Even went into the newspaper business across the river at the *Post*.

Knuckles was deeply proud of that. From caveman to newsman in one generation, he thought. When he told the guys at the Alibi that his son was promoted to editor, though, the only comment was from Frank. "So what's a guy like that do all day? Typing?" Where do you even start with that?

He liked to imagine his son talking with the other editors and reporters about great literature and art. But Jacob said it was not like that at all. "They're all know-it-all neurotics," he said. "If I made the mistake of mentioning that I was reading *War and Peace,* someone would have to say, 'I read it twice,' and then someone else would say, 'I read it in

Russian.' They're like crabs in a bucket, crawling all over each other to win some phony prize in the Cracker Jack box. Probably because the pay is so bad. I'd rather have a beer with you and the guys at the Alibi."

But Jake was a fine writer and a good editor. It made Knuckles proud to read the paper every day, front to back, knowing how hard all those people worked to produce something that only cost a dime and was as useless the next day as a cancelled stamp.

"Hey, Myron, you retired too soon," Knuckles said after a while, pushing his newspaper closer to the bright "Blatz Bohemian Style Beer" sign and looking down his nose through his reading glasses. "Says here the convention business has never been better in Cincinnati. They're doing more business than Vegas without the Sin City carnival attractions. Headline says, 'No Dice But Cincinnati is on a Roll.'"

"Those chamber of commerce hustlers lie like cats and dogs," Myron said. "If that's what they call business, I don't want it. These guys now, they come to a convention and they bring their *wives*. Can you believe it? It's all, 'Take me to Shillito's,' and, 'Take me to Lazarus, can you wait for me?' Hell, if I wanted to wait while a woman shops I would spend some time with my wife."

"No swells to give you fifty-dollar tips to find the Wilder women?" Knuckles prompted, knowing Myron was just warming up.

"I haven't seen a fifty in so long I can't remember if the face on it is General Custer or Robert E. Lee. The guys who come across the river these days have no class. They wear tight sailor jeans and windbreakers and have mustaches like child molesters. No offense, Steve. They're all looking for the strip clubs, nervous and jumpy like a kid buying his first *Playboy*. No offense, Steve. They give off a bad *ambience*.

"The last year I was working, I swear I didn't see a guy in a tux but once, and that was Rickles working at the Beverly Hills. People say he's funny. Yeah, about as funny as a double amputee on roller skates if you ask me. I start to tell him the dime tour highlights of Newport's attractions and he says, 'Hey, buddy, do you know how to keep your mouth shut?' I figure here it comes, he wants me to find him a hooker. So I says, 'Sure I can.' And he says, 'Show me.' And he leans back and that's that, not another word. Silent as God's library the rest of the way. I got a lousy 50-cent tip from that chiseler. He's squeezes a penny so hard he gives Abe Lincoln an Excedrin headache."

"They call him the 'Dean of Mean,' right?" Steve asked.

"No, his first name's Don," Myron shook his head. "But when it comes to mean, Milton Berle makes Rickles look like Saint Francis of the Sissies."

"You want funny," said Frank when they stopped laughing. "How about that raid last month. The FBI sent sixty-five agents to bust a canasta party in a Mound Street apartment. Sixty-five."

"Yeah," said Knuckles. "And nearly all the charges were dismissed. Sixteen arrested and only three prosecuted."

"This is a fine state of affairs when the FBI says it won't testify or produce evidence when it made the arrests," Myron said, reading the judge's comment over Knuckles' shoulder in his spot-on voice of W.C. Fields.

"Biggest FBI raid ever, they said. Now they're pretending it never happened," Knuckles said. "Sort of like the old days, but back-ass-wards. Back then they pretended it never happened *before* they busted down any doors. Saved everyone a lot of inconvenience."

"It's a sad state of affairs indeed when the Effed Bee of Eye has to scrounge around for gambling arrests like a wino digging in the backseat of my cab for spare change," Myron nodded.

"Hey kid," he said, "hit me again with something cold and foamy. You got any more of that salami torpedo left? You don't have any special herbs and spices on it, do ya? Did I ever tell you about the time I picked up James Bond? He was working across the river for United Fruit, see, running those Marx Brothers revolutions in Central America, and he told me this wild story about how the CIA and the mob tried to kill Castro with an exploding cigar..."

Steve, who had indeed heard the story before, plugged a dime in the juke box from his tip jar and keyed the numbers for a recent hit by Ray Charles. "Here we goooo again..." Ray crooned. Steve smiled and wondered if anyone else got the joke.

Everyone rolled their eyes at Myron's story. It was just too hard to believe, even in crazy 1968 when it seemed like almost *anything* could happen. Assassinations, riots, cities burning, crazy longhairs burning draft cards in the streets, good Catholic girls barely out of high school taking their shirts off at rock concerts, dancing to music that sounded like troglodytes beating hollow logs with clubs while guitars screeched like barbecued cats...

But Myron's CIA story was closer to the truth than anyone knew at the time.

As Myron liked to say, "Those mob guys never got Castro. They're a lot better at killing our own president."

Swatting flies with a sledgehammer

Late in 1967, while 70,000 protesters marched in Washington against the War in Vietnam, the FBI was busy organizing a surprise raid in Covington, Newport and Dayton, Ohio. Thirty-eight IRS agents went along to hit the 845 Bar in Covington and four targets in Newport: Mikes 101 Bar, the Newport Billiard Lounge, the Spotted Calf and the C and L Café. The federal agents seized horse-betting sheets and gambling paraphernalia.

In June of 1969, while the polluted Cuyahoga River caught fire in Cleveland, police raided a bingo parlor in Newport and a basement crap game in Covington.

In August 1969, while the Beatles were crossing Abbey Road, the FBI raided a sandwich shop in Newport. No gamblers were arrested, but the agents confiscated $3,000 worth of gambling equipment with help from Newport Chief of Detectives Pat Ciarfardini and Police Chief Edward "Buzz" Gugel, son of former chief George Gugel.

Two months later, police struck again using sledgehammers to bust down the doors at the Bachelors Club in Newport. They arrested two women. One was 83. That raid was led by Campbell County Commonwealth Attorney Frank Benton, who vowed, "We're not going to let this happen."

The decade that began with a bomb explosion in quiet Fort Thomas came to a close with cap-gun raids by G-men who were flogging a dead horse.

Poet T.S. Eliot captured the spirit in *The Hollow Men,* his 1925 tribute to Joseph Conrad's *Heart of Darkness.* He described a journey of broken, condemned souls on their way to "This broken jaw of our lost kingdoms."

This is the way the world ends,

This is the way the world ends,

This is the way the world ends,

Not with a bang, but a whimper.

A footnote on the 'perfect crime'

When Palestinian Sirhan Bishara Sirhan shot Bobby Kennedy in a Los Angeles hotel kitchen on June 5, 1968, it was the first example of Middle Eastern terrorism against the United States, or the perfect crime by the mob to scapegoat another "lone gunman."

Or perhaps both.

Sirhan was an unstable, troubled outcast who willingly confessed that his motive was hatred of Kennedy for pledging military aid to Israel. He had warned his trash collector not to support Bobby Kennedy because, "I plan to kill him."

After the shooting, as he was pinned to a table while his gun was wrenched from his hand, he said, "I did it for my country," meaning Palestine.

In diaries found at his mother's home, he wrote about his "unshakeable obsession" to kill Kennedy, who was campaigning for president in the California primary. "Kennedy must fall," he wrote. "We believe Kennedy must be sacrificed for the cause of the poor, exploited people." And, "Kennedy must die before June 5."

According to his lawyers, Sirhan started acting strangely after a head injury at a horse track where he worked. He pleaded guilty to the murder, tried to fire his lawyers and begged to be executed. The judge denied his demands and ordered a trial. He was found guilty.

But there are still loose ends, rabbit holes and troubling evidence.

Witnesses said Sirhan approached and shot Kennedy from the front, at a distance of at least three feet. But the autopsy report said the fatal injury was a gunshot wound that entered behind Kennedy's right ear, where powder burns showed it was fired from just one or two inches.

Three shots hit Kennedy in the head, right rear shoulder and back, and more shots and ricochets injured five bystanders.

Ballistics analysis initially said all the shots came from Sirhan's eight-shot, .22 caliber Iver-Johnson Cadet revolver. But a second analysis concluded that some of the bullets that were recovered came from a second gun, and that at least nine shots were fired—too many for Sirhan's gun. A 2005 audio analysis counted 13 shots in the crowded kitchen.

Bullet holes in a doorframe, shown in TV videotape, may have provided key evidence, but the doorframes and whatever they contained were removed and destroyed immediately after the shooting.

Sirhan consistently claimed he had no memory of the shooting. He was sentenced to life in prison. In 2016, at yet another failed request for parole, he and his lawyers offered a new story. With the aid of a Harvard doctor who specialized in memory recovery, they said he had been "programmed" as part of a conspiracy. After 60 hours of interviews with the doctor, Sirhan claimed to remember an attractive woman who gave him a drink in the hotel pantry, then triggered him with a post-hypnotic suggestion to shoot Kennedy, like the brainwashed soldier in the *Manchurian Candidate*.

He claimed he remembered nothing between the drink and finding himself choked and restrained on the table where Kennedy's bodyguards took his gun and held him for police.

Sirhan was stabbed by another inmate in 2019, but recovered and remains in prison.

The shooting was revisited in 1975, when an independent investigation by the Los Angeles Board of Supervisors interviewed 6,000 witnesses and collected thousands of pages of evidence. It concluded that "there is no evidence that Sirhan did not act alone."

But as the 1979 House Committee on Assassinations reported, the mob was known to use unstable "cutouts" to take the fall for their dirty work:

"In each case, the persons recruited to carry out the acts could be characterized as dupes or tools who were being used in a conspiracy they were not fully aware of. In each case, the intent was to insulate the organized crime connection, with a particular requirement for disguising the true identity of the conspirators, and to place the blame on generally nondescript individuals."

When he was arrested for killing President Kennedy, Lee Harvey Oswald protested, "I'm just a patsy." It became his epitaph. Jack Ruby made sure Oswald did not live long enough to explain.

If Sirhan Bishara Sirhan was also "just a patsy," the mob had learned from its mistakes in the killing of JFK. Bobby was the Kennedy the mob hated most. Some had vowed he would be next after his brother. The room where Bobby was shaking hands was packed with supporters, campaign aides and hotel workers. A second gunman could have easily escaped in the chaos after the shots, as Robert Kennedy lay fatally wounded on the kitchen floor, speaking his final words—"Is everybody okay?"—before he slipped into a coma.

If so, it joins the JFK assassination as another ultimate cold case and perfect crime.

During his 1960 campaign for the presidency, John Kennedy visited Newport leading a motorcade in an open convertible that ominously foreshadowed his assassination in Dallas three years later. The roots of his blood feud with the mob began in Newport.

Photo courtesy of Nick Rechtin

Part V — 1970s

1.
Reaping the Whirlwind

Porn king Sammy Wright flees from a photographer on the streets of Newport. He owned the Cinema X adult theater. When it was closed, police found hidden cameras and pictures of police and prominent citizens secretly photographed watching hard-core porn such as *Deep Throat*. Kenton County Library archives.

211

When Sheriff Ratterman and the feds fumigated Sin City in the 1960s, some of the vermin escaped through cracks under the doors and scuttled across the bridges to infest Cincinnati.

The biggest was Larry Flynt. He was born and raised in Kentucky, in dirt-floor poor Magoffin County, southeast of Newport. He ran away at age 15 and served in the Navy on the *U.S.S. Enterprise* aircraft carrier that picked up John Glenn's space capsule in 1962. He said he got his start in the nightclub business with money from his mother's dive bar in Dayton, Ohio.

He would have fit right in among the underworld "police characters," pimps, strip-club operators, small-time hustlers and porn peddlers in Newport.

By the time he opened his Hustler Club in Cincinnati in 1970, anyone who walked in must have wondered if the whole thing had been jack-hammered out of the ground in Newport and dropped by a crane into a rundown block of the downtown business district.

Timing was everything. The romantic era of peace and love was being shoved aside by lust and hard drugs. Romantic *Knights in White Satin* was replaced by a *Black Sabbath* screamer who bit the heads off doves and bats. The protesters who pushed down the barricades of traditional values were finding that nobody was left to push back. The "over 30" generation that endured the Depression and won World War II was cresting the hill of middle-age, worn out, bone-weary of hand-to-hand combat with their own sons and daughters.

As the rebellious boomer generation charged ahead to find new fences to knock down, author Tom Wolfe called it "The Great Re-Learning."

In 1987 he wrote a parable about what he had seen in 1968:

"At the Haight-Ashbury Free Clinic there were doctors who were treating diseases no living doctor had ever encountered before, diseases that had disappeared so long ago they had never even picked up Latin names, diseases such as the mange, the grunge, the itch, the twitch, the thrush, the scroff, the rot. And how was it that they had now returned? It had to do with the fact that thousands of young men and women had migrated to San Francisco to live communally in what I think history will record as one of the most extraordinary religious experiments of all time.

"The hippies, as they became known, sought nothing less than to sweep aside all codes and restraints of the past and start out from zero. ... Among the codes and restraints that people in the communes swept aside—quite purposely—were those that said you shouldn't use other people's toothbrushes or sleep on other people's mattresses without changing the sheets or, as was more likely, without using any sheets at all or that you and five other people shouldn't drink from the same bottle of Shasta or take tokes from the same cigarette. And now, in 1968, they were relearning ... the laws of hygiene ... by getting the mange, the grunge, the itch, the twitch, the thrush, the scroff, the rot."

Lessons learned at great cost through centuries of advancing civilization were scorned and thrown on the ash-heap of history. Marriage was "oppression." Children "didn't need" dads. Drugs were "self-discovery." Sexual experimentation and casual promiscuity were "healthy." Porn was "instructional" and "therapeutic." Abortion was a new constitutional right of convenience. "Different strokes for different folks," was the new anthem. "Anything goes."

Larry Flynt's nightclubs were a metaphor for the downside of the 70s, dark in every sense of the word. His brother told a reporter that low lights in their strip club were more of a necessity than a vice. "When you opened it up in the daylight and let the sunlight in, it looked like a toilet," said Jimmy.

Because it was.

When Hamilton County Prosecutor Si Leis threatened to prosecute Flynt's strip club in Cincinnati on obscenity charges, Flynt bragged to him that he could arrange to have the prosecutor's good friend, Cincinnati Police Chief Carl Goodin, sitting in the club anytime he wanted. Leis called the bluff. Sure enough, Chief Goodin was there on display when Leis showed up.

Flynt was busted by Leis for public sodomy and discharging a firearm during a sex act in his bar. That led to indictments of Chief Goodin and six officers on his vice squad in 1975, for extortion and bribery. A letter from nine police officers accused Goodin of soliciting bribes and throwing "prostitution parties."

The scrofulous grunge that was always contained across the river like Cincinnati's bedroom secret had spread like a sexually transmitted disease. Leis said in 1997, "If Larry Flynt had not been stopped, he would have corrupted the whole town. Adult bookstores. Massage parlors. Adult movies. And yes, corruption. His start-up money came from organized crime in Cleveland."

When Hollywood made a First Amendment saint of Flynt in *The People vs. Larry Flynt*, the national and local media mocked Cincinnati for being a church-lady town, too uptight and puritanical to get with it and appreciate all that the smut peddler had done to defend every American's constitutional right to buy crude, degrading, demeaning porn.

Anything goes.

But the sophisticates who defended Flynt either forgot or never understood how Cincinnati had lived for decades next door to its dysfunctional neighbors across the river. The Queen City had seen firsthand how hard it was to exterminate corruption, vice and organized crime once it burrowed into the woodwork in Newport and Covington. Leis was not going to let that happen in his city.

The battle was long and ugly. Flynt tried to frame Leis by sending strippers and a photographer to bust into his hotel room at a prosecutors' convention—taking a "frame-up" page from the Ratterman saga, that he hoped to publish in his *Hustler* porn magazine. It could have destroyed the sheriff and discredited the crusade against porn. But the former Marine Leis shoved the strippers and the photographer back into the hallway and locked the door.

"We won," the sheriff said, looking back 20 years later. "Cincinnati is safe, a good place for a family."

Most cities went the other way. Nearly all of them had their own local "sin strips" that sprouted like weeds in declining, litter-strewn downtowns. The mini-Times Square carnivals of seedy topless clubs, adult movies and porn stores. In the 1970s, even college campuses had regular movie nights for triple-X porn in the dorms. At Michigan State University, the student newspaper ran ads for regular showings of *Deep Throat*, *The Devil in Miss Jones* and *Behind the Green Door*, along with want-ads seeking students to "audition" for roles in locally made X-rated porn.

The 1970s became known as "The Golden Age of Porn." Film critic Roger Ebert gave favorable reviews to hard-core porn movies to show he was "cool" with the new "porno chic" fad.

By the end of the decade, the FBI arrested and indicted 45 major pornographers as part of a two-year undercover investigation. The $4 billion a year porn industry was almost completely controlled by organized crime, said FBI Director William Webster. Si Leis was right.

Roger Young was the FBI's lead investigator on that MIPORN investigation. He told the Catholic News Agency, "There's no such thing as 'just' an obscenity case, because they ran into child pornography, stolen property, illegal weapons, money laundering, prostitution—many, many violations."

"One pornographer assigned to me was a 'made' member of the Colombo [organized crime] family, Anthony Perraino, who was the originator of the *Deep Throat* movie back in the '69-'70 era, and had continued on with his pornography business and developed it in the San Fernando Valley."

An X-rated hangover

"You ain't never gonna believe it, Knucks," Myron said, tossing his jacket on an empty barstool and taking a seat. "The wife asked me to take her to see *Deep Throat*. My *wife*. The woman who raised my son, God rest his soul. The woman who hasn't missed mass on Sunday since Christ was a carpenter's apprentice. And how did she get this genius idea? She says she read in *Parade Magazine* that Jackie O'Kennedy went to see it along with all the other egghead nitwits in New York."

"What did you tell her?" Knuckles asked, shaking his head.

"I told her you couldn't drag me to see that garbage if Old Blue Eyes himself was bonking the dame. I told her Jackie O must be half-a-moron for marrying Jack and that fat Greek, and all the brains of all the intellectualoids in New York City couldn't fill a shot glass. I told her she would have a cardiattack infartshun before she got through the credits."

Knuckles laughed. "I guess wild old Newport was ahead of its time after all. I read the other day that more people recognize the woman in that movie than Henry Kissinger."

"Kissin-what?" Myron joked. "Maybe instead of cleaning up Sin City, Bobby should have invited his sister-in-law for a tour. I can think of a half-dozen stops that would beat the pants off anything showing at Cinema X."

"You got the right idea staying away from that place," Knuckles nodded.

"Yeah, I might get stuck to the seat."

"It's not just the raincoat regulars. From what I hear, you will wind up in Sammy Wright's photo album. He has hidden cameras aimed at the audience. City commissioners, judges, police, you name it, they're all in Sammy's photo album."

"That figures for an ex-con Purple Gangster like Sammy. I wonder what he's paying Mayor Johnny TV to keep the raids away. Cops are on the take. Downtown looks like hell—worse than it did when the real mob was in charge. With the casinos gone, Newport has all the crime with none of the charm. No celebrities, no glamor, no nightlife, just an X-rated hangover."

"Amen, brother," Knuckles said, lighting another cheroot and shaking out the match. "Downtown will never recover as long as it has the strip club clap. Newport's like that guy in the movie *Walking Tall*. You know, he gets elected sheriff and tries to clean up a bunch of gangsters in a sleazy bar—sorta like this one come to think of it." He looked around the Alibi Club as if to confirm it, nodded and continued.

"But this sheriff Buford, he doesn't know what he's up against. Like Ratterman. They gang up on him and he takes a helluva beating. Every day while he recuperates he whittles this great big stick like an ax handle for Paul Bunyan, waiting for his chance to finally walk back into that bust-out joint and get even. Then the day finally comes. He goes back to the bar, pulls the screen door open and steps inside—and some guy in a black robe from the Supreme Court runs up to grab the club out of his hands. So they beat the hell out of him again."

"Hey, that's not how that movie ended," Steve the bartender objected.

"No, that's how Newport ended."

"Perfect," Myron nodded. "The way those justices defend the porn mob, it almost makes you wonder what they're doing under those robes."

Newport fights back

Newport led the nation in battling sleaze during the "Golden Age of Porn" in the 1970s, and won a major victory when the Cinema X adult theater finally closed in 1982. Kentucky Views

While Cincinnati battled Larry Flynt, Newport waged its own war against another powerful porn tycoon known as the reclusive "Howard Hughes of porn." For the first time, city voters began to tip toward the reformers. They removed the pro-porn "liberals" led by Mayor Johnny TV Peluso and elected a team who promised to exterminate downtown's "sin strip" on Monmouth Street. The new commissioners started by prosecuting a seedy adult bookstore and X-rated movie theater.

But nearly every victory was reversed by the U.S. Supreme Court. The same court that invented a constitutional right to abortion in 1973 also ruled repeatedly to protect the porn industry.

The Monmouth Street Novelty and Bookstore and Cinema X theater opened in the heart of downtown Newport in 1970, owned by Midwestern porn king Harry Virgil Mahoney of Durand, Michigan, who got his start with a drive-in porn theater known as "The Durand Dirties." His empire covered Michigan, Ohio, Indiana, Illinois and Kentucky with massage parlors, peepshows, strip clubs, adult bookstores and X-rated theaters.

In 1973 the FBI raided Cinema X in Newport and seized the hard-core movie *Deep Throat* ("The first stag film to see with a date," said critic Roger Ebert). Defense lawyers argued it had "redeeming social value" as a teaching tool in sex therapy, because Americans were "ill informed" about sex. Juries rolled their eyes when told that Americans, whose movies, advertising and pop culture were steeped in sex, needed training films. They didn't buy it, and neither did a judge who watched the movie. He described it this way:

> "The film runs from one act of explicit sex into another, forthrightly demonstrating heterosexual intercourse and a variety of deviate sexual acts, not 'fragmentary and fleeting' … it permeates and engulfs the film from beginning to end. The camera angle, emphasis and close-up zooms (give) maximum exposure in detail of the genitalia during the gymnastics, gyrations, bobbing, trundling, surging, ebb and flowing, eddying, moaning, groaning and sighing, all with ebullience and gusto. There were so many and varied forms of sexual activity one would tend to lose count of them."

The jury found no redeeming value and ruled the movie was obscene. U.S. District Judge Mac Swinford fined "Howard Hughes" Mahoney $72,000 and ordered three months of jail time.

But then the Supreme Court overturned the case and changed the rules—raising the bar for porn prosecutions and lowering standards for decency. "Contemporary community standards" that allowed towns like Cincinnati and Newport to decide what they would tolerate were eliminated. The old standard of "no redeeming value" was no longer enough. Prosecutors would have to prove a book, movie or magazine was "utterly without redeeming social value."

The Supreme Court also undermined efforts to shut down strip clubs by ruling that "mere nudity" was protected "speech."

Undaunted, a local jury found *Deep Throat* obscene again and "utterly without redeeming social value." But again, the higher courts yanked away the football and overruled the verdict.

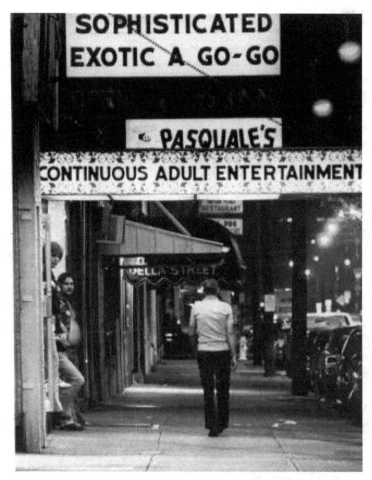

The Sin Strip in Newport in the 1970s.
Kenton County Library archives.

Still, Newport did not give up. While many in Newport still longed for the old days when the mob made the city hum, a slim majority of voters wanted to clean up festering police corruption, extortion, crime, prostitution and other side effects, such as "white slave" trafficking for prostitution by the Seventh Sons motorcycle gang. The reformers were often mocked as uptight "prudes." A headline about a Cinema X raid caught the tone: "Too Sexy for Police."

The pro-porn crowd made a comeback in 1980, when Peluso and his gang recaptured the city commission. "It was a bloodbath" said Ken Rechtin, who was city ombudsman and liquor control agent at the time. As Johnny TV retaliated against anti-porn city officials and clean cops, "Half a dozen were terminated immediately."

But outside the city, Campbell County Attorney Paul Twehues continued to battle porn and prostitution, helped by the Kentucky State Police and the FBI.

After he served prison time for running a brothel as Wilder Town Marshal, Big Jim Harris opened a strip club that was raided by Kentucky State Police.
Kenton County Library archive

In 1980, raids of several clubs included the arrest of "Big Jim" Harris (again), the ex-con owner of the Jai Alai Piano Lounge at 904 York Street. The former Wilder, Kentucky town marshal who had moonlighted with his own whorehouse and extortion racket, had served a stretch in prison and was now up to his old tricks. Twenty Kentucky State Troopers and ten Newport Police arrested eight women, Harris, and a former president of the Newport Fraternal Order of Police. Troopers said women in the club offered them sex acts if they bought a $55 drink.

During the raid they caught one naked couple in the act and seized bedspreads, sheets, hygiene products and an extra-large inventory of paper towels. Ultraviolet lights revealed the club was practically painted in body fluids.

Porn merchant Sammy Wright and his wife, Mary Dell, had their strip club raided along with others. A University of Louisville thesis by Michael L. Williams, *Sin City Kentucky: Newport, Kentucky's Vice Heritage and its Legal Extinction, 1920-1991*, found that in 1982 there were 16 clubs in Newport, such as the Kit Kat Club, the Dream Bar, Dillinger's, the Pink Pussycat, Nite Life Lounge, Trixie's, Talk of the Town, the Brass Ass, the Brass Bull and Sparkle Plenty.

Rechtin's brother Nick Rechtin, who became a community activist to clean up Newport in the 1970s, says, "I counted 17 strip joints in the city on Monmouth in the late 70s. They were mostly bars decorated with Christmas lights in which women took their clothes off. There were some better ones—like the carpet joints versus the bust-out joints in the old days. It all went back to the Glenn Rendezvous, the Tropicana, the Yorkshire, places like that."

Ironically, Peluso sowed the seeds of reform by applying for federal urban renewal grants. The application required participation from neighborhood associations, and "that legitimized grassroots groups," Nick Rechtin said. A Citizens Advisory Council was formed, which set reform in motion.

Peluso's gang wanted to "polish the rotten apple," Nick Rechtin recalled. A consultant told citizens that eliminating porn would be a mistake; Newport should turn its vice into virtue, "like Bourbon Street in New Orleans."

"The advisory council said 'Go to hell. We've had enough of this crap. We don't need it and don't want it,'" Nick Rechtin recalled.

The battle was symbolized at the north end of Monmouth Street, where the Committee of 500 reform group had its headquarters—directly across the street from brothels, bars and a gangster gambling joint. Then again, it was almost impossible to find a place in downtown Newport that was not surrounded brothels and bust-out joints.

In 1982, Peluso lost and reform Mayor Irene Deaton took over with a new city commission that launched raids on sex clubs to back up County Attorney Twehues and the embattled Newport Police, who were no longer handcuffed by Mayor Peluso and his pro-porn cronies. It was a turning point.

The battle drew national attention. Visiting for a rally in 1984, President Ronald Reagan joked that he had heard Cincinnati was so straight "that you used to have to cross the river into Kentucky to have a good time." The crowd roared, but Newport leaders didn't laugh. They continued to battle.

And slowly, the strip clubs were pushed out by relentless prosecution and enforcement of liquor law violations for "disorderly premises" and a new anti-nudity ordinance. Strippers tried see-through Band-Aids and pasties to beat the nudity ban, but by 1993 only two strip clubs remained.

When the Cinema X was finally shut down in 1982, city officials found hidden cameras and photos of many faces recognized by the mayor.

Newport was finally leaving its ugly past behind—with no help from the Supreme Court.

Mayor Deaton, Twehues, Commissioner Steve Goetz, early reformer Charles Sarkatsannis and others had to overcome threats, mocking headlines, bribe offers and hugely expensive, frustrating legal battles to prevail. But Newport became safer, healthier, wealthier and cleaner because they had the courage to stand up against the mob, the media, the Supreme Court and the smut peddlers.

Newport led the nation in fighting porn. But it was a long, uphill battle. As late as 1990, TV talk show host Phil Donahue's studio audience cheered a Newport stripper while Newport Mayor Steve Goetz argued that Donahue was exploiting serious community development problems for schlock entertainment.

"I'm embarrassed about the negative image of Newport," Goetz said after his TV appearance. "Monmouth Street is not all it is."

Nick Rechtin says he is still amazed at the perseverance of Goetz and other leaders. "The cleanup was far, far more profound than liquor licenses, strip bars and gambling. It revolved around changing the indigenous attitude."

Newport remains "schizophrenic," he says. "Johnny TV gave away free things, patronage. The battle was between the newcomers versus longtime residents. There are still holdovers to this day who think things were better in the old days. The Peluso name is still respected in Newport."

Peluso was a decorated veteran of World War II, taken prisoner at the Battle of the Bulge. When he died in 2015 at 92, his obituary said, "He was well known for purchasing hundreds of pairs of shoes for the children of Newport and delivering hundreds of baskets of food for those in need during Christmastime."

As of 2020, two Pelusos still led the city: Mayor Jerry Peluso and Commissioner Frank Peluso. But it had become a much different city. The promise of Mayor Goetz in 1990 came true: Newport shed its embarrassing past and became far more than Monmouth Street, which now ends at the city's shopping, dining and entertainment trophy of development, Newport on the Levee.

Ken Rechtin saw the battle from the front row, as a reformer, a victim of Johnny TV's firings, a city commissioner and county commissioner. He returned to the city commission in 2017. "At one time, probably 90 percent of our police force was on the take," he said. "Hell, almost all of them had their hands in it somewhere. It was expected. To have come from that to where we are now, we've come a long way."

A tsunami of crime

The national porn epidemic of the 1970s opened a Pandora's Box of sick culture, but it was just the "itch and the twitch" compared to the malignant cancer of violent crime.

According to FBI statistics:

Property crimes nearly tripled between 1960 and 1979, from 2,000 per 100,000 people to 5,500.

Murders doubled in the same period. Rapes more than doubled from 1960 to 1970, then doubled again to 76,000 in 1979.

Drug arrests exploded from 20 per 100,000 in 1965 to 380 in 1973—multiplied by 20 in eight years.

Women exercised their equal rights to be represented everywhere in the 1970s—including crime statistics. Crimes by women rose 74 percent between 1960 and 1970. But at the same time, prostitution arrests dipped by 43 percent.

Some in the press were puzzled and befuddled. A famously obtuse *New York Times* story even wondered how crime rates could decline as prisoner populations increased. Crime went *down* when more criminals were locked up? How could that be, the *Times* wondered.

But the crime wave of the 1970s was no Raymond Chandler mystery. Supreme Court rulings by the liberal 1960s Warren Court handcuffed police and made enforcement more difficult. (When President Eisenhower said, "I have made two mistakes and they are both sitting on the Supreme Court," he meant Chief Justice Earl Warren and Justice William Brennan.) Race riots of the late 1960s demoralized police, along with widespread youth rebellion and protests against the Vietnam War. An increasingly liberal media indulged criminals with "root-cause" excuses—like the joke about an ACLU lawyer who finds a bleeding mugging victim and says, "We have to find the man who did this. He needs help."

But the crime wave of the 1970s was no Raymond Chandler mystery. Supreme Court rulings by the liberal 1960s Warren Court handcuffed police and made enforcement more difficult. (When President Eisenhower said, "I have made two mistakes and they are both sitting on the Supreme Court," he meant his appointments of Chief Justice Earl Warren and Justice William Brennan.)

Race riots of the late 1960s demoralized police, along with widespread youth rebellion and protests against the Vietnam War. An increasingly liberal media indulged criminals with "root-cause" excuses—like the joke about an ACLU lawyer who finds a bleeding mugging victim and says, "We have to find the man who did this. He needs help."

The crime spike was also a predictable result of the new guilt-free, no-rules, anything-goes morality, just as it had been in the Prohibition era when gambling, prostitution, corruption and violence came to the party arm-in-arm with bootleg hooch.

Riots in the late 1960s left law and order splintered like broken glass in the streets. Police in some cities abandoned whole neighborhoods that were too dangerous and volatile to patrol. The spreading drug culture spawned a menagerie of crime while a plague of extremely addictive crack cocaine was imported by gangs and organized crime.

Organized crime supplied a third of all the heroin in America, most of it from Mexico. The mob was also involved in smuggling illegals across the border. By no coincidence, Moe Dalitz built a house in Nogales, Mexico in 1974, and divided his time between Las Vegas and Mexico.

The mob had found its new bootleg liquor: drugs.

The mob keeps its secrets

Ironically, while law and order seemed to be disintegrating everywhere, the U.S. Senate decided to focus on *organized* crime. In 1975, the Senate's Church Committee summoned Chicago mob boss Sam Giancana to answer questions about CIA plots to kill Castro.

Giancana had boasted that "one of these days I'm gonna tell everything." He had plenty to tell.

But on June 19, the night before his interview by Senate staffers, a police detail assigned to his Chicago home was inexplicably called off. An intruder entered the house, found Giancana in the kitchen preparing dinner, and shot him to death, twice in the back of the head and six times in the neck and mouth—an underworld message for "rats" who talk too much.

Less than a month later, on July 16, 1975, the mob continued to clean up loose ends. Another mobster involved in the Cuba plots, Handsome Johnny Roselli, was found dead, stuffed into a floating oil drum. He had been tortured and was wrapped in heavy chains. Both of his legs were broken.

The drum bobbed to the surface off Miami Beach near the Fontainebleau Hotel where he had recently met with Florida and Cuba mob boss Santo Trafficante. It was also the same place where Roselli and other mobsters had met CIA agents to cook up their pulp-fiction schemes to kill Castro.

At the time he was killed, Roselli had played his CIA-Cuba card to avoid deportation, threatening to "tell all" about CIA efforts to assassinate a foreign president. His lawyers told the feds that Roselli could also offer evidence of a conspiracy to assassinate JFK.

In declassified FBI reports, agents said Roselli, the Las Vegas bully, was so frightened of Trafficante that he would not even mention his name, and became visibly nervous and agitated when anyone else did. But whatever secrets he had were sealed up in that oil drum with his mangled body.

Next on the hit list was Jimmy Hoffa, who disappeared near his home in Michigan on July 30, 1975, just two weeks after Roselli was found dead. Hoffa was trying to retake control of the Teamsters from Frank Fitzimmons, who had become useful tool for Moe Dalitz and other mobsters. Hoffa had served five years of his 16-year prison sentence when it was commuted by President Nixon in 1971, and may have been suspected of "ratting" to the feds for an early release. In any case, he knew too much. He was last seen at a restaurant near Detroit, where he had a meeting with two mobsters, Anthony Provenzano and Tony Giacalone.

Sam Giancana, Johnny Roselli and Jimmy Hoffa were all silenced within six weeks. All were unsolved mob hits. And all were implicated in the conspiracy to kill JFK and plots to kill Fidel Castro—along with Santo Trafficante of Miami and New Orleans boss Carlos Marcello.

Marcello, who was Sicilian, had a sign in his office that explained the Old World code of *omerta*: "Three people can keep a secret… if two are dead."

The new version for Marcello and Trafficante: "Two can keep a secret if three are dead."

The year after all the loose ends were cleaned up with the killings of Giancana, Roselli and Hoffa, Moe Dalitz threw himself a big birthday party in Las Vegas.

Bomb City, USA

Cleveland sounded like a battlefield in 1971 as a mob war broke out between the Irish gangs and the Italian mafia. It was waged primarily with car bombs, like the one that killed *Arizona Republic* Reporter Don Bolles in Phoenix in 1968.

The "Trojan Horse" bomb was a Cleveland specialty. A car packed with explosives would be parked next to the target's car. As the victim got in the car, the bomb-packed vehicle would be triggered from a safe distance by remote control.

There were so many bombings Cleveland became known as "Bomb City, USA." The Federal Bureau of Alcohol, Tobacco and Firearms set up a branch office in northeast Ohio and doubled the staff there just to keep up with the mob bombs and battles.

In 1976 there were 37 bombings in the Cleveland area. More than a dozen mobsters were shot, beaten to death or blown up, as the Italian Mafia led by James "Jack White" Licavoli battled for control against Danny Greene and his Irish mob.

One of the final shots in the Cleveland gang war was a Trojan Horse car bomb that blew up Greene, aka "The Irishman," in 1977 as he arrived for a dentist appointment in a Cleveland suburb.

Amateur hour

But that was just Cleveland. In 1971 and 1972, the FBI recorded 2,500 bombings in America. By far most were not mobsters but "amateurs"—radical leftist hippies, freaks and revolutionaries such as the Symbionese Liberation Army, the Weather Underground, splinter groups of the far left SDS, and the Black Panthers, among others.

So-called "protest bombings" targeted military bases, ROTC buildings, banks, armored cars, campuses and Wall Street. San Francisco had so many bombings it was nicknamed "Belfast by the Bay."

In 1975 the U.S. State Department was bombed, damaging 20 offices but causing no injuries. The Weather Underground boasted that it was responsible for 25 bombings in one year, the FBI reported, including bombs at the U.S. Capitol, the Pentagon and a New York City Police station.

Only a few of the bombers were prosecuted after the Supreme Court ruled that wiretap evidence was inadmissible. One pair of Weathermen bombers, Bill Ayers and Bernadine Dohrn, went underground until 1980, when they emerged unrepentant, suffering almost no consequences. They even became close friends with future President Barack Obama; investigative reporter Jack Cashill found and reported convincing evidence that Bill Ayers was the ghostwriter of Obama's first book.

Dohrn, a former cheerleader who had attended Miami University near Cincinnati, pleaded guilty to misdemeanor charges and eventually became a law professor at Northwestern University's Children and Family Justice Center. Ayers boasted about his participation in bombings of the U.S. Capitol, New York City Police Headquarters and the Pentagon, yet became a professor of education at the University of Illinois at Chicago.

Two murdering bombers became celebrity professors of law and education, and pals of a President. The irony is as thick as smoke.

The domestic terrorist bombing spree of the 1970s is a bizarre and surprisingly forgotten page of American history, as if the whole nation had concussive amnesia. But it helps to explain the huge demand for "law and order" that elected President Richard Nixon in 1968 and 1972, and his replacement, President Gerald Ford—who personally experienced the violence of the 70s when he was nearly killed twice by two women "revolutionaries" in a 17-day period—a member of the Charles Manson gang and a woman who said she was trying to spark a violent overthrow of the government.

It also provides context to the lawless anarchy and violence of the far left that has spread like a hereditary disease, as groups such as Antifa and Black Lives Matter have picked up the city-burning torch carried by SDS, the Black Panthers and the Weathermen—coached and taught by the old radicals who failed in the 1970s.

Hot time in Old Kentucky

While the leftist radicals preferred bombs, the Newport gangs chose arson. As old gambling clubs became strip clubs, nightclubs and restaurants, mobsters moved in with a familiar offer to "buy it or burn it."

Northern Kentucky nightclub fires were nearly as common as bombings in Cleveland.

On March 19, 1970, the Galaxie Club in downtown Newport erupted in flames. Firefighters fought the blaze for three hours as it spread to a volatile paint store next door. The Galaxie owner immediately blamed arson, but refused to say why. The charred remains had previously been the Stork Club, the Silver Slipper, the Bongo Club and the Stardust Club.

The Galaxie Club was rebuilt and reopened. By the following September, police arrested an exotic dancer there for indecent exposure. The busted stripper was Morganna, who later became famous as the "kissing bandit" when she ran onto the baseball diamond to smooch Pete Rose during Cincinnati Reds games. Rose eloquently responded, "You crazy (bleeping) broad. Are you out of your (bleeping) mind?"

The Cabana Restaurant and Bowling Lanes in Erlanger, Kentucky burned down in a six-alarm fire in July 1971.

The upscale White Horse Restaurant in Covington burned down in January 1972. The fire started in the basement, of "undetermined origin."

Arson was suspected in a fire that burned out the Pink Pussycat nightclub on Christmas Eve, 1975. It was described as a "quick, unstoppable fire." All the valuable liquor had been removed from the club, a typical signal that owners had been warned by the mob to sell or burn.

On August 14, 1973, another notorious landmark of the Sin City Days, the Lookout House in Fort Mitchell, was burned, causing a loss of $2.5 million. Five fire departments fought the blaze for four hours as flames shot 50 feet in the air. Arson investigators found the presence of a flammable liquid accelerant in the basement.

In its glory days and wild nights, the fabled Lookout House had been owned by gangster Jimmy Brink until he was forced out by the Cleveland mob. After gambling was shut down in 1961, it was purchased in 1962 by twin brothers Richard and Robert Schilling, who got their start with a drive-in hamburger stand in Fort Mitchell that they kept open 24 hours a day, 365 days a year.

The Schillings remodeled the notorious old Lookout House, added seating and turned it into a popular posh restaurant and nightclub, featuring big bands, comedy acts, fashion shows, lounge singers and top-notch entertainers.

A critic wrote in 1963, "The fantastic business that this club has done in its first year makes crow-eaters out of many persons who predicted that this plush restaurant would never make it. It also removes any doubts that this area will not support a large, first-class supper club."

But the Schillings had union trouble. In 1964, a Democratic Party dinner at the Lookout House was picketed by the Northern Kentucky Labor Council because the Schillings ran a non-union business. A fight erupted and an assistant county attorney was arrested for assault.

Richard Schilling sold the Lookout House for $2 million after his brother died in 1969. By the time it burned down four years later, it was owned by the Ohio Real Estate Investment Corp.

For a few years it had been the main attraction on the Dixie Highway "Gourmet Strip," which flourished until Ohio changed its laws to allow Sunday liquor sales, which dried up the weekend booze pilgrimage from Cincinnati. By 1973, the Lookout House was advertising B-list entertainers and burlesque strippers and was undergoing remodeling. There was no doubt that the fire was arson.

The next nightclub to burn was Newport's raunchy Brass Ass nightclub, in January 1974. The club was a frequent target for prostitution arrests. Arson investigators said it had been saturated with gasoline before the fire. They suspected the mob.

The Brass Ass owner, Vance Raleigh, was also among a half-dozen victims of mob murders in the 1970s in the Newport area. He was killed in a 4:00 a.m. shootout with a West Virginia ex-con who also owned a strip club.

Among the others who were killed:

Nightclub owner and gangster Sammy Eisner. His police record included at least 33 arrests for prostitution, assault, burglary, resisting arrest, shooting with intent to kill, and armed robbery. He was gunned down in August 1972 in what was called "a gangland slaying." He was shot three times with two different guns. The fee for the hit was rumored to be $10,000.

An ex-con with a long police record was found in the Ohio River by water skiers in the summer of 1973. Gerald Arthur Johnson, 32, was identified by his fingerprints. He had been bound with cords, and a rope tied to a boat anchor was wrapped around his body. The police called it an apparent execution murder. He had been shot in the chest by a .38 caliber gun.

Notorious numbers racketeer and killer Screw Andrews "fell" from an upper-story window while hospitalized at St. Luke Hospital. Screw had recently suffered a stroke or may have been experiencing the onset of Alzheimer's disease, making him a hazardous custodian of mob secrets. His wife said Andrews told her he wanted to go home, then jumped out the window. But stories persisted that three large men showed up at the hospital and told the nurses on the floor to take a break. When the nurses returned, their patient was gone. Editors and reporters finally could use one of their favorite words: Screw Andrews was defenestrated.

2.
The Second Fire at Beverly Hills

When Dick Schilling sold the Lookout House, he took the $2 million and put "every last dime" into another glamorous old casino that had fallen on hard times: the Beverly Hills Country Club.

Schilling bought the club and 17.6 acres on the hilltop in 1969 for $420,000 from Hy Ullner, who was described in news stories as "a popular Cincinnati business leader and showman." Schilling put $20,000 down and Ullner held a $400,000 mortgage with annual payments of $80,000.

Although Cleveland mob boss Moe Dalitz had adamantly insisted in 1951 and again in 1961 that he had no connection to the Beverly Hills Country Club anymore, the records showed he was lying, as he so often did. Ullner had purchased the abandoned club in 1967 for "an undisclosed amount," the newspapers said. The deed lists that amount as $10. The trustee at the time was Cleveland mob accountant Alan Geisey, who was wiretapped by the FBI as he discussed the maintenance costs of the Beverly Hills club with Dalitz in Las Vegas in 1962. The attorney handling the sale in 1967 was Dan Davies.

Before he sold it, Ullner had big plans to turn it into a dinner-theater attraction that would be "frosting on the cake" for Cincinnati's convention business. But the frosting went sour, the club flopped and it was closed again.

Schilling saw it as a tarnished jewel that could be purchased at a pawn-shop discount. Just before it had closed in 1961 after the Ratterman crackdown, the Beverly Hills had been remodeled at a cost of $250,000 (more than $2 million in 2020).

On the night it closed—October 20, 1961—the house orchestra played *My Old Kentucky Home* and *Auld Lang Syne* at 1 a.m. Then the lights were turned out for seven years of darkness. A $2,000 chandelier and

229 spotlights that lit the stage were shut off and the staff of 250 was sent home, out of work. Southgate lost $26,000 a year in taxes. A new wine cellar, stocked with 87 varieties, was liquidated.

The Beverly Hills Country Club was a time capsule from Newport's glorious, notorious past, rich with history and stories, locked up and silent but still maintained by the mobsters who loved it and got their start there.

"The name Beverly Hills was known all over the country," Schilling said, announcing his purchase. "That name alone was worth a million dollars to me."

He shared his plans to add 11 banquet rooms, kitchens, fountains and new furnishings to accommodate 3,000. It was scheduled to open in September 1970.

Then on June 21, 1970, as the Beverly Hills renovation was nearly complete, it was gutted by an early morning fire that left only the front rooms of the building standing. Historic records and priceless pictures from the old club were lost.

It was undoubtedly arson.

The Kentucky State Police investigation found "no petroleum hydrocarbons present" in the evidence that they examined. But apparently, they did not examine very much.

Burn patterns on the floor and carpets in the bar showed dark scorch marks where fires were started with a flammable accelerant in four separate places. Doors had been forced open. And then, as if to make sure everyone knew it was arson, two emptied five-gallon gas cans were left in the club, charred, still sitting near the origin of the fire.

None of the workers who had been on the site recognized the gas cans. There was no reason for them to be in the middle of the club unless they were brought there to start the fire.

Electric power and natural gas were shut off or not connected and were eliminated as causes, Southgate Fire Chief Ray Muench reported. Muench said he got a phone call at home at 3:00 a.m. by an unidentified man, who told him the Supper Club was going to burn. The fire was reported at 3:17 a.m.

In his report to the National Fire Prevention Association, Chief Muench was blunt: "This fire was the work of an arsonist." He complained that his own report had been stalled by incomplete and delayed work from the Kentucky State Police. He speculated that the motive for arson was labor troubles, because Schilling was using non-union workers, just as he had at the Lookout House.

There were also rumors that the mob wanted the club back and burned it because Schilling refused—just as they had burned down Pete Schmidt's original Beverly Hills in 1936.

In their book *The Beverly Hills Supper Club: The Untold Story Behind Kentucky's Worst Tragedy,* the most comprehensive encyclopedia about the fire of 1977, Robert Webster, David Brock and Tom McConaughy describe Dick Schilling's possible loans from Ben Kees. They found evidence of organized crime connections to Ullner and Kees, who was a regular at Schilling nightclubs and was described by Dick Schilling as "like family."

Brock, who worked for the Schillings from the age of 13, said the first time he met Kees he instinctively feared the man and was reprimanded by Schilling for not helping Kees out of his car.

"Ben Kees was the guy who ran vending in Northern Kentucky for 30 or 40 years," Brock said. "Mob guy. Slots, cigarette machines, pinball machines, pool tables. The first time I saw Ben Kees I was scared to death. I was only 17. It was just his demeanor, the way he looked and carried himself. He used a wheelchair, and when he pulled up in his car and started to get out, I ducked back into the club.

"Later, Mr. Schilling called me into his office and Ben Kees was sitting there with him. He asked, 'Do you know who this man is?' I said, 'Yes, Ben Kees.' He said 'He's a friend of mine. Next time he needs help, you will help him out of his car.'

"I said, 'Yes sir,' but I was glad I never had to."

In 1951 Kees was caught funneling syndicate cash into local political campaigns to defeat anti-gambling reformers. In U.S. Senate testimony, he was described as "one of the slot machine men" who tried to bribe or intimidate reformers.

In 1952 Kees was arrested with several gangsters in an FBI raid of Kentucky Amusement Company, where 829 slots were seized. The company was previously owned by Jimmy Brink, owner of the Lookout House before it was taken by the Cleveland mob.

Kees was described in news reports as one of the "big shots" in the local gambling business. He owned taverns, restaurants, grocery stores and liquor stores, and ran concessions at recreation centers in Cincinnati and Northern Kentucky, including Devou Park, where the Schilling brothers got their start selling hotdogs.

Brock's instinct was right. Kees was strange. His Dixie Delicatessen sold octopus, muskrat, buffalo, whale skin, fried grasshoppers, dried honeybees and unborn snakes, a local newspaper reported.

Rising from the ashes

A Campbell County grand jury was assigned to investigate the $700,000 fire at the unfinished Beverly Hills Club. It found arson was "strongly suspected," but shed no light on a motive. That was the end of it. The Kentucky State Police closed the case as a fire of "undetermined" cause.

Schilling rallied and vowed a month later that it would rise again, bigger and more beautiful than ever. Few doubted it, given his history of hard work and success.

He toured Las Vegas for ideas, imported extravagant chandeliers from Europe and bought the most elegant furniture, paneling, draperies and artwork he could find.

His new Beverly Hills would be like nothing anyone had seen before.

The club re-opened on February 10, 1971. Some of the old personality remained, including the trademark oval bar installed by Schmidt in 1937. It was lit with a golden halo from a ceiling cutout with recessed lighting. Those who gathered at the bar stepped into a flattering glow that was like a highball from the fountain of youth.

In the following months and years, Dick Schilling doubled the club's footprint with a huge modern kitchen and two large banquet rooms— the Cabaret Room and the Garden Room—doubling the old club's capacity to 3,200, not including almost 300 employees. By 1977, it was 54,000 square feet with 19 rooms—1.5 acres under a single roof.

But the remodeling was done in disjointed, start-and-stop phases, slapped together with whims and impulses like a children's tree fort: $170,000 for the kitchen; then another $187,000; then two more projects at $13,000 and $84,000.

Schilling used an unlicensed architect and treated blueprints as mere suggestions. He hid construction from local and state inspectors so he could avoid permits and inspections. He revised the architectural plans to delete exits and paid an unemployed architect to falsely certify that his shortcuts were legal and safe.

When he did have permits, most of the finished work was never inspected or approved by fire marshals.

An investigation in 1979 found that the Cabaret Room was expanded in 1974 without architectural plans. And even those were never submitted to the state Fire Marshal, as required by law, although Schilling claimed they were approved.

The Southgate building inspector who tried to keep up with Schilling's constant construction was a former bricklayer who was given no training, no car, no travel allowance and paid only $200 a year. He did not even have a current copy of state codes.

When the inspector tried to insist on more exits, he was ignored. In 1976, Schilling's new Garden Room blocked two of the Cabaret Room exits that would have led directly outdoors.

State and local inspectors complained that Schilling bypassed them again. "The garden room was 90 percent finished before we got the plans," said one inspector—and they only got to look at those blueprints by threatening to take him to court.

The Southgate Fire Chief raised concerns as far back as 1970, when he sent a letter to the mayor of Southgate. Nothing came of it.

When inspectors visited before the club re-opened, they found ten major safety violations. "Our concern is about fire hazards," the report said. Their list included inadequate exits, combustible building materials and an open circular stairway that could feed fire to the second floor.

But Kentucky State Fire Marshal John Calvert, a political appointee, overruled the field inspector and expedited approval of a permit to open, giving Dick Schilling a certificate of occupancy just one day before the grand opening. Calvert claimed he had found a misplaced file that showed the club was safe and all the problems were corrected.

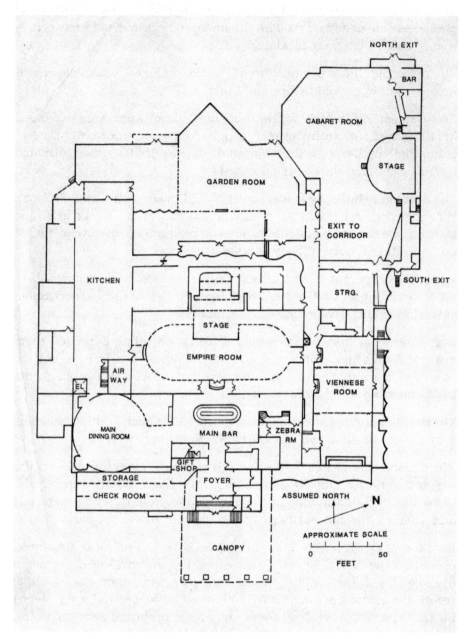

A floor plan shows the expansion by Dick Schilling.
Kenton County Library archives.

His letter to the Southgate Fire Department said, "After finally receiving plans for Beverly Hills I immediately sent an inspector to the site. I

236

received my inspector's report on said building and after visual inspection and discussion of these corrections with Mr. Schilling I have been assured that the corrections under discussion would be taken care of."

That was either corrupt or naïve. Schilling had no intention of making changes that would force him to tear up his new club and delay the opening. But Calvert's letter was enough to mislead the local fire department, the mayor of Southgate and even a grand jury investigation.

Before the club opened, local newspapers raised questions that were so serious a judge assigned a grand jury to investigate, warning about fears of a "holocaust." But the grand jury relied on Calvert's letter and found no problems—another example of the "Newport Eye."

Schilling promised the public and the grand jury that he would create an employee fire brigade to make sure guests were safe. He did not. His broken promises and Calvert's dereliction of duty would be fatal for 165 people. Schilling's Beverly Hills Supper Club was a firetrap.

Remodeling continued in spurts and pauses, whenever Schilling had the whim and the wealth. More remodeling and new construction was still in progress—without a permit—when the Supper Club burned down in 1977. Yet the club had never been inspected after 5:00 p.m. when it was crowded, as required by law. Inspectors said they were unable because their workdays ended at 4:30 p.m.

There was a small electrical fire in 1974, put out with fire extinguishers before the fire department arrived. Yet the new Zebra Room was remodeled without permits in 1975, using combustible paneling and materials, with lighting that violated fire safety codes.

Electrician Jerry Kremer described how it was done. "Mr. Schilling provided all the materials that were used in the Zebra Room," he told investigators after the fire in 1977. Wiring "was not run through conduit as specified in the code."

Kremer said he told Schilling it was wrong, but Schilling refused to install conduit because it was "too expensive." Investigators asked Kremer if he could have done it properly anyway, to avoid criminal violations of fire and safety codes.

"No, no, no, no," he answered. "You don't dig Schilling here. His sons don't even get a free hand and they run the joint. I mean, he has his own ideas and you had to wire accordingly."

Other electricians confirmed Kremer's account. Schilling's orders were not confined by permits, codes or architectural plans.

Dick Schilling gives instructions to prepare for a big show at the Supper Club. The Cabaret Room featured stars that were headliners in Las Vegas and Hollywood. The Cincinnati Enquirer

Grand opening

The first big show in February 1971 featured Frank Sinatra, Jr. at the "Beverly Hills." It was soon billed as "the Showplace of the Nation," and the Schilling family gave it a new name: "The Beverly Hills Supper Club," sometimes known locally as "The Hill."

Jeff Ruby, who would build his own group of restaurants in Cincinnati, Columbus, Louisville, Lexington and Nashville, inspired by the glamorous Supper Club, was there for opening night. As a hotel manager at the time, he knew the Schilling family and was able to get VIP seating.

"The way Dick Schilling did things was first class. He brought that kind of class to Cincinnati. I've done the same with my restaurants, so yeah, he did inspire me. We respected each other."

He says one of his proudest moments was when Dick Schilling visited his newest Cincinnati restaurant, Jeff Ruby's Steakhouse, before he died in 2002. Ruby recalls Schilling saying, "Jeff, I wouldn't have done a thing different. This is incredible."

"We're in the business of making people feel good about themselves," Ruby said. "A lot of things are important—location, designer, chef, décor. But the only thing that's *really* important is making the *guests* feel really important. Like they are the most important person in that restaurant.

"The food at the Supper Club was not that great, but when you went to the Cabaret Room for a show, dinner and drinks, you felt like you were in Vegas."

The resurrection of the Beverly Hills was celebrated on Easter in 1971 with a menu that drew big crowds, as churches emptied and families lined up in their Sunday suits and Easter dresses. "Filet of Sole: $2.95. Roast Prime of Beef: $5.65. Filet Mignon, Tender Heart of the Beef: $6.95."

Reporters emptied their dictionary of superlatives to pour compliments on the new nightclub. It was plush, posh, swank, luxurious, lavish, opulent, ornate, glittering, flashy, extravagant and elegant.

It was the "classy" place to go, the "in" place to see and be seen, with 14 banquet halls, eight bars, a gift shop run by the owner's wife, Theresa Schilling, and a kitchen staffed by 60 cooks, commanded by Chef Charles Chandler. Chandler and his crew boasted that they could feed 3,200 guests at one seating.

Interior decorator Harry Backus, who designed the famed Maisonette restaurant in Cincinnati, which had America's longest five-star rating when it closed in 2005, decorated the new Beverly Hills Supper Club with a palette of rich gold and deep burgundy. The trademark oval bar, burned down to bare steel bones in the 1970 fire, was restored in tufted gold. Curving brick interior walls hung with mirrors and artworks beckoned guests to explore the back of the club.

The north-south Hall of Mirrors led back to the glass-walled Garden Room that overlooked manicured and sculpted hedges that echoed European palace gardens. Classic Roman and Greek-style statues loitered around fountains and flower beds. Views from the nearby Fountain Room were equally spectacular.

A massive chandelier in the main dining room was so elaborate it took the staff a half day to hang and balance it and another fill day to attach all the prisms. A small stage in the Empire Room, in the center of the building, provided a venue for bands, banquets and meetings.

But the biggest draw was the vast Cabaret Room's lineup of star-studded shows that rivaled any of the glittering names in lights on the Las Vegas strip. It could hold nearly a thousand, and tickets for even the biggest stars were less than $10.

When local newspapers sent reporters as "critics," the reviews were chronically negative, panning the shows to flaunt their pseudo-sophistication. But the public paid no attention. They loved the entertainers and flocked to the Supper Club like pilgrims on a mission to Hollywood holy land.

In 1973, future Rock & Roll Hall of Famer Little Richard vamped, strutted and sang *Tutti Fruitti* in a powder blue tux with a mirror-studded vest and white go-go boots. ("Limp-wristed" and "narcissistic," *The Cincinnati Enquirer* sniffed.)

The sarcastic wit of Phyllis Diller and the raunchy blue comedy of Redd Foxx followed a few weeks later. Rhythm and Blues singers Lou Rawls and Al Green came to the "Showplace of the Nation" the following year.

That summer of 1974 also brought an ominous surprise: Southgate Police Chief John Shay found a small wooden box with a glass front and a clock ticking away inside, sitting about halfway up the driveway to the Supper Club. The bomb squad from Newport blew it up and found no explosives inside, but it was otherwise a "working bomb," the police chief said. The Schillings told him they had no idea why anyone would plant a phony bomb in the driveway.

Someone was sending a message. But any concerns were lost in the excitement of the spectacular club, which hid sloppy wiring, fire code violations and combustible materials behind a veneer of luxury, like a candied apple full of worms.

In 1971, *The Cincinnati Enquirer* reported, "Proprietor Dick Schilling seems to have overlooked nothing to make his establishment a 'showplace of the nation,' but he already is planning additional changes to make it even better."

By 1975, the shows were bigger and more dazzling than ever.

Jerry Lewis drew huge crowds. He was followed by the comedy team Rowan & Martin (the same Dan Rowan who romanced Sam Giancana's girlfriend). One of the biggest hits that year was the sultry Hollywood dancer Joey Heatherton, whose after-show parties were legendary.

The sentimental hit of 1975 was the homecoming of Dean Martin, who had once worked as a croupier in the original Beverly Hills Country Club in 1942-43, when illegal gambling was the main event of Newport nightlife. In an interview, "Dino" recalled how he and Jerry Lewis had gotten their start as a comedy team at Pete Schmidt's Glenn Hotel Rendezvous, in the wild old days when the mob ruled Sin City.

Those days were gone. Dick Schilling was the new boss of his Supper Club kingdom. When he wasn't pitching in to help out, he held court for guests, wearing expensive suits, spotless white shirts, flashy gold cufflinks and a gaudy gold ring set with diamonds. It was all part of the show—the infectious illusion that drew Supper Club guests like moths circling the hot lights of glamor.

Schilling could say like Sinatra, "I Did it My Way," and he wasn't shy about letting people know it. He had the hottest nightclub east of Las Vegas.

"Any time a waiter spills something on a woman's dress," he said, "she never fails to say she bought it special for this occasion."

That was often true. A night on The Hill was all the excuse couples needed to show off new dresses, neckties, sports coats, suits and hairstyles.

It was like the adage about a priceless bottle of wine: You don't need a special occasion to open it; the day you pull the cork *is* the special occasion. Dick Schilling's Supper Club *was* the special occasion.

"At least after a night out at Beverly Hills, they know they've been some place," Schilling would say.

The sprawling, constantly expanding Supper Club was a personification of its owner and creator: a stubborn, hard-driving man who overcame setbacks and never stopped remodeling reality to keep up with his own big ideas.

His next project was already being planned in 1977, to add a motel, a convention center and a disco club to his 17-acre hilltop empire.

But the ghosts of the club's cursed past watched from the shadows, where tragedy waited behind those paneled walls and chandeliered ceilings.

3.

Fire on the Hill

Dick Schilling in front of his new Beverly Hills Supper Club before it was remodeled and expanded. The club opened in 1971 and immediately became the Showplace of the Nation, the finest nightclub with the best entertainment in the Midwest. Courtesy of Northern Kentucky Views.

Great restaurants and nightclubs make more than meals and music. They woo the senses. Perfume, cologne, sizzling steaks, soft lights and bright colors, music thumping like a racing heart, exotic cocktails, frosted glasses, linen, silk, silver, crystal, deep carpets....

At the Beverly Hills, truck drivers, bankers, moms and kindergarten teachers could imagine the better life everyone dreams about, treated like royalty for a night before returning to Monday's diesel, paperwork and crying kids.

The staff and owners loved their work and found joy in making guests happy with fine food, relaxing drinks, dazzling shows, smiles, laughter and the personal attention that made anyone feel witty, attractive, welcome and important.

But Dick Schilling was not done yet. He had yet another Next Big Idea to make everything better and more profitable.

'Till death do us part...'

"Incomparable... in every way," the full-page Sunday newspaper ad promised breathlessly in 1976. "...Your wedding at beautiful Beverly Hills!"

Schilling's plan was to fill his sprawling banquet rooms with another unforgettable attraction: a simple little white chapel, complete with stained-glass windows and antique-white pews for 120 wedding guests, "situated in beautifully landscaped Formal Gardens."

Like a reformed drunk who found Jesus, the notorious old club on the hill that had been the backdrop for bankruptcies, armed robberies, bombings, beatings, muggings, murders, arsons, hangovers, one-night stands, affairs and untold divorces was now... the new home of holy matrimony. A nightclub with its own church.

The one-stop wedding package was an immediate hit, as couples put their names on waiting lists to exchange vows in the chapel or outdoors in the garden. Everything was included: planning, rehearsal dinners, drinks, bridal showers, menus, champagne, wedding cakes, bachelor and bridesmaid parties...

"And you can know the exact costs in advance," the ad promised. "For the reception, Beverly Hills offers 18 banquet rooms—from the picturesque Garden Rooms overlooking the Formal Gardens to the elegant Monaco Parlours. Accommodations are available for 20 to 1,000 ... right down to the wedding cake."

Saturday, May 28, 1977 was a busy day. Dick Schilling was at his vacation home in Fort Lauderdale, Florida recovering from surgery, leaving his sons in charge. Four weddings were lined up, circling the hilltop like airliners waiting to land and taxi down the aisle. It was Memorial Day weekend, the kickoff of the peak June wedding season. Getting married on a beautiful spring day in the flowering garden or the dollhouse chapel was every bride's dream for a storybook ceremony.

The reservations list that day was also jammed with anniversaries, birthdays, dating couples, office parties and families celebrating graduations, retirements, job promotions and the simple joy of springtime. Young couples staked their claims on window tables with a view of the gardens or the city lights, to pop the question or announce their engagements. Husbands surprised their wives with a night at Beverly Hills for their anniversaries.

There was an Afghan Hound Owners' Club party of 90 in the second floor Crystal Rooms, and a Cincinnati Choral Union party of 120 right across the hall. A senior-citizens' Roadrunners traveling club had booked a charter bus from Louisville for dinner and a show.

A group of doctors had the Viennese Room. And 400 bankers from the Savings and Loan League of Southwest Ohio and Northern Kentucky would banquet in the Empire Room.

Hundreds more families and couples had dinner reservations to enjoy the three-day Memorial Day weekend.

More than 2,000 tickets had been sold for two shows that night in the cavernous Cabaret Room by entertainer and singer John Davidson, first at 8:30, then a late show at 11:30. Davidson's shows at the Supper Club the year before had been a big hit, especially with the ladies. His perfectly styled, collar-length, razor-cut hair was clean cut and all-American by the scruffy long-hair standards of the 70s. The former Sears catalogue underwear model had become a national celebrity as an actor on *Love Boat*, *Love American Style*, *Fantasy Island*, *Sonny and Cher's Comedy Hour* and many other TV shows and movies. But he was best known for his earnestly sincere double-talk answers that bamboozled the contestants on *Hollywood Squares*. Everybody's mom loved John Davidson.

His warm-up act was a ventriloquist comedy team that lampooned politicians and current events, Teter and McDonald.

Davidson's final performance at the Supper Club that weekend was described in ads as a family show, and he drew hundreds of moms, dads, aunts and uncles with their kids along. They packed into cars, station wagons, vans and charter buses all over Ohio, Kentucky and Indiana for a big night they would never forget.

Two buses were on the way from Dayton, Ohio carrying a AAA tour of 82 people for the show in the Cabaret Room. Only 26 would survive.

James Crane, 19, and his fiancée Tammy Kincer, 18, of Waynesville, Ohio had reservations to celebrate his new job, her high school graduation with honors, and their engagement. Both would be killed.

Another group of 37 had reservations to celebrate the retirement of elementary school teacher Ona Mae Mayfield. Her son Clark, 35, who was head football coach at Jacksonville State University in Alabama, came home for the dinner. Clark was killed along with a dozen others in the group from rural Wayne Township, Ohio.

Also killed were Donald and Dorothy Koontz. They left behind four children at home on their farm.

If "a house is a machine for living in," the Beverly Hills Supper Club was an entertainment factory with an assembly line of kitchen stovetops, grills and ovens, food pantries, prep tables, glassware, silverware, plates and saucers, heating and air conditioning, hostess stations, bars, cases of liquor, beer and wine, elegantly set tables, spot-lit stages, conference rooms, restrooms, lighting sconces and chandeliers, dishwashing sinks, food-service carts, cleaning equipment, trumpets, trombones, violins and other band instruments for a 30-piece house orchestra...

And that afternoon, the factory was humming. Waitresses, busboys, managers, bartenders, hosts and hostesses, cooks, dishwashers, stage managers and owners worked at full throttle to make sure banquet rooms were ready and each reservation "turned over" on time to make room for the next.

Dick Schilling often worked 12- and 14-hour days, and Rick, Ron and Scott, his wife, Theresa, and Rick's wife, Margie, all did the same. The Schillings would plunge in to wash dishes, carry trays, serve food and drinks, mop-up spills—wherever they were needed.

So did many staff members who felt like part of the Schilling family. Servers often stayed well after 3:00 a.m. As soon as the last guests had weaved out the doors at "last call," they worked to prepare rooms, set up tables and polish silver for the next night.

David Brock, who had been part of the Supper Club family since he started working for Schilling at age 13, arrived at work that day around 10:30 a.m. He had landed his job with help from an older brother who also worked for the Schillings. Their home was just a short walk away.

"Dick Schilling was almost like a father to me," he would often say later. By 1977, Brock had been working as a busboy at the Beverly

Hills Supper Club for five years and loved it. Although only 18, he was one of the most trusted and valued employees on the staff, and was assigned that night to work in the Cabaret Room.

But first Brock was asked to set up the Zebra Room, where a small wedding party of about 25 guests would have their dinner and reception after a ceremony in the chapel.

In the old Beverly Hills Country Club of the syndicate days, the Zebra Room had been an unnamed break room where dealers went to smoke, grab a sandwich and swap stories about celebrities, high rollers and big losers. It was one of the few rooms spared by the fire in 1970. But even after the rebuilding in 1971, it remained an afterthought "junk-drawer," part utility closet and part coat rack, nicknamed the "Zebra Room" by busboys as a joke.

But as the new Supper Club took off, constant construction and remodeling couldn't keep up with the growing crowds. On some nights, cars lined up all the way down the hill and back along Route 27. The club's parking lot could hold 1,000 cars, but still overflowed. As capacity was stretched, groups had to be turned away. Waiting lists for special events stretched to more than a year. So the Schillings turned the old break room into a plush but small dining room, sandwiched between restrooms and the hostess station just inside the front entrance. They kept the exotic name.

As Brock started work, he went to the Zebra Room to set up tables at 11:00 a.m. To his surprise, two men were working there. "They wore gray jumpsuits with no names," he said later. The men stood on ladders, doing something behind the drop-ceiling panels. When he asked when they'd be done, they brushed him off and told him to come back later. He had plenty of work to do, so he went to help set up the Empire Room and the Cabaret Room.

'Something isn't right'

Waitress Shirley Baker arrived at work at about noon. She had started working for the Shillings three years before, at age 18. Like Brock, she got the job through family: Her mother and two of her aunts were waitresses and all of them enjoyed working for the Schillings. "They treated us like family," Baker said. "I loved it. It was beautiful and I enjoyed it so much."

Shortly after she was hired, her mother took her to the basement to find her a fresh uniform. Shirley looked around and was dazzled by what she saw. "There were roulette wheels, card tables like for blackjack and other games. They all looked brand new. I asked, 'Mom, what is all this?' She said, 'It's gambling equipment. They used to gamble here.'"

As she learned the history of the old club, she was thrilled and fascinated. "I felt honored to work there. I thought, 'This isn't a job. This is more like a playroom.' I have so many great memories of that place."

One of her favorite nights at work was the New Year's Eve party at the end of 1976. "I had a girl I worked together with, and a busboy, and we had 20 tables. At the end of the night we put all of our tips together and divvied it up and we went home with more than $500 each." A guest at one table tipped her $200 just to sit down at their table for a few minutes and sneak a drink with them.

On her 21st birthday, her mother arranged to have her work in the Cabaret Room where Frankie Valli and the Four Seasons were performing for sellout crowds. During a break in the music, Valli announced, "I hear we have a birthday girl here tonight."

Shirley thought, "Oh, man, this is neat, somebody has my birthday."

But when she looked around, everyone was pointing at her. "He came down and took my hand and led me up on the stage and sang to me. I was so embarrassed."

She met Jerry Lewis, Ricky Nelson and Connie Stevens, who gave her an autographed picture for her husband's birthday, then asked for a wine list and bought Shirley and her husband a $150 bottle of champagne to take home.

She also met Joey Heatherton ("not real friendly"), Milton Berle ("mean"), Redd Foxx ("he had a dirty mouth, boy did he ever") and dozens of other stars.

"I wouldn't have traded that time for anything," she said.

After she punched in on the time clock in the kitchen that Saturday at noon, Shirley went directly to the Zebra Room to set it up. It was assigned as "her room" to work in and manage for the night, and she had been told that the four o'clock wedding party was coming early for pictures.

"As I went into my room there were two men in there. One was tall, the other one short and heavier. I asked, 'What are you doing?' They said,

'Oh, we're working on the air conditioning unit. We're working on the wiring.' They had all the outlets, sconces and wall switches pulled out with the wires hanging."

As she left she saw something else that seemed odd. "I looked down the mirrored hallway toward the Cabaret Room in the back, and I saw two ladies and a man there, with a little girl who was sitting on the floor playing."

The group was in the Hall of Mirrors that connected the front of the club to the Garden Rooms and Cabaret Room in the back. They were using towels and a ladder to wipe down the walls from ceiling to floor with a bucket of milky-white liquid, she said. They wore rubber gloves.

About halfway down the hall she turned left to cut through the Empire Room to get to the kitchen. She picked up the things she needed and returned to the Zebra Room. The two men were still there. This time the tall man was still on the ladder, but the stocky man was wiping the back walls down with a towel, using what looked like the same liquid she had seen in a bucket in the hallway.

She asked, "How much longer are y'all going to be in here?"

"We'd get done quicker if you would leave us alone," one of the men replied.

She asked again what they were doing, and was told they were cleaning the walls so that the patrons would not be overcome by fumes. She thought, That's not right. Cleaning crews on a busy Saturday makes no sense. And wiping down the walls in the Zebra Room after working on the air conditioning? Wiring and chemicals don't mix.

She shook her head and told them, "I'm going to get someone and find out what's going on." The men suddenly stopped what they were doing and stared at her. The room got quiet.

"The short, heavy man said, 'Little girl, if you know what's good for you, you will get your ass out of here.' The tall man came toward me. He was evil looking. His demeanor was like, 'Don't mess with me.'"

She hurried away, again using the Hall of Mirrors where she saw the crew still wiping the walls, using a ladder. "It was the exact same stuff they were using in the Zebra Room. It had no smell to it at all."

Looking for someone to help, she found two busboys. One said he would try to find one of the Schillings. The other, Mark Johnson, went back with her to the Zebra Room. "By the time we got there, it was like nobody had ever been there," Baker said. The crew in the hallway was gone too. It was 1:45 p.m.

David Brock had also been back to the Zebra Room to check on progress of the men, once at 11:45 and again at 12:30. The first time he returned, he found them still reaching into the ceiling near a chandelier at the front of the room. He told them he had to set up the room, and they again told him to come back later.

At 12:30 he told the men he had to get the room set up by 2:00 p.m. or he would get in trouble. He asked them what they were doing.

"Air conditioning," he was told. "We'll be done soon."

Brock left. At 2:00 p.m. he returned to find the men gone, so he pitched in to help Shirley Baker with wedding party preparations. They got done just before the bridesmaids arrived for pictures.

Baker and Brock were each troubled by the strangers washing walls and yanking wires, but they were too busy to stop and ask questions.

But later, and for the rest of their lives, they would be haunted by what they saw that morning. When they finally met again 30 years later and compared notes, the pieces of the Zebra Room puzzle finally fell into place.

But on that busy Saturday they pushed aside their concerns and went back to work. Soon the club was filled with parties and guests.

Sometime around 5:00 p.m., wedding guests dining in the Zebra Room heard a muffled bang, as if a firecracker had gone off somewhere behind the ceiling. Two more thudding, muffled explosions were heard that evening near the Zebra Room, between 5:00 and 6:00 p.m.

Guests also reported a strange smell, described as dead fish, dirty socks, sour milk, bad meat or a musty, burning odor. Some said it was like the stench of a slaughterhouse.

The Zebra Room was getting unusually warm. A party for the Cincinnati Choral Union fashion show in one of the Crystal Rooms directly above it noticed that butter on their tables was melting into puddles.

Wedding guests in the Zebra Room complained that it was uncomfortably warm and getting hotter, but most assumed it was because there were so many people in such a small room. Oren Hall of Elyria, Ohio rented the room for the wedding. "We started to sweat and thought the air conditioning was off," he said later. The reception broke up early because of the stifling heat.

As more families and couples drove up the long driveway to the Supper Club at the top of the hill, a few noticed a thin black column of smoke coming out of the roof near the front of the building, over the Zebra Room. They recalled it later, but didn't mention it to anyone that night.

Just before 7:00 p.m., guests in the main dining room, across the entryway from the Zebra Room and the hostess station, noticed a haze in the air, but dismissed it as cigarette smoke. In the 1970s, *everyone* smoked, especially in restaurants or wherever drinks were served. A smoke before dinner with drinks. An after-dinner cigarette. Even during dinner. There were ashtrays on every table, holding Marlboros, Kools, Winstons, Camels or Salems that sent wispy smoke-signals to gather near the ceiling.

As dinner groups came and went, the hostess who sat just outside the Zebra Room complained that she was uncomfortable. Her eyes were watering and burning. She was long accustomed to the usual cigarette smoke. This was something different, more irritating. It made her skin itch.

'Like a party every night'

Wayne Dammert, the banquet captain, arrived five minutes early and clocked in for his usual shift, from 6:00 p.m. to closing. Nobody there that night knew the club and its vivid history better than he did.

In the glory days of the underworld, Dammert had worked as a dealer at the old Beverly Hills Country Club, flipping aces and jacks at one of those blackjack tables Shirley Baker had seen collecting dust in the basement.

Dammert grew up in Edgewood, Kentucky, just southwest of Newport. Fresh out of the Navy in 1957, he met a Beverly Hills Country Club boss while playing golf. "He said I should apply for a job, so I did. The first night on the job I stood right next to Jerry Lewis as he lost a quick $700 at the blackjack table. By the third night I was dealing cards. They showed me a couple of skills, but there was no real training."

He was there for the party on the night Screw Andrews got out of prison. He knew the regulars, including Red Masterson, Tito Carinci and Sleepout Louis Levinson. His boss was John Croft, who was one of the owners of the club on paper. Gangsters Sam Tucker and Sam

Schrader made occasional visits, keeping an eye on the club for the real owners, Moe Dalitz and the Cleveland mob. "You had to be on your toes when those guys came in," Dammert recalled.

There was a push-button switch to set off an alarm if a raid was spotted, so gaming tables and equipment could be hidden in minutes. "Most of the guys who worked there were like me, but there was Mafia there too. We were tied in with the Desert Inn in Las Vegas. The Beverly Hills was a big thing, a very nice nightclub. I saw people win and lose thousands of dollars."

He played golf with Tony Bennett and met Frank Sinatra, Dean Martin, the Andrews Sisters, Perry Como and dozens of other stars while working at the club. He also met his wife, Betty, a former Rockette from Radio City Music Hall in New York. She had toured the world and been part of the June Taylor Dancers featured on *The Jackie Gleason Show*. She was working in the chorus line at the Beverly Hills Country Club when he met her at a boating party on the Ohio River in 1958.

When most of the dealers, dancers, bartenders and mob bosses migrated to Las Vegas in 1961, some of their friends became managers at the Sands, the Stardust, the Dunes and the Desert Inn. But Betty and Wayne stayed put.

"Betty wanted to stay, so we stayed," he said.

He left the Beverly Hills Club in 1960 before it was closed down in the 1961 crackdowns by Sheriff George Ratterman and the feds. He called bingo games briefly at the Merchants Club in Newport, working for Red Masterson and Screw Andrews. But the place made him nervous. His instincts were right: It was raided and Andrews was arrested shortly after he left.

"I drove an airport limo for a while, worked at GE in the service shop and became a draftsman at GE." He was working in another drafting job in 1970 when he heard that the Beverly Hills was going to re-open.

He met with Dick Schilling, who had been a regular guest at the old Beverly Hills. "He knew who I was. They hired me first as a waiter, then banquet captain. I saw it as a nice extra job."

Soon he fell in love with the club again. "Going to work was like going to a party every night."

Dammert calls his life "somewhat adventurous." Others might call it cursed or blessed, depending on their perspective. He has witnessed or been first on the scene at dozens of accidents, plane crashes and fires. Death and injuries seem to follow him like stray cats.

When he was a teen, he watched as a girl got out of the car he was riding in and was struck by another car going so fast it threw her 50 feet and left the shape of her body molded into the hood. She lived.

He was first on the scene of a fatal jet crash in Cuba while he served in the Navy, and sorted through the grisly wreckage to find the mangled remains of the pilot before the ambulances arrived.

His list of what he calls "interesting occurrences" stretches to double digits, far beyond the law of averages: fatal car wrecks and plane crashes, a deadly bus crash, a helicopter crash, pedestrians struck by cars... and Wayne Dammert is there in scene after scene.

But none of those experiences prepared him for what he would see and go through on that Memorial Day weekend at the Beverly Hills Supper Club.

'My God, there's a fire!'

As banquet captain for two large parties in the upstairs Crystal Rooms, Dammert literally had his hands full. The Choral Union needed more than a hundred dinners served at 7 o'clock during their fashion show. The Afghan Hound Club across the hall was expecting dinner for 90 at 8:45.

While he was in the kitchen at 8:25, hurrying to pick up items for the second dinner that was falling behind schedule, Shirley Baker was finishing up service for the Zebra Room and asked him to bring her the bill for the wedding party that was wrapping up.

Dammert went to the back of the building for the check, then to the front of the building to get it added up. When he took it to the Zebra Room a few minutes later, one of the guests asked him if the air conditioning was broken because the room was so warm. Dammert thought it felt fine. As he left at 8:30 he noticed "absolutely nothing unusual" in the Zebra Room, he said later.

Back in the upstairs Crystal Rooms, he saw that salads needed to be served, so he returned to the kitchen on the service elevator.

At the Zebra Room, Baker closed the doors as the last guests left, and took a quick break in the restroom at 8:50.

In the Cabaret Room, Brock cleared tables of empty glasses and dishes as the warm-up act was just coming onstage.

At 8:55, two waitresses who were sisters, Roberta and Marsha Vanover, went to the Zebra Room to find tray stands, and were alarmed to see dark smoke near the ceiling in back. "When I opened the doors, it just roared out at me," one of them said later. She ran to get help and met Rick Schilling and busboy Mark Johnson coming the other way, running toward the Zebra Room.

Eileen Druckman, whose hostess station felt so toxic she said it made her nail-polish bubble, had already sounded the alarm. About the same time the Vanover sisters opened the doors, she smelled smoke in her cubicle that was just outside a set of doors at the back of the Zebra Room. As she opened one to investigate, she was engulfed in a cloud of eye-stinging black smoke. She ran to a nearby bartender, shouting, "My God, there's a fire!"

In the Cabaret Room at the back of the club Brock and the rest of the crowd had no idea anything was wrong. Teeter and McDonald were on a roll, dropping punchlines that spread ripples of laughter.

Dammert, returning to the second-floor Crystal Rooms on the service elevator, carried a large stainless-steel bowl of salad in his hands as he turned down the hall, pushed through the swinging doors and was met by a wide-eyed, frightened waitress, Fran Oaks. "Wayne, there's a fire in the Zebra Room!" she said in an urgent whisper.

Directly below them, Rick Schilling emptied his fire extinguisher into the Zebra Room and quickly saw the fire was out of control. He shouted, "Get everyone out of the building!"

His wife, Margie Schilling, used a phone at the bar to report the fire at 8:59, as the staff told patrons to find the exits and leave.

"I was in the bathroom when the fire started," Baker said. "They got me and two other ladies out. The only way out was through the Empire Room. The smoke was already thick and black. When I turned around on my way out I could see smoke at the door."

As dazed and panicked guests stumbled from the Supper Club, the fire spread quickly to the Cabaret Room in back. Some, like off-duty fireman Peter Sabino, went back in to rescue people who were trapped there. Kenton County Library archive

As she went out the door, she noticed that a busboy's jacket was smoking and smoldering and yanked it off him. By the time she circled the building to get to the Garden Rooms in the back, the whole place was in flames. "I could see the fire in the Hall of Mirrors. It was like someone put an industrial fan behind it and just blew it down that hall."

Walter Bailey, who would be described in the press as "a guardian angel in busboy's attire," heard about the fire and went to check it out. After seeing smoke roll out from the Zebra Room, he hurried to the Cabaret Room and ran into Brock.

"Walter told me there was a fire," Brock recalled, "but he told me the wrong room. I was standing outside the Cabaret Room. I turned back to the Garden Room to make sure people could get out. Then I went back to the Zebra Room. I was standing there yelling, 'NO! NO!' as I saw (busboy) Buddy Bethel come running down the stairs and kick the doors in."

Bethel, who was Shirley Baker's cousin, was bravely rushing to put out the fire before it could spread—or so he thought. He had no way of anticipating what would happen next.

As long as the room was shut, it could not get enough oxygen to feed the smoldering fire. But that changed in a split-second. "Those doors were eight feet high," Brock recalled. "When they opened it was like a freight train of flames and smoke. It tried to suck Buddy in and we had to grab him. The door handles were too hot to do anything. It just exploded out of that room."

What Brock saw was identified later by a senior research engineer at the Center for Fire Research in Washington, D.C., who analyzed the Supper Club fire down to the composition of carpets, carpet pads, ceiling tiles, paneling, furniture, chair coverings and foam padding.

"During the time attempts were being made to extinguish the fire within the Zebra Room, flash-over occurred," the report by Richard Bright said. He defined that as "simultaneous ignition of all combustible materials within the room."

Those materials included polyurethane padding, nylon and wool carpets, polyvinylchloride (PVC) acoustical tiles, wood, plastic, Naugahyde imitation leather made from PVC, rubber, linens and various other substances that produced deadly gases and byproducts such as cyanide gas, along with choking smoke and carbon monoxide, which "produces confusion and disorientation ... and ultimately, death."

"This furnace-like fire had only one immediate flue or vent available to it and this was the pair of doors at the north end of the room," Bright's report continued.

Witnesses said the cloud of superheated smoke that came out of the room when the doors were kicked open moved at astonishing speed. One of the witnesses was uniquely qualified to describe what he saw when he testified at a U.S. House hearing in December 1977.

Peter Sabino, a captain with the Cincinnati Fire Department, had arrived with his family at 8:45 and stood with them in the hallway near the Zebra Room as they waited for a table in the main dining room. They were about to have dinner, then go to the 11:30 show in the Cabaret Room.

"We were standing in the hallway and I heard loud talking coming from over in the Zebra Room area," Sabino recalled. "A couple of waitresses ran past us, kind of frantic looking, and our hostess started moving our line—about 18 or 20 people. She said, 'We have a problem, everyone will have to get out.' That was about ten minutes to nine or nine o'clock. We got outside, and I told my family to wait while I went back to find out what was wrong.

"Being a fireman, I thought possibly if I pulled some drapes down and some tablecloths, I could (use them to) hold it until the fire department arrived. So I found a waiter and identified myself. We were proceeding down this hallway, and I felt heat on my face."

Re-entering the building through the Garden Rooms at the back of the club, he looked down the Hall of Mirrors toward the Zebra Room, about 80 feet away. "I could see flames in the ceiling area down there. Between the time I felt the heat on my face and was on the floor, crawling out with the waiter, it was about 15 or 20 seconds. This heat came out—it was a tremendous amount of heat, and there were about 18 or 20 inches of fresh air on the floor in this area. I could see the glass doors and we just headed for the doors" that exited from the Garden Rooms.

"I heard a lot of screaming coming from what I now know was the Cabaret Room. We got out and saw smoke pouring out of the doorway. So I crawled into this area where people were piled up, just laying on top of each other—all you could see was a pile of arms and faces and they were screaming and reaching.

"So I started pulling people off the pile. Two men crawled in behind me and passed the people back outside. I took as much as I could."

Sabino worked until he could not stand up, breathe or even lift his arms.

As the first waves of more than 500 firefighters arrived, he worked alongside them until morning.

"I fit in with the rest of the people," he said. "I was out for the night and did not really look for the fire hazards and life hazards that did exist."

One element of his testimony would be critical: He estimated that the fire roared from the Zebra Room, down the Hall of Mirrors and into the Cabaret Room in just 15 to 20 seconds.

'You should leave'

As Brock yanked Bethel back out of the Zebra Room furnace, Walter Bailey walked down the center aisle in the crowded, noisy Cabaret Room and approached the stage, where the puzzled comedy team stopped in mid-sentence and handed him a microphone.

**Walter Bailey and his mother after the fire. Survivor Jeff Ruby
was so grateful for Bailey's warning in the Cabaret Room
that he gave him a job at one of his restaurants and helped
him through college.** Kenton County Library archive

Although only 18, barely out of high school and too young to vote, Bailey took charge. His mother said later she wasn't surprised because Walter had helped raise his three younger brothers. "He's been a father figure to this family since his father died three years ago. He's chipped in money and helped me bring up the boys. I'm so proud of him."

As Bailey took the microphone and began to speak, it was 9:08, no more than eight to ten minutes after the fire was discovered and the 911 call was made. Later, Kentucky Governor Julian Carroll would tell a U.S. House hearing that the Schillings failed to warn Cabaret Room guests for 20 minutes, based on the Investigative Report to the Governor by his hand-picked team.

But Special Prosecutor Cecil Dunn re-examined the evidence more thoroughly in 1979 and concluded that "there was a lapse of time of approximately eight to ten minutes between discovery of the fire ... and notification" to the Cabaret Room.

Dick Schilling had no fire brigade. His workers had no idea what to do and had not been drilled to warn and evacuate a crowd. There were no fire alarms to pull. But thanks to Walter Bailey's courage, the Cabaret Room crowd was warned in less than 10 minutes.

Bailey climbed on the stage, took a microphone from Teter and McDonald, and calmly asked the crowd to look for exits. He pointed out the green-lit signs where doorways in the right and left corners at the back of the room opened onto the Hall of Mirrors. "There's a fire in a small room on the other side of the building," he said, calmly and without drama despite his nervousness. "I don't think there's any reason to panic or rush. You should leave."

He handed the microphone back and walked deliberately back toward the exits. Some in the crowd got up to leave; others stared at him as if he were crazy; a few laughed, took another drink and waved him off, figuring it was all part of the comedy act.

As people in the Cabaret Room tried to understand what they had just heard, reactions slowed by the fog of alcohol, a rolling, boiling cloud of death was hurtling down the hallway, headed for the crowded room.

Most of the victims in the Cabaret Room never had a chance. Split seconds of indecision were fatal.

Bailey jumped onto a long green couch and began directing people through the exits, guiding them away from the fire toward the back of the building, through a hallway that led outdoors into the gardens behind the Garden Rooms. As he saw that most of the crowd was calmly filing out, he went to a control room to switch on the house lights, then turned to go back up the Hall of Mirrors to the front of the building, to see if the fire was under control.

He was stopped in his tracks. "I saw this big cloud of smoke coming down the hall at me real fast," he said later. Almost immediately, the most obvious and accessible exits from the Cabaret Room were blocked.

From the Bright report: "As the smoke, flames and hot gases left the Zebra Room, they were propelled across the ceiling (at) high velocity." The tornado of smoke, superheated fumes and toxic gases turned the corner, filled the Hall of Mirrors and "sealed off the most familiar exits from the Cabaret Room," Dunn reported.

Smoke arrived first—soot-black, churning with byproducts from burning plastic and polyurethane. It reached temperatures of 1,500 to 1,800 degrees. Melted glassware found in the kitchen showed temperatures there reached more than 1,400 degrees, investigators said.

"It was the blackest smoke I'd ever seen," said one survivor. "Up until that time, everything was orderly. There wasn't any chaos, no screaming, no panicking or anything. It was when people saw the smoke and the fire that they became panicky and they started screaming ... and you wouldn't be human if you didn't scream then, because they were dying."

As panic shot through the crowd like electricity, people in the back of the shuffling herd began shouting and urging the ones in front to "Get going!" and "Move it!" A single gulp of the lung-scorching smoke was agonizing and deadly. "The people after us were just falling out the door," a survivor said, "I mean literally falling all over the ground. It was terrible."

At the front of the Supper Club Brock watched the inferno shoot down the Hall of Mirrors into the Cabaret Room like a flamethrower and ran to the Empire Room. "There were about ninety people still there from a savings and loan group. We got them all out through the kitchen."

Most left at the first warning. But as in the Cabaret Room, some paid no attention until smoke filled the room, then they scrambled for the exits. Among the bankers was their speaker for the evening, future Ohio Governor Bob Taft.

Brock raced through the Empire Room to the kitchen, then through the kitchen and the Garden Rooms in the back, where the crowd from the Cabaret Room was still trickling out through the narrow hallway like water from a kinked garden hose.

"A woman came running through the room," he recalled. "She was on fire and just threw herself through the doors. We put her out with our busboy jackets. She lived. There was a guy taking pictures there and someone grabbed his camera and smashed it, saying, 'You're not taking pictures of these bodies.' By then we had 60 to 80 dead people out there on the lawn."

'Thank God there was light'

On the second floor, Dammert knew he was in trouble as soon as Fran Oaks told him, "Wayne, there's a fire in the Zebra Room!" He'd been trained to fight fires in the Navy and was well aware that the flames under his feet would quickly incinerate the Crystal Rooms. He put down the salad bowl and ran into the dining rooms. "I started yelling as loud as I could, 'Everybody out the back! Everybody out the back!

Everybody out the back!'

"I knew there was no way these people could exit by the staircase. The Zebra Room was directly at the bottom." The grand "Cinderella staircase" and its red carpeted runners spiraled down to a fountain at the landing next to the Zebra Room. It was cited as a fire hazard in 1971, but still was wide open, with nothing to stop flames from racing to the second floor.

With Fran Oaks directing guests to a hallway that led to another stairway down to the kitchen, Dammert got everyone out of the first set of Crystal Rooms where the Afghan Hound Club was meeting, then went back to the Choral Union rooms. Choking on thick black smoke, he was having trouble seeing but knew the rooms well because he had set them up. He made it as far as the doorway in back that opened onto a hallway. Across that hall were dressing rooms where women had changed for the fashion show.

"When I opened the door about four inches I felt a terrific blast of heat coming from the hall. It was tremendously hot and I knew the fire was completely out of control and that there was no way I could get into that hall or the dressing rooms on the other side."

He had no way of knowing that two women would die there. One was Charlene Mathews, who had worked with Dammert to organize the dinner and fashion show. A few days later, they would be the last two victims found in the scorched wreckage.

Dammert slammed the doors shut and ran out of the room, stumbling over chairs and banging his shins. As he got out to the exit hallway he was stunned to see that the crowd was still stuck in the hallway, not moving at all. "I knew the fire was roaring up those (spiral) stairs and was going to consume the second floor in short order."

Smoke was pouring into the hallway, people were struggling to breathe and nobody was moving. Some crawled on their hands and knees to gulp smoke-free air, pressing napkins over their faces. But somehow, everyone remained calm. About 75 people were trapped.

Dammert recruited a few men to try to break through a door on the left wall that opened onto a flat roof, but the heavy plywood was padlocked solidly and would not give. Then the lights went out.

"It was pitch black, they could hardly breathe and they were jammed in together in darkness with a huge fire working its way ever so quickly toward them," Dammert recalled.

A few men yelled, "Keep calm!" Somehow they did.

The lights flickered on again, a last fluttering flash of hope, then went out permanently. In a booth in the Cabaret Room at the other end of the building, lighting technician Stuart Coakley was frantically resetting circuit breakers as they popped and blew open. While others fled, Coakley stayed to keep lights on that helped people find exits, saving countless lives. But the circuit for the upstairs rooms was fried.

In the smoke-filled darkness, as he tried to breath and began to confront the certainty that he was going to die, Dammert saw another kind of light. "Quite suddenly, a picture of my family flashed in front of me, a large color picture," he recalled. It had only been minutes since he had first learned of the fire; now he was trapped, hopeless. Yet there, almost real enough to touch, were his wife and children, smiling, happy. He decided God was telling him to get out or he would leave his family with no one to take care of them.

He immediately started moving. Shouldering his way through the crowded hallway, he hugged the wall down the right side where there was a stairway down to the kitchen. He didn't know what he would find. Air? Light? Or flames, smoke and death?

"When I got to the top of the stairs I could see light. Thank God, there was light!"

He started directing the trapped crowd down the stairs and followed them to the bottom. As they pushed open a door they were amazed to find the kitchen was still brightly lit and free of smoke. Cooks, chefs and dishwashers stood on tables, calmly directing people out the back to a loading dock, then down a few steps to the ground.

Dammert figured out later that someone closed the back stairway to let other rooms evacuate through the kitchen. As Dammert stepped outdoors and gasped for fresh air, he looked around and could not quite grasp what he saw. There were bodies strewn across the grass, faces and hands blackened by soot... they were not moving.

Meanwhile, in the screaming crush of the Cabaret Room, people fought and scrambled for their lives, tripping on furniture, stepping on bodies both dead and alive. Waitress Janetta Johnson described the scene to a hearing in the U.S. House six months later.

"All of a sudden I heard a big swoosh like a pressure release type of thing and I looked over my left shoulder. I saw the smoke and fire come into the room. The smoke was so black it looked like crude oil in midair, just rolling. People began to scream and shout and push. ... I screamed, 'My God, there really is a fire!'

"I jumped on a chair, then a table, then into the crowd and grabbed a man's collar and he pulled me through the door. My blouse was burned, my hair was singed, and it was just like a blast of smoke that came out back of me.

"As I came out, I turned to look and the people weren't screaming anymore. The smoke had covered them all up."

With smoke and flames blocking the exits to the Hall of Mirrors and the Garden Room, there were only two ways out for hundreds of people still trapped in the Cabaret Room. There was a northeast exit in the front corner of the room, to the right of the stage, blocked by a jumble of spare chairs, tables and a service bar. And a southeast exit in the opposite front corner at stage left. It led to a poorly marked, smoke-clotted hallway, then outdoors down a treacherous set of steps made of open steel grating.

There were no exit signs. Aisles were blocked by tables that had been pushed close together on the terraced levels to exceed the room's capacity. "There were chairs crammed in the aisleway," Johnson said. "There were eight people sitting at tables where normally there are six. Aisleways were almost nonexistent."

She described her escape from the southeast exit. "Once you got past the double door you could not see the single exit door at all. There was nothing directing you which way to go. In fact, there is a little closet there and there was a red and white exit sign painted over this door. I understand some people were found dead in there. It was just a closet, you could not get out."

Brock, who had run to the back of the building, would have nightmares for the rest of his life about what he saw behind the Cabaret Room. "People were trapped against two exits at opposite ends of the room, on either side of the stage. The doors were each split into inward and outward openings. People got jammed up against the ones that would not open outwards and began stacking up until they blocked the exits entirely. They were stacked there like cordwood, eight or nine bodies deep.

"We started carrying them out as soon as we could. When we grabbed them by the arms, it was like grabbing hot wax. That's how hot it was."

Walter Bailey led hundreds out of the Cabaret Room, then went back in to rescue more. "I had to go back in," he said a couple of days later. "I wanted to do what I could. I knew where the doors were."

A bartender who narrowly escaped the Crystal Rooms ran to the back of the building to help firefighters and other staffers drag out victims still trapped inside. As the roof of the building burned off, the fire was vented to the sky and the smoke cleared enough to see the horrifying scene he described:

Volunteers and firefighters risked their lives in the smoke-choked inferno to drag out people who were trapped in logjams near the exits. One said it was so hot, 'grabbing their arms was like grabbing hot wax.'
Kenton County Library archive

"There was a woman… and she was out of this thing except there was about six people—there was enough people where we couldn't get her out at this time because they were on her legs, the back of her legs. She was clear of this thing, but she had all this weight on her and we just about pulled her arms out of their sockets and we couldn't move her."

Some victims were suffocated by the smoke, others were poisoned by the gases, some were crushed by the stampede and some were burned so badly that no fingerprints could be collected to identify their remains. Death was random. One woman found in the pile of bodies looked as if she had not been touched—except the back of her skull had been burned through.

Janete Zorick was stuck in the crowd, shuffling slowly toward the doors with her husband, George, a Kroger truck driver and volunteer firefighter in their hometown of Mack, Ohio. As they saw smoke roll into the Cabaret Room, George began cursing. "My God, the smoke is rolling," he told her. "It is a working fire. We have just a few minutes to get out and this damned place has no sprinklers."

They had come to the Supper Club with George's father, 52, and his aunt, Irene Muddiman, 48. Zorick's father, George, Jr., told his son, George III, "You go ahead. I will bring Irene."

"George asked people to move a little faster," Janete Zorick recalled after she was released from the hospital with lung damage. "There was a swooshing sound similar to a small explosion and it became very hot, and there was a yellow glow. A woman screamed and that's when the panic set in. I was knocked down several times and (was) walked on. My husband drug me up and threw tables out of our way. He told me not to look behind me, and he picked me up and carried me down a couple of levels, jumping tables to bring me to the exit.

"At this point I could not go any farther and he threw me out of the exit. This exited into a room or a hall. I could not find a way out, and neither could other people because there were no exit signs. There were people on the floor already. One woman was screaming and I tried to help pull her out but she was too badly burned to get up. When I turned to my left I was hit by flames. Some man told me to grab his belt and he would find a way out. The smoke and flames were so intense I tried to cover my face with my dress to breathe, and all my jewelry started to melt on me. I must have become unconscious because the next thing I remember was my husband pulling me up by the armpits saying, 'I've got you honey, you are going to be okay.'

"He went back in for his dad and aunt and I never saw any of them again."

One of the first to get out was the star John Davidson, who held a door for others until it got too hot. Among the last to get out from the southeast exit was Jeff Ruby. Because of his friendship with the Schillings, he and his group of three couples had seats front row, center stage. "The best seats for a show, the worst for a fire," he said later.

When Walter Bailey took the stage and announced the fire, Ruby and his group were directed to the northeast exit. He was still carrying his Jack Daniels Black Label whiskey on the rocks. "I figured I would take my drink along, wait out on the grass until it was over, and return to the show. That's how it came off to me."

But as they were herded toward the exit on the left side of the stage, "It looked like a thousand people trying to get out that door." It reminded him of the mass of people who clog the exits at the end of a Bengals game—without the exits.

One of his friends shook his head and said, "We'll never make it." Ruby started looking around for another way out. "And then I saw Scott Schilling, all 350 pounds of him, and he's running for his life, coming from the front of the house, and I saw smoke."

Ruby cursed, put down his drink and said, "This is for real.'"

He turned around and led his group toward the southeast exit on the other side of the stage, brushing off orders to stay with the crowd. "We got into a hallway. My girlfriend had her face pressed up into the back of my gray suit. People started pushing from behind, all panicking. I yelled, 'Stop pushing. Stay calm, the only way we get out alive is if there is no pushing.'

"Everyone was coughing, we couldn't see anything through the black smoke. Then I saw daylight—the greatest sight of my life. It was the front yard where the sign said 'Showplace of the Nation.' That's when I said, 'We're gonna make it.'"

As he looked back at the doorway, the comedy team came stumbling out with their ventriloquist dummies bobbing along on their shoulders. "Those dummies coming down the steps through the smoke, it was just so eerie. It was surreal."

Behind them, people were dying. They tripped on chairs and tables in the dark, dove for the exits, fell and trampled each other. The lucky ones lost consciousness, overcome by smoke and carbon monoxide. The unlucky ones were still conscious as they fell, pinned in the logjam of writhing bodies, screaming for help as the flames filled the room. Some were dragged out before the fire reached them, but many could not be saved.

The ones who got out would tell investigators later, "People were fighting each other like animals." As smoke and flames rolled into the room, "That's when people went berserk."

They described the inhaled smoke as "a really hard, deep burning sensation." The fire came in as if "the whole room exploded." Elderly people who could not keep up in the stampede for the exits were left behind, or clogged the doorways. People jumped on tables. One panicked man began throwing chairs into the crowd. Near the doors, people were stumbling, falling on top of each other, being trampled and crushed. "You had to fight to stay in line. Otherwise you would have been ground up against the wall somewhere."

Dammert described a friend he worked with, Paul Smith, who played violin in the house orchestra. Smith escaped and looked fine. "But even though he was out of the building, after a short while he dropped dead."

The bartender continued his account to investigators:

"And then there was a man that was on top, he was a heavy guy and he was reaching his arms up, and so I thought he was all right. I had him wrap his arms around my neck and I pushed up against the floor as hard as I could and I moved the guy about this far, about two feet. And about this time he was out of it. He didn't have enough strength to help me and I didn't have enough strength to lift him, and he just looked at me and shook his head... you know. There was nothing I could do."

He found a young girl on top of the pile. "She wasn't screaming or anything, but she was in fine shape." As he tried to carry her out, her leg was caught around a table leg, "and I couldn't pull her out."

Dammert ran to the front of the building and grabbed an axe from a fire truck. He found a fireman to bring a ladder to the flat roof on the side of the building. They climbed up and used axes to easily break through the plywood door that seemed so solid when he was trapped on the other side a few minutes earlier. As the door fell open, huge gouts of black smoke poured out and both realized there was no hope to go in and search for victims on the second floor.

Back on the grass near the entrance Dammert found a young woman who was unconscious and helped load her into an ambulance. He directed the driver through the traffic snarl of arriving firetrucks and ambulances and then knelt and tried in vain to save another woman with mouth-to-mouth resuscitation as her husband watched her die.

He finally gave up, turned to the man and said, "Your wife is with God now. Please be brave. God love you." He took the distraught husband's coat and draped it over the woman's head and shoulders.

The long driveway up the hill was clogged with vehicles and dazed, wandering survivors as hundreds of firefighters from dozens of fire departments on both sides of the Ohio River arrived to fight the blaze all night, working desperately to rescue victims.

Southgate Fire Chief Richard Riesenberg was frustrated at the demands of the press and politicians who wanted photo-ops while he was directing rescues and concerned about the safety of his crews. Here he answers questions while Kentucky Governor Julian Carroll looks on. Kenton County Library archive

Adding to the confusion were TV, radio and newspaper reporters flocking to the scene, demanding to talk to someone in charge. That was Southgate Fire Chief Richard Riesenberg, who was frantically working to save the lives of trapped victims and his own firefighters. "Every one of them tried to put words in my mouth," he said later of his brief press conference in front of the burning building. They wanted to know about "thousands" tapped inside. "They didn't want to know the truth. They wanted to make it even more spectacular."

When one of them blocked his path to demand access as a First Amendment right, the chief replied with two words he would not repeat for the record. Sometime after midnight, when it was clear no more people could be saved and further attempts could get firefighters killed or injured, he gave the heartbreaking order to pull back and let it burn.

Again and again, witnesses talked in awed tones about the incredible speed of the fire and the way it erupted from the Zebra Room and hurtled down the Hall of Mirrors toward the Cabaret Room, as if it were something alive, an angry monster seeking out the biggest crowd of helpless people to burn and suffocate.

**Survivors who made it outside gasped in disbelief when they
saw the bodies that were spread on the ground near the chapel.**
Kenton County Library archive

Dammert and others saw head dishwasher Willie Snow, bartender
Joe Kennedy and the youngest Schilling son, Scott, frantically pulling
bodies out of the tangled piles blocking exits. "They worked until
complete exhaustion forced them to stop," Dammert recalled. Ron
Schilling also worked all night, risking his own life to rescue victims
and pull out bodies.

Snow, a big man, was carrying two at a time. "In Willie Snow's case, he
had to be ordered to stop before he himself would have died," Dammert
said.

Bodies were sprawled in the grass as if they were casualties on some surrealistic battlefield. Many had soot-covered faces, hands and clothing. In some cases, survivors were tortured by their evening wear made of polyester "miracle fibers" that were popular in the 1970s. The synthetics melted in the extreme heat and fused to the flesh. One witness described a husband trying to peel away his wife's melted skirt as her skin came with it.

Dammert helped to carry a woman's body to the chapel, which was being used as a command post. When he got there, he was stunned to see more than a hundred corpses lined up on the lawn. He went from body to body, saying a prayer over each: "Please, God, take this soul into the kingdom of heaven." Soon he was joined by a waitress and two priests who offered their own prayers for the dead.

Later as he sat down to gather himself, he saw a policeman tackle a man, pin him to the ground and put handcuffs on him. The cop told him the man was looting the pockets and purses of the dead.

As the huge Supper Club began to collapse in explosions of flame, flying cinders and smoke, Dammert watched over the bodies to make sure nobody else tried to steal from them. Then he finally decided he had had enough. He found a policeman who was leaving and asked him to take him away... anywhere, just away.

The kid who grew up fascinated by fires, the sailor and blackjack dealer who had seen so many accidents, crash scenes and near brushes with death, had seen too much. He could not stand to watch the club he loved burn to the ground with friends, coworkers and guests inside.

When he finally reached a place where he could phone home, he was overwhelmed by the sound of his family cheering on the other end of the line. Betty and his two little children, Ron and Lisa, had been worried sick, afraid he was dead. They had no way of knowing that their vivid faces in that blacked out, smoke smothered hallway had saved his life and the lives of so many others.

When he finally got home, he stayed up all night and long into the morning, unable to close his eyes, afraid of what he might see in his dreams. Instead, he watched TV coverage of the fire. "I didn't sleep much at all that night. And, for that matter, for a lot of nights thereafter."

4.
The Day After

As if there could never be enough tears for the dead, the sky wept steadily on Sunday, drenching the blackened, scorched ground with a hard rain. The spring thunderstorm helped firemen finally squelch the smoking wreckage, but only made the search for victims more soggy and treacherous.

"The fire of undetermined origin raged for seven hours before the flames began to subside," an FBI agent reported from the scene that morning.

It was a day of looking, searching and asking why.

As the gray light of dawn exposed the horrific scene, exhausted firefighters went back into the building to rake through scorched shoes,

twisted chairs, burned purses, soot-blackened dishes, broken glassware, warped steel and melted silverware like something from a Salvador Dali painting. They tore through collapsed roofing, tangled electrical wires and charred framing lumber to search for human remains.

Thanks to the valiant efforts of rescuers, 137 bodies had been dragged out of the flames during the night. Another 28 would be found in the following days.

Some of the charcoal-black bodies

Southgate firefighters were on the scene for 93 hours.
When they could take no more, they collapsed for a brief break, then went back to work. Kenton County Library archive

were fused together or welded to furniture and pieces of the building, burned beyond recognition. They were found huddled together, piled on top of each other, "stacked like cordwood," witnesses kept saying— like the petrified victims of Pompeii who clung to each other in their final moments.

Fire Chief Riesenberg had been one of the first on the scene the night before, driving the lead firetruck. As he first glimpsed the billowing gray smoke rising from the top of the hill he thought, "Oh my God, we got the big one."

After fighting the fire all night, he came back the next morning. "We were there for ninety-three hours," he recalled at a survivors' reunion in 2020. "The next day I was up there I said, 'There are people still in there. We have to get them out.' We found one body broken in two. There were headless bodies. There was one woman by herself at a table. She had dropped her rosary. A firefighter found it on the floor and gave it to me. There was nothing wrong with it, but it had been through that fire. You can draw your own conclusions.

"I just couldn't stop myself from crying. I still choke up when I think about it."

Thirty-four victims died in the southeast hallway where Ruby, Janete Zorick, Janetta Johnson and others escaped. Twenty were found trapped in a closet that looked like an exit. Three of those bodies wore tuxedos—members of the orchestra.

At the opposite side of the stage in the northeast corner of the building—"stage right" from the performers' view—125 bodies were recovered. Many had been unable to find their way past a service bar, stacks of chairs, a cashier's stand and dishwashing station to reach the doorway to the back lawn.

"I guess I'll always see them piles of people," said survivor Ed Payne, who had worked feverishly during the fire. "People who made it to the doors got out. When the lights went out, that's when people started piling up. They started diving out the doors and falling down the steps. That's when we started to pull them out. We was just grabbing them and pulling them out onto the lawn."

He was lucky to have "bad seats" near the back of the Cabaret Room, near the exits. "They turned out to be the best," he said. "We just went there for a weekend to remember, and we got one that we don't want to remember." Payne and his brother joined busboys and waiters to plunge back into the building as the fire raged. "I don't think it will ever leave my mind."

"There was no way to describe the heat," another survivor said. "It was a horrible, engulfing heat. You could not breathe at all. And it was extremely dark because of the smoke."

The local coroner was overwhelmed by the sheer number of dead. Coroner Fred Stine did only 10 random autopsies and declared that all the victims died of smoke inhalation and/or carbon monoxide poisoning. That was the kindest thing to say for the grieving families. Nobody wanted to imagine their loved ones burning to death. But investigators said further autopsies would have revealed death by cyanide gas, caused when chair padding and other synthetics burned.

Stine said he didn't have the resources to handle 165 autopsies. He was haunted by the tragedy for the rest of his life.

As the worn-out firefighters sorted through the grisly rubble on Sunday, a few of them collapsed from exhaustion. Finally, at 6 p.m., they were all sent home to rest. The search was suspended as the rain continued to soak the ashes.

Fire investigators, detectives, firemen and a team from the FBI carefully sifted through the wreckage to find the remains of victims. Many were missing limbs, burned beyond recognition or welded to furniture. Kenton County Library archive

Meanwhile, a team from the FBI Disaster Squad tried to identify bodies that were recovered and taken to the makeshift emergency morgue at the Fort Thomas Armory.

Their careful list of clothing and possessions was heartbreaking in its inventory of the ordinary.

Gold watch, Timex. Wedding band with inscription. Shoes, men's loafers. One woman's shoe, blue, with platform heel. Car keys, Ford. Kroger tie clip. Cigarettes, Kools. Cricket cigarette lighter. Rose Blossom lipstick. Glasses. Sunglasses. Credit cards. Photos of kids. Comb. Religious medals. Gold cross. Picture of Jesus with a name written on the back.

The corpses wore dresses, pantsuits and polyester double-knit suits. Scars, "good teeth" or dental work were noted where fingerprints were impossible. "No hands," said cryptic notes on several victim cards.

Roy O. Butler, Body 136B, was 50. His I.D. card showed he was a member of the Ashland, Kentucky Auxiliary Police Department. He had $17 in his wallet. "Burned beyond recognition," the agents reported. "No lower body."

There was inevitable confusion. Judy Bohrer, 28, of Cheviot, had to be exhumed and re-buried when it was discovered she had been mis-identified as Evelyn Shough, 62, of Dayton.

Rose Mary Dischar, 38, a pretty and popular waitress who was working in the Cabaret Room, was Body 147. Her fingers were missing along with half of her skull. She was last seen crying for help, trapped behind the crowd in the Cabaret Room. She left behind five children, who had been abandoned by their father a few years before.

Stuart Coakley, 37, who had stayed behind to keep the lights on, was a chemistry teacher at Notre Dame Academy in Park Hills, Kentucky. He worked part time at the Supper Club, to set up and direct stage lighting during shows. He escaped, then went back to rescue others and never came out again.

Death was random. From Ohio, it took victims from Dayton, Trenton, Columbus, Ironton, Waynesville, Williamsburg, West Carrollton, Kettering and numerous suburbs and neighborhoods of Cincinnati.

Kentucky's victims came from Louisville, Lexington, Covington, Crittenden, Ashland, Dover and dozens of other towns and cities in Northern Kentucky.

Others were from Indiana, California, Tennessee and Alabama.

Tiny Cynthiana, Kentucky, about 50 miles west, lost an entire farm family: Willard and Fredericka Fryman, their teenage daughter, Tracy, and son, Martin Scott, all died in the Cabaret Room.

Sheila Ann Dwyer's brother James was photographed leaving the morgue after identifying three bodies: Sheila; his mother, Rosemary; and another sister, Mary. In the picture that was published in newspapers across the nation, he is held up by his elbows between a priest and a friend. His head is thrown back, eyes clenched shut to blot out what he has just seen, mouth open in an aria of heart-wrenching horror and grief.

The FBI reported that Sheila, 22, had eyeshadow, lip gloss, two pairs of sunglasses and receipts for gas and dry cleaning in her purse. The three Dwyers had driven up from Lexington to see John Davidson.

George Zorick, 32, who rescued his wife then went back for his father and aunt, was Body 138B. He wore a blue blazer with red stitching, light blue pants and a white shirt. He was charred along his left side, but two rings were recovered: a 1963 class ring from Western Hills High School, and a silver ring inscribed, "Kroger Safe Driver Award." As a firefighter in the small town of Mack, Ohio, he had always stressed and taught fire safety, his daughter said. His wife, Janete, missed his funeral while she was hospitalized in critical condition. "He was a hero," she said later.

Bodies were loaded onto National Guard trucks and taken to a makeshift morgue in a gymnasium for identification by family members. Kenton County Library archive

Bright, Indiana, hardly big enough for a stoplight, lost five residents, all friends: Gary Littrell, 29; his wife, Sharon, 26; Robert Sykes, 30; his wife, Lora Jean, 29; and Rosalie Schuman, 33. Schuman's husband, Ron, survived but was badly burned. Ironically, all three men were members of the Bright Volunteer Fire Department.

Robert Kettman, an executive at the Keebler Company, and his wife, Susan Ann, had just moved to Cincinnati from Ft. Wayne, Indiana six months earlier. Both were killed in the fire. But that was not the end of Kettman family tragedies. They left behind three orphaned daughters: Pamela, 8; Christi, 7; and Cari, 2.

On Sunday morning the girls still were unaware of what had happened. A family friend and an aunt, who knew Robert and Susan were missing, distracted the kids by taking them to breakfast, then to a farm to pick strawberries. As they filled pint baskets, the girls were excited about the strawberry pie their mother would make.

When they went home that afternoon, the street in front of their home in Withamsville, Ohio was lined with cars. "I thought we were having a party," Pam recalls. It was a wake. Her parents had been confirmed dead.

"Christi and I were playing in the backyard and were called into the living room. We were sat down on the fireplace hearth and they told us our parents were dead. Christi and I and Cari, who was just waking up from her nap, were surrounded by my dad's family and acquaintances who told us our mom and dad were never coming home."

While the adults discussed the children's future, the girls fled to the basement to watch coverage of the fire on TV. All around them were reminders of their mom and dad: shelves their dad had built, part of his unfinished project to remodel the basement into a rec room; coffee cans covered in black, gold and white contact paper, made by their mom to hold the girls' toys and treasures.

"It was so odd to see our family's church photo on the TV screen. It was as if time had stopped," Pam recalled. "How could it move forward without them?"

After their parents' funeral, the girls were sent to live with an aunt and uncle. It was not a happy home. "My aunt made us feel like our parents had done everything wrong," Pam said. "My parents never spanked us. But my aunt had a paddle on her wall. It was terrifying."

Christine struggled with defiance and grief. She was singled out for abuse. So the girls were split up and shuffled off again, as the older two were sent to live with friends of the family. At first it was an improvement. But then a boy who was about their ages "became like a predator," Pam recalled. "We had to kick him to keep him away."

It was much worse for Cari. During a marriage counseling session, their aunt and uncle revealed that Cari had been sexually abused by the uncle for years, starting when she was 11. At age 14, social workers sent her to live with Pam, who was 19. The uncle was sent to prison.

Pam said families should plan for the worst. "When parents die, children are left exposed to things," she said. "It's so important to have adults care for you whom you can trust. Life can change so fast."

At the end of that first day after the fire the press reported that 81 people had been injured, including four firemen, one of them seriously. The total for injuries would grow to 116. The death list would settle at 165, not including at least two unborn infants.

Each body number told a story of hopes, dreams, experiences, victories and defeats—an unfinished book of life. And there were hundreds more stories about survivors—tales of heartbreaking, devastating damage.

Some had severe burns and smoke-injured lungs; most were scarred by indelible images of what they saw, what happened, the loved ones they lost, what they did or did not do in the panicked hell of the burning Supper Club. Haunted by survivors' guilt, they would always wonder, "Why me?" and "What else could I have done?" Some died years later of lingering injuries, left off the official list of victims. A few took their own lives.

Four days after the fire, on Wednesday, the officials on the scene declared to the press that all the bodies had been found. But within hours, a cloud of flies pointed to two more bodies in the wreckage: Lenora Hill Gentry and Charlene Matthews, both of the Cincinnati Choral Union. Matthews organized the fashion show and dinner. Both women had been trapped in a dressing room on the second floor. Their remains were found in the Viennese Room below, where the second floor had collapsed. One witness said he saw them come out, then go back in to retrieve the money they had collected to pay the bill. "The evidence leaves little doubt that these victims once exited the building in complete safety and returned to rescue money," said Special Prosecutor Cecil Dunn in his 1979 report.

An unidentified woman is helped up the stairs to the morgue to identify a member of her family. The bodies were draped in sheets on the basketball court. Many had to be identified by personal belongings. The county coroner was so overwhelmed he decided after a few autopsies that all had died of smoke inhalation.
Kenton County Library archive

As families arrived to identify bodies, the gymnasium-morgue echoed with screams, gasps and anguished sobs. Six refrigerated semi-trailers loaned by Kroger, headquartered in Cincinnati, were parked nearby to preserve the bodies that were tagged and identified.

"I was in the military in World War II, and I am no stranger to carnage," Kenneth Lance told a reporter. "I was on four beaches in the Pacific, but over there the guys were alone. Here they are surrounded by their relatives. It is a more traumatic situation. It is heart-rending to see people identify their mothers and fathers, and in some cases their sons and daughters."

The FBI team noted: "The possibility of this case being a criminal matter has not been ruled out."

Yet there was little effort to preserve evidence in and around the Zebra Room where the fire started. On Sunday, as the ashes were still smoking, a 50-foot crane began removing the collapsed roof of the club that had fallen into the Cabaret Room, to help clear the way for searchers.

Shortly after that, a bulldozer began moving the rubble. In the days immediately after the fire, debris was pushed from room to room by heavy equipment, and the Zebra Room area was flattened and destroyed.

On the same day the last two bodies were found, newspapers reported that arson had been ruled out. Kentucky State Police Commissioner Ken Brandenburgh pointed to napkins that had been stacked in the Zebra Room and said, "We're getting very close to determining how the fire started."

He could not have been more wrong.

An unidentified staff member at St. Elizabeth Hospital sorts through the personal belongings that were recovered by searchers after the fire. The scorched and soot blackened purses, eyeglasses, shows and car keys were divided into separate stacks and boxes to aid in the identification of bodies that were burned beyond recognition. Kenton County Library archive

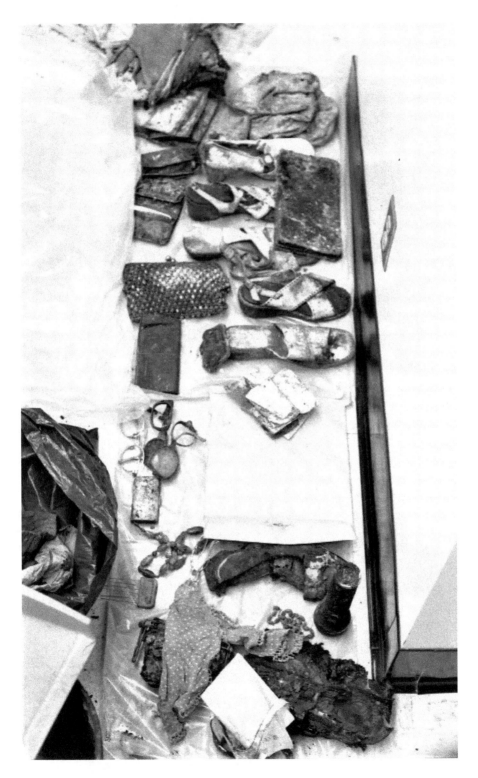

5.
Sifting Through the Ashes

When Wayne Dammert returned to the hilltop on the day after the fire, he was sickened by what he saw. The hallway where he and 75 people had been trapped was gone, with only a doorframe left standing and tables dangling over the edge of the upstairs wreckage.

Wayne Dammert barely survived the fire, then went back the next morning to crawl through the wreckage in the Zebra Room. He's still troubled by what he saw that day. Kenton County Library archive

The acrid, sooty reek of burned wreckage saturated the hilltop, mixed with odors that nobody wanted to think about. As he walked to the front of the building he met a fire inspector and offered to show him the layout. With a state police photographer, they entered the Zebra Room area just hours before it was obliterated by heavy equipment. "We were the first people to enter this room after the fire," he said. "We crawled over the rubble of the collapsed ceiling where the Zebra Room had been. I stood in the exact place where the fire roared out."

He could still make out the remains of the room as he had left it the night before, when he took the bill to Shirley Baker's wedding party. Only the metal frames of tables and chairs were left standing. The paneling and doors were burned away, leaving blackened studs to show the bones of the room. Charred fire extinguishers sat at the entrance where they had been abandoned during the frantic initial attempts to control the blaze.

He was amazed to see tray stands still stacked with unbroken dishes and silverware, left as tables were cleared. The ceiling had collapsed into the center of the room, leaving the sides less damaged.

As he followed the fire inspector and climbed over a tangle of framing and furniture, he saw something that still bothers him: "One wall between the studs was all black, but the ones next to it were both white, unburned. The one that was black had the sconces and wiring that went to the basement. The investigator didn't have anything to say about it. We just looked at it."

Before he could explore more, a state police trooper found him and sent him to a hotel in Fort Mitchell to answer questions from Kentucky State Police investigators. "By the time I got back, I was very surprised to find that they had moved the big crane from the back of the building to the front and they were tearing out the front walls of the Zebra Room. They had torn the whole front of the place off and it was all gone. They bulldozed and cleared it out fast. Especially the basement. They cleaned everything out of there so fast."

That same day one of the first news stories about the fire blamed it on an exploding generator under the Zebra Room. The story said that when Ron Schilling had tried to put the fire out, "the generator exploded and Schilling was blown across the room."

The generator did not explode and did not cause the fire. But if the fire did start under the Zebra Room, as Ron Schilling thought, that blackened wall flanked by unburned sections was an important clue leading directly to the basement.

The Zebra Room where the fire started was among the first targets of demolition. Investigators who suspected arson were dismayed at how soon the evidence was destroyed and covered up. Kenton County Library archive

Exactly when the Zebra Room was torn apart and buried by bulldozers has been disputed. Dammert said he saw it happen on Sunday and Monday. Official reports said the demolition was done to uncover remains. News stories said the crane and a bulldozer on the site for Dick Schilling's convention center project were used Sunday morning "to remove the collapsed roof from the east half of the building where most of the dead were entombed." That half of the building included the Cabaret Room and the Zebra Room.

"As soon as heavy construction equipment could be made available from the search for victims at the rear of the complex, the front wall of the Zebra Room was opened to allow examination of that area," said the Investigative Report to the Governor, published four months later, on September 19.

Whatever the reason, within hours or a day at most, the origin of the fire and any evidence in and below the Zebra Room was destroyed and buried.

The Kentucky State Police had arrived the night of the fire to "secure

An aerial view shows the front of the building and destruction of the Zebra Room next to the covered main entrance. Kenton County Library archive

the scene," officials said. Kentucky Governor Julian Carroll arrived at 3:30 a.m. as the fire still burned. Two investigators from the National Fire Prevention Association arrived on Sunday morning as the ashes were cooling. Three more joined them and continued to investigate for weeks.

But none of them secured the possible crime scene of the Zebra Room.

Former Kentucky State Fire Marshall Rodney Raby was one of the first there, along with the state's top arson investigator, Deputy Fire Marshall Clell Upton, now deceased. "Clell believed it was arson from the beginning," Raby said later. "Clell told Governor Carroll it was arson, but the governor told him to back off. The state police took over from that point on and we were not listened to. It made no sense at all. They destroyed the whole scene. The fact that we were not allowed to investigate makes it even more obvious that it was arson."

At first, officials said the "prevailing theory" was that the fire started in the basement, under the Zebra Room. But that was quickly corrected. By Wednesday, June 1, the Kentucky State Police had ruled out the basement as the site of origin, because barboy Marc Mathes said he was in the basement at 9:00 p.m. and "didn't see any fire or smell any smoke." One investigator even told reporters the basement was "untouched by flames," which was false, as photos would show.

The official version quickly settled on a new theory: The fire was "electrical in origin."

Governor Carroll let it be known that he held the Schillings responsible, and appointed a team to investigate: Kentucky State Police Commissioner Ken Brandenburgh; the governor's Chief Executive Officer Jack Hall; and State Fire Marshal Warren Southworth. A few days later the governor added Ovid Lewis, a law professor at Northern Kentucky University's Chase Law School, as chief counsel to study liability.

The governor's team was first among many investigations. It set the framework of the media version that endures today, but it was by far the most tainted and suspect. Except for the law professor, Lewis, the rest of the team was cursed with scandal.

Fire Marshal Southworth was a no-show for the initial meetings and it soon became clear why. When the report was released in September he was suspended, fined and then fired by the governor for "failing to carry out his legal duties." The report showed that Southworth, his chief deputy and a field investigator were directly implicated in approval of the permit that allowed the Supper Club to open in 1971, while ignoring code violations that made it "an electrician's nightmare."

Brandenburgh

Kentucky State Police Commissioner Brandenburgh was forced to resign in disgrace two years later. The story behind his removal made headlines for years. In 1979, State Police Trooper Eddie Harris was shot and killed. The suspect, Clyde Graham of Elizabethtown, was tracked down in Illinois and killed by State Police Sergeant Eugene Coffey. Brandenburgh's foot-dragging report on the shooting finally announced that Graham had struggled with Coffey and the trooper was justified in shooting him twice in the chest. But an investigation by Attorney General (later governor) Steve Beshear found that Graham had been shot *in the back* and the chest, and there was no struggle. Brandenburgh's report also covered up excessive force by troopers who arrested members of the fugitive's family. Beshear said the truth was "deliberately concealed or not discovered as a result of gross incompetence." That meant Brandenburg may have tampered with evidence to justify Graham's killing.

He was always an odd choice to lead the Kentucky State Police. He was appointed by Governor Carroll in 1976 at the age of 34, with no evident police experience. He had been the vice president for business affairs at Transylvania University in Lexington, which had an enrollment smaller than a large high school.

The governor's assistant Jack Hall was accused of overreaching to "direct" the meetings and manipulate findings to fit Governor Carroll's blueprint. The report had to be rushed so Carroll could present it at a special U.S. House hearing in Cincinnati on September 19, 1977. Meanwhile, the Campbell County Attorney who would have to prosecute any criminal charges was left in the dark. He was handed the report on the same day the media got it.

"In a lot of areas of the report, statements were taken out of context, completely out of context. And a lot of investigative conclusions were drawn from the statement of only one person out of 50 ... the one the investigator wanted to get in," said Robert Lawson, a University of Kentucky law professor who wrote the book on *Kentucky Rules of Evidence*, and also wrote *Beverly Hills: Anatomy of a Nightclub Fire* (1984).

Richard Bright was sent to the fire scene by the National Bureau of Standards to help the governor's investigation. "This was an extremely unusual investigation in that locals did not take part at all," he said later. "The state was not conducting the investigation. There was really no one in charge." The state police collected 10,500 pages of interviews with survivors and employees, but shared almost nothing. "We were able to read only one eyewitness statement," Bright said. "If we had better access to witness statements, we may have been able to come to a better conclusion. And they started bulldozing the place before I even arrived."

Governor Carroll held a press conference near the fire scene to release the report and quoted it as gospel the next day at Congressional hearings led by Cincinnati Democrat Tom Luken. Both events were staged for maximum publicity, just two days after John Davidson had returned for a concert attended by 8,000 to raise money for the children of victims.

The governor's words were incendiary: "conspiracy," "fraudulent," "illegal," "complete and total disregard for human life by the owners." His calls for criminal indictments of the Schillings made big headlines. But Governor Carroll and the other grandstanding politicians were wrong about many of the facts, as later investigations would show.

Kentucky governors and scandals mix like bourbon and sugar in Derby Day juleps. But Carroll filled the scandal glass until it spilled over the top. After he left office it was discovered that his son and daughter had been paid $500 a month by a businessman whom Governor Carroll had appointed to the University of Kentucky Board of Trustees—the equivalent of Kentucky knighthood. He pleaded the Fifth Amendment to avoid testifying when his chairman of the state Democratic Party, Howard "Sonny" Hunt, was convicted of taking insurance commission kickbacks. Carroll was given half of an Oklahoma oil well without investing a dime, by two men who made millions on no-bid contracts with the state. And one of his aides, Henry Vance, was sent to prison in 1988 for planning and providing a gun for the murder of a Florida prosecutor.

By 2017, Carroll had served in the Kentucky Senate for a dozen years, telling voters he was the "moral choice" who stood for traditional family values. As a distinguished state senator, he was redeemed. "Forgotten were the convictions and indictments of his aides in the years following his time as governor," *Louisville Courier-Journal* Columnist Joseph Gerth wrote.

But then one day the past caught up. It was revealed that Carroll had been caught on a tape years earlier, soliciting sex from a troubled young man. "The image he had so carefully cultivated—particularly after the federal investigations trashed his gubernatorial legacy—came crashing down," wrote Gerth. "At best, the former governor, who was profiled in a 1977 book called *Julian Carroll of Kentucky: The inside story of a Christian in public life,* will be remembered as a hypocrite and a dirty old man."

Or perhaps worse. *The Bluegrass Conspiracy* by Sally Denton (1990) tells a wild story of a gang known as "The Company," that trafficked guns and drugs from Lexington's Blue Grass Airport in the 1970s.

It quotes from a classified report by the ATF, describing the gang's activities: "...the smuggling and domestic trafficking of narcotics and dangerous drugs; the infiltration and hidden control of gambling casinos domestically and internationally; the trafficking and smuggling of firearms and military hardware; the acquisition and diversion of large amounts of currency; contract assassinations; **arson for profit**; business scams; and the corruption of public officials..." [Emphasis added.]

The ATF report said the gang worked with organized crime leaders, pornographers, international drug cartels, casino operators, law enforcement officers, "prominent political figures" and "La Cosa Nostra crime families."

Denton's book says: "A review of Governor Julian Carroll's official phone records reflected hundreds of phone calls from the governor's office to the residences (of the three gang leaders) every month since 1977." Carroll left the governor's office in 1979.

Governor Carroll and his handpicked team of investigators—except for Ovid Lewis—made a remarkable lineup of crooks, liars, political hacks and hypocrites, all chosen to investigate Kentucky's worst tragedy. But their Investigative Report to the Governor became the "first draft of history" in the press.

Following that report, there were five more official investigations:

- Hearings by the U.S. House (1977)

- A Campbell County Grand Jury (1978)

- The National Fire Prevention Association (1978)

- Special Prosecutor Cecil Dunn (1979)

- The Kentucky Office of the Inspector General (2009)

The reports all concluded that the "likely" origin of the fire was "electrical in nature." But they also unanimously conceded that the cause was unknown and undetermined.

The Report to the Governor: "Due to almost complete consumption of (the Zebra Room) it has not been possible to develop a more specific conclusion as to origin, source or cause."

Campbell County Grand Jury: "The Jury feels it would be very hard pressed and possibly inaccurate to point to the source other than to that it appeared to be electrical in origin somewhere in the Zebra Room itself."

The NFPA: "The precise electrical equipment (lighting fixture, switch, receptacle, outlet or fixed wiring), or the form of heat of ignition (short circuit arc, arc from faulty contact or heat from electrical fixture) could not be determined during two weeks of intensive investigation."

"However, the theory that the fire originated in the basement was reasonable... There was evidence of fire in the basement under the main bar area." The primary argument against that theory: employees who passed through the basement did not smell smoke or see fire. But if the fire rose through air ducts, smoke and heat could go unnoticed in the basement.

Special Prosecutor Dunn: "There is substantial disagreement... (but) the specific form of ignition, the circumstances under which it occurred, and its exact location could not be determined."

The biggest obstacle to proving criminal liability, Dunn said, was that even after "Kentucky State Police interrogated virtually every employee at the Club extensively about the electrical system in and around the Zebra Room," they could *not* find "credible evidence with which to prove **that the fire was caused by defects or deficiencies in the electrical system**." [Emphasis in original.]

Grand jury says no

Carroll blamed the Schillings for "a 20-minute delay" in warning the Cabaret Room. But a Campbell County grand jury disagreed. The grand jury heard from more than a hundred witnesses, reviewed almost a thousand written statements, and "was able to hear testimony from many witnesses that had never been contacted by the State Police, and had access to materials and evidence that was found after the initial investigation was concluded." On August 2, 1978, after five months of work, they found "no delay in the notification of guests and patrons," and "insufficient evidence" to charge Dick Schilling or anyone else.

Carroll had promised indictments, so he was incensed when the grand jury announced that it "did not find any evidence that would tend to raise the possibility of indictment." He responded to public anger—that he had inflamed—by appointing Dunn as special prosecutor.

Carroll made it clear to Dunn: He wanted a "second opinion" from a new grand jury that would indict Dick Schilling and perhaps officials in the Kentucky Fire Marshal's office.

There were plenty of reasons to blame Dick Schilling.

The Investigative Report to the Governor, the NFPA and the special prosecutor listed a catalogue of Schilling's negligence, lies, broken promises, code violations, shortcuts, overcrowding and strong hints of corruption.

The most reliable estimate of "gross overcrowding" in the Cabaret Room during the fire was 1,011, Dunn said. The Governor's Report chose 1,360. The NFPA estimate was 1,300. But even the lowest guess was far beyond the club's own maximum Cabaret Room capacity of 756, and double the 511 allowed under NFPA rules.

One guest who survived described tables jammed so close together he was unable to slide into his chair. "We were disgusted," he said. "You couldn't get through the aisles. We told the waitress we would stand in the door because there was no place to sit."

Waitresses said they could hardly squeeze through aisles to serve drinks.

Investigators agreed that the total crowd in the entire Supper Club that night was about 3,000 to 3,400, double the allowed capacity of 1,511.

The building had only 16.5 total exits, which was 11 short of the 27.5 required. Some of the exits were obstructed, even hidden; in many cases, there were no signs. "The crowd was notified too late, without sufficient egress," the reports said.

Fire training was "practically nil," an employee said. "I was not instructed what to do... nothing, you know, you just try to get out and hope that everybody else does."

Among 518 survivors from the Cabaret Room who were interviewed, about 90 percent said it was less than five minutes from Walter Bailey's warning to the rolling black cloud of smoke that poured into the room. About a hundred people made it out through the exit near the Garden Room before that door was blocked by smoke. For the rest, the situation was hopeless.

Although Schilling spared no expense on showy chandeliers and mirrors, his building materials were combustible and released poisonous gasses when they burned, the NFPA found. Interior finishes fed the fire. "Widespread use of wood framing and lack of separation devices" directly contributed to the loss of life. If fire resistant doors had been installed on the Zebra Room, they could have bought at least an hour of containment to get everyone out safely.

There was no alarm system. A sprinkler system that could have saved lives was not clearly required by code at that time. After the fire, Kentucky lawmakers made many changes to upgrade inspections and curb patronage that allowed incompetence and corruption in state agencies. Sprinklers and fire alarms were required.

State and local fire and building inspectors had been warned and knew about hazardous code violations, but had done nothing. A state senator said he visited the club before the fire and was so alarmed he notified the state Fire Marshal's staff that "something bad might happen there." But, "Lo and behold, they already knew about it," he reported. He was told that the inspector was "hampered by somebody over him in carrying out and enforcing what he thought was right."

That "somebody" was the Fire Marshal in 1971, John Calvert, who issued a permit to open despite hazardous code violations. He wrote, "I have been assured that the corrections under discussion will be taken care of." One of the deputies in his office later said he knew the permit was handled outside normal channels because it had none of the customary log numbers to show it was reviewed properly.

But that posed another roadblock for indictments, Dunn said. Schilling was let off the hook because "inspections were grossly insufficient." The strongest case against Schilling was to charge him with reckless homicide, but proving it would be unlikely, Dunn decided. The first grand jury had already determined "there was negligence involved (but) this negligence was not criminal in nature."

Dunn pointed out that Schilling's own family was in the club, along with his friends and employees. To imagine that he would knowingly risk the lives of his sons, daughter-in-law, wife, grandchild, friends and himself "defies all but irrational belief."

Schilling's shortcuts, dodged permits, sloppy remodeling, closed off exits and gross overcrowding were "immaterial acts of carelessness."

The State Police Commissioner said he had no doubt that Schilling "cut corners and did whatever was necessary to make a buck."

But after Dunn reviewed all the other reports—including 680 interviews by 30 investigators, 10,000 pages of testimony and 1,100 surveys sent to survivors—the special prosecutor concluded: "Nothing is to be gained from additional efforts to pursue criminal prosecutions."

Everyone was guilty, so nobody was guilty. It was an accident.

The Kentucky Inspector General's re-investigation in 2009 seemed designed to smother growing suspicions about arson. Although it confirmed strong evidence of arson, it concluded that the arson theories were faulty. Among the reasons cited: Kentucky State Police had asked a 16-year-old busboy "whether he had heard that the fire was set by organized crime." He said "No."

Without finding any proof to back it up, all of the investigations agreed more or less with the NFPA: "The only possible source of ignition that could be located within the concealed spaces was electrical in nature."

Unless it was arson.

6.
Down in the basement

"I saw a lot of things that were strange there.
Especially in that basement."
— **Former Kentucky Fire Marshal Rodney Raby**

A wall of the Zebra Room in the left foreground. Behind it is the
'Cinderella' spiral staircase that led to the second floor.
Kenton County Library archive

In the days following the fire, survivors were shocked, traumatized, trying to make sense of what happened as their lives were changed forever in one night. Most were interviewed by the Kentucky State Police.

Shirley Baker said she tried to tell the investigators about something that bothered her. She had arrived at work one morning with co-worker Judy Holiday. While she waited for Judy to stop in the restroom, she overheard a conversation in the bar.

"Ricky and Scott and Ronnie (Schilling) were inside the bar, and two men were sitting there at the bar. I heard them ask Ricky, 'Will you be willing to sell?' Ricky said, 'No, we're making money. Why would we sell? We're getting ready to build a motel and convention center up here.'"

Baker said one of the men asked, "Would you consider taking on partners?"

"We don't need any," Rick Schilling replied.

"I saw him hand Ricky a piece of paper. Later, I found out it was a blank check. They said, 'Put any amount on there that you want.'"

But as Baker watched, Rick shook his head and refused, saying, "I already told you, we're not selling and we're not taking on any partners."

Baker recalled: "The smaller man, who was kind of heavy, told Ricky, 'Well, did you ever stop to consider that if you won't sell and you won't take on partners, did you ever think you wouldn't have it long, either?'"

As she tried to reassemble her life after the fire, that scene came back to her with new meaning. "I started thinking about it. Those were the same two men I saw working in the ceiling of the Zebra Room."

David Brock and others at the club confirmed the story. Brock said he was told by Rick Schilling that the men offered him a blank check.

Like Baker, Brock was troubled but scared. The investigators asked him a few questions about organized crime but did not seem interested. And he was afraid that anyone who would kill 165 people would not hesitate to silence a talkative busboy.

Baker said the state police brushed her off when she told them the story. "They stopped the tape and told me they didn't want to hear it. They said they knew it was the wiring."

Baker, Brock, Dammert, Raby and various survivors are part of a small but dedicated group that has fought for more than 40 years to find the truth. They are not governors, assistants to the governor, fire marshals, state police commissioners or prosecutors who prepared the official reports. They have no political power, no easy access to the press. Their stories were never taken seriously by the police, the politicians, the press and the courts, where a civil case blaming faulty aluminum wiring was settled for $50 million, making it official: it was electrical.

But they were there. They are witnesses. Their stories match up and they have not changed the details over four decades. They have worked relentlessly to prove the Supper Club fire was arson, and have uncovered persuasive evidence.

If they are right, the fire on May 28, 1977 was not just the second worst nightclub fire in U.S. history. It was also one of the nation's worst mass murders and America's most deadly unsolved crime.

"If that is the case, this would be one of the largest mass murders in American history, ranking right behind the terrorist acts in Oklahoma City and New York," said Glenn Corbett, professor of fire science at John Jay College of Criminal Justice in New York City and technical editor for *Fire Engineering* magazine.

The evidence for arson

Before the Zebra Room was bulldozed and buried, Raby and other investigators climbed down to the basement underneath it to take a look. A Kentucky State Police photographer took more than 1,500 pictures at the scene. But many are missing, destroyed or never released.

What Raby and Clell Upton and a few others saw in that basement below the Zebra Room was confirmed many years later when Brock tracked down the photographer and Brock's co-author Tom McConaughy sued the Kentucky State Police to get access to the pictures.

"I spent two years suing them to get the truth," McConaughey said. During that time, his respect for the KSP evaporated. "They lied when they had no reason. They said there was no damage in the basement. I did a Freedom of Information request for the photos and they said there was no basis for my request."

Yet the Kentucky State Police were glad to help the FBI recover a priceless souvenir from the fire. An FBI memo, dated December 11, 1981, obtained by an FOIA request, describes how a KSP detective from the Dry Ridge Post "continuously pursued" a request by the FBI's Gambling Section for four years, to finally obtain "for training purposes" one roulette wheel that had been found in the basement.

"These roulette wheels were handcrafted in wood and were made over 20 years ago," the memo said. "The newer roulette wheels are now made of plastic and sell for over $22,000."

One of the same roulette wheels that dazzled Shirley Baker when she reported for work at the Supper Club is now somewhere at the FBI's Quantico office, perhaps in some boss's office, or even someone's home—a sentimental keepsake from a fire that killed 165 people.

The KSP roulette-wheel detective deserved a commendation, the memo said: "In light of his efforts and persistence to insure [sic] the securing of a roulette wheel, which is priceless, it is felt a letter from the (FBI) Director is appropriate."

But the KSP was not so enthusiastic about pictures of the fire. In late 2011, McConaughy's lawsuit was finally decided in his favor, and the KSP was forced to finally release about 300 of the 1,500 pictures taken at the scene.

As Raby said, they show "strange things."

Clearly visible in the basement are heavy-gauge red and blue wires that have been stripped and pushed directly into a wall outlet. At first the hazardous wires were blamed on Schilling's shortcuts. But an insurance inspection five months earlier had found nothing wrong. Photos also show fountains of soot on the basement walls, leaving a pattern that indicates flames shooting upward. A nearby air-handling duct has a hole the size of a manhole, revealing soot-caked walls inside the ductwork. The edges of the hole are curled back, either cut out or blown out by an explosion. Nearby equipment shows soot and burns, making claims that it was "untouched by flames" preposterous.

Brock said fire investigators who reviewed the photos agreed there was an intensely hot fire in the basement. His theory after examining the pictures: "The fire started right there. There were two tanks nearby, like fish tanks, set up to feed some kind of liquid into the air handling system, and a timer for the igniter. It ran up through the ducts into the Zebra Room directly overhead, into the ceiling, and spread from there. It burned for two hours. The rest of the basement is almost untouched. There are burn marks on one wall where it flashed upstairs: the dark parts show 1,500 degrees, the white parts show more than 2,000 degrees."

Corbett, who helped investigate the Trade Center terrorist attack on

9/11/2001, has studied the Beverly Hills Supper Club fire. "I'm not prone to conspiracies," he said. "The most compelling thing to me when I looked at the paperwork was the surprising deficits in the original investigation.

"In the 1970s, aluminum wiring was the topic *de jour* for fires. But nobody showed there was aluminum wiring anywhere near the Zebra Room where the fire started. And one of the biggest issues is that the area of origin was destroyed pretty quickly. That raises red flags to me."

Evidence of fire damage in the basement raised more alarms, he said.

In 2009, Kentucky's Office of the Inspector General dismissed arson claims but did confirm two stories that indicate the fire was not an accident:

1. In a phone interview, the report said, Rick Schilling's wife, Margie, "Stated that she received a letter composed of newspaper script stating, 'We burned you down once, we'll burn you down again. You keep building, we'll keep burning.' She could not determine if the letter came the day of or the day after the fire, and did not recall to whom she had given it. She said that she heard men talking outside her home during the night after the fire. Thinking they were about to break in, she yelled that she had a gun and the men dispersed."

    Brock said he and others heard about the note at the time. "I contacted Mrs. Schilling the next morning after the fire. They didn't get home until 2:00 a.m. She said she checked the mailbox and there was a stack of mail. There was one without a seal or postmark. Inside it was all taped-on letters that said, 'We burned you once, we will burn you again. You continue to build, we will continue to burn.'"

    The 2009 report said Rick Schilling was interviewed and denied that it happened.

2. That investigation also confirmed a story by hostess Eileen Druckman. In three depositions in the civil litigation and one statement to Kentucky State Police, she told a consistent account about "two air-conditioning men who caused an explosion in the laundry room" under the Zebra Room a week before the fire. "She also stated that the men were laughing as they came up the stairs from the basement."

The 2009 investigation also contacted Shirley Baker, who had finally given up trying to tell investigators about her suspicions. After the fire, she found another job. But then, she said, the threatening phone calls started.

More than 40 years after the fire, in an interview for this book, she recalled what happened. Near Christmas in 1978 she picked up the phone and a man on the line said, "You think we went away. Think again. We know where you are. We know where your husband works and where you work…"

It was the first of several calls, she said. "He gave me details of everything, about my son, where he was going to school. He told me if I didn't keep my mouth shut and say what they wanted me to say, my family would disappear."

A few days later, her son's teacher told her that two men had come around to ask about him.

Baker believes she was a target because of what she saw and heard at the Supper Club bar when she eavesdropped on two men trying to buy the club. After more than a dozen threatening calls, she moved to Lexington in 1981 to get away.

When they re-connected at a 30-year reunion, Dammert, Baker and Brock began comparing what they saw and heard before the fire.

Brock told about being contacted by a young woman who said she was the little girl who came with the crew that wiped down walls in the club before the fire.

Baker told about the threatening phone calls, and what she overheard in the bar.

Dammert told about the strange burn patterns in the Zebra Room that he saw before it was destroyed.

They each said they had been told by a lawyer who sued on behalf of victims to keep their mouths shut, because, "There's no money in arson."

The Master of Disaster

Stan Chesley, who became famous on *60 Minutes* as the original "parachute lawyer" and "Master of Disaster," liked to be known as the pioneer of the class action suit because he launched his career from the ashes of the Supper Club. He became an international litigator in famous cases: the MGM Grand fire in 1980 (85 killed); the Union Carbide gas leak in Bhopal, India in 1984 (almost 4,000 killed); Dow Corning breast implants; tobacco companies....

Chesley rushed to the scene of the fire almost before the ambulances left. He and other lawyers filed so many lawsuits that Campbell County Judge John Diskin had to get a waiver from the Fire Marshal for all the paperwork in his office. Chesley named hundreds of defendants. When all but a few were eliminated by settlements and dismissals, he targeted the electrical wire industry. Half of those companies settled out of court.

Famous litigator Stan Chesley launched his career on the ruins of the Supper Club. He rushed to the scene to dig through the wreckage looking for lawsuits. Kenton County Library archive

Chesley's first lawsuit blaming aluminum wiring was rejected by a jury. But eight years later the Federal 6th Circuit Court of Appeals in Cincinnati set aside that verdict because one of the jurors had experimented with aluminum wire at home during the trial. The second trial lasted almost three months. A fire inspector for the Consumer Products Safety Commission testified that aluminum wiring was not the cause, but the jury's verdict on July 16, 1985 blamed it anyway. The gruesome pictures of victims presented by Chesley were persuasive. Of the $50 million awarded in damages, victims got about half.

That example of excessive fees was cited as Exhibit A in the battle for tort reforms to cap attorneys' fees. But trial lawyers used those huge fees wisely, to contribute generously to the Democratic Party, buying votes to block reforms. Chesley turned class actions into an industry that made him wealthy enough to become a top fundraiser for President Clinton. He and his wife, Federal Judge Susan Dlott (appointed by Clinton), were among the lucky VIP donors who were invited by the Clintons to stay overnight at the White House, which was auctioned like a bed-and-breakfast weekend on a PBS fundraiser.

But in 2013 Chesley's fame and power went sideways. He was disbarred in Kentucky and publicly shamed for looting settlements and cheating the victims he represented in the fen-phen diet drug class-action lawsuit. Chesley and other lawyers had used a crooked Northern Kentucky judge.

Judge Joseph Bamberger awarded less than half of the $200 million settlement to victims and gave as much as $104 million to the lawyers, while the lawyers paid him more than $5,000 a month.

The Kentucky Supreme Court disbarred the judge for actions that "shock the conscience," and said Chesley "knowingly participated in a scheme to skim millions of dollars in excess attorney's fees from unknowing clients." Suddenly his previous cases came into question. A *Wall Street Journal* editorial called him a "legal scoundrel" with "a remarkable ability to make money from human suffering." To avoid disbarment in Ohio, he resigned from practicing law.

But before his fall, Chesley was skilled at schmoozing reporters to get flattering coverage. His civil lawsuit blamed the Supper Club fire on aluminum electrical wiring, and that became the media's story too.

Shirley Baker, who knew the Zebra Room very well because she often worked there, never believed it. During the civil trial she spotted something odd about Chesley's evidence. "He had a board that he said came out of the wall in the Zebra Room and had outlets on it. But the one he had, the outlet was too high. They were actually close to the floor. His was midway up. It was not a real piece of the Zebra Room."

The evidence for arson

Tom McConaughy sued the Kentucky State Police to finally pry loose photos taken in the basement under the Zebra Room. They showed severe damage to the air handling equipment, that indicated an explosion and an intense fire. Scorch marks and soot on the walls and ductwork disproved claims that there was no fire in the basement.
Courtesy of Tom McConaughy

Brock has worked harder than anyone to prove the fire was arson, devoting four decades and countless thousands of dollars to his odyssey. "I never have let it go," he said.

When he heard Rick Schilling was about to toss out records from the Chesley lawsuit, Brock immediately drove to the law firm to rescue 29 boxes of documents and photographs.

He pored over them, assembling the case that he presented in his book with Robert Webster and Tom McConaughy: *The Beverly Hills Supper Club: The Untold Story Behind Kentucky's Worst Tragedy.*

Brock and McConaughy say thousands of photos and records have been lost or concealed by the Kentucky State Police.

The case for arson includes:

- Men working in the ceiling of the Zebra Room immediately before the fire, followed by flames "shooting out of the ceiling" as the fire was discovered.

- "Strange things" in the photos of the basement, including damage to the air handling equipment on scorch marks on the walls that indicate an intense fire despite Kentucky State Police claims that the basement was untouched by the blaze.

- A threatening note and phone calls.

- The eyewitness account by Cincinnati Firefighter Peter Sabino, who said the speed of the flames down the Hall of Mirrors could only be explained by use of an accelerant. Sabino told the KSP investigators, "Fires that are accelerated act this way. I have never, in all my life, seen a normal fire travel like this."

- Reports of a crew wiping down walls in the Hall of Mirrors with a "milky" liquid that may have been an accelerant.

- Reports of eye-stinging fumes and strange "dead fish" or "slaughterhouse" odors in and around that hallway and the Zebra Room.

- Brock, McConaughy and Webster concluded that the accelerant on the walls that killed flies in midair and caused physical distress for hostess Eileen Druckman was probably liquid graphite extender, a highly flammable, toxic lubricant. A technical report on liquid graphite extender says, "Vapors can flow along surfaces to a distant ignition source and flash back."

- When the Pink Pussycat Lounge in Newport was destroyed by arson in late 1975, investigators described the fire as "rapid and furious." Their tests showed the club had been saturated in a "lubricant oil."

- Just weeks before the Supper Club fire, two unidentified men working in the basement caused an explosion, then came up the stairs laughing, according to Drucker.

- The conversation in the bar witnessed by Baker.

- Brock's account that he was told by a tearful Dick Schilling that, "They burned me out." He says that after Schilling rushed to the scene from Fort Lauderdale, he told him, "Don't talk to anyone about it. Let the lawyers handle it all." Brock had no doubt it was arson. But, "Their mistake was the timer," he said. "They set it on p.m. when they wanted a.m." If the fire had been ignited early on Sunday morning, the club would have been empty.

Another piece of evidence emerged in research for this book. In an FBI report from 1977, obtained by an FOIA request, a man said he was told the Supper Club was going to be burned 18 days before the fire. The report said that two weeks after the fire, an informant (name deleted) walked into the Norfolk, Virginia FBI office and "stated that on 5/10/77, while on a flight from Norfolk, Virginia to San Francisco, California he became engaged in a conversation with an individual who identified himself as (name redacted) of Arjay, Kentucky, along with several associates."

[Arjay is southwest of Harlan, Kentucky, near the Tennessee border.]

The report continued: "The topic of the fire that destroyed the Cocoanut Grove in the 1940s led to a further conversation on why (name redacted) thought the Beverly Hills Club of Southgate, Kentucky should meet the same fate."

[The Cocoanut Grove Club in Boston burned in 1942, killing 492.]

"(Name redacted) mentioned the owner of the Beverly Hills is a Mr. Schilling who was a Mafia-connected figure living in Northern Kentucky. (Name redacted) also mentioned the name (redacted), whose name came up in the conversation as an individual who would like to see Beverly Hills go up in smoke. (Name redacted) was another name mentioned who was a college student working at Beverly Hills.

"Since the Kentucky State Police (KSP) have an active investigation regarding the cause of the Beverly Hills fire, the above information was furnished to Detective (redacted) of the KSP on 6/21/77. (The KSP detective) advised his department would definitely investigate this incident since the alleged conversation took place a few weeks prior to the fire."

OPTIONAL FORM NO. 10
JULY 1973 EDITION
GSA FPMR (41 CFR) 101-11.6

UNITED STATES GOVERNMENT

b6
b7C

Memorandum

TO : DIRECTOR, FBI   DATE: 7/11/77

FROM : SAC, LOUISVILLE (32-297) (C)

SUBJECT: FIRE AT BEVERLY HILLS SUPPER CLUB
SOUTHGATE, KENTUCKY
5/28/77
IDENTIFICATION MATTERS

The assistance of the FBI in the matters of identification, with local authorities and officials was concluded on or about 6/15/77.

On June 17, 1977, Louisville Division in receipt of a letter dated 6/14/77 from Norfolk Office, the contents of which are summarized as follows:

On 6/13/77 a ████████ (whose credibility has not been established), appeared in the Norfolk Office of the FBI and stated that on 5/10/77, while on a flight from Norfolk, Virginia to San Francisco, California, he became engaged in a conversation with an individual who identified himself as ████ of Arjay, Kentucky, along with several of █████ associates. The topic of the fire that destroyed the Coconut Grove in the 1940's, led to a further conversation on why ████ thought the Beverly Hills Club of Southgate, Kentucky should meet the same fate. ████ mentioned the owner of Beverly Hills as a Mr. SCHILLING who was a Mafia connected figure residing in Northern Kentucky.

████ also mentioned the name ████ whose name came up in the conversation as an individual who would like to see Beverly Hills go up in smoke. ████ was another name mentioned who was a college student working at Beverly Hills.

Since the Kentucky State Police (KSP) have an active investigation regarding the cause of the Beverly Hills fire, the above information was furnished to Detective ████

2 - Bureau
1 - Louisville

VWB/jns
(3)

REC-93 95-216821

JUL 18 1977

Buy U.S. Savings Bonds Regularly on the Payroll Savings Plan

The FBI's 'anonymous tip' memo.

'Those who forget history...'

There was plenty of evidence of arson that was overlooked or dismissed by the official investigations. On a much smaller scale, it was similar to the Warren Commission whitewash: Eyewitnesses were brushed aside because their accounts did not fit the "official" findings. Many who were in Dealey Plaza on November 22, 1963 never believed there was one "lone gunman." And many who worked or dined in the Supper Club on May 28, 1977 have never believed the fire was caused by an electrical short.

In both cases, they were ignored. But anyone who took more than a glance at the context of history would immediately suspect the mob. In both cases.

The criminal record of that hilltop where the Beverly Hills Supper Club burned should have been a red flag for arson by organized crime. Sin City mob crimes were routinely covered up by law enforcement and elected officials, all the way to the state capitol in Frankfort.

Kentucky governors and local judges, police chiefs and prosecutors had been regular guests at the Beverly Hills and other local casinos. And the fire in 1977 was a horrific rerun. The old club was burned and bombed in 1936. The new Supper Club was burned in 1970 and threatened with a dummy bomb in 1971.

The Lookout House, owned by Dick Schilling before he sold it to buy the Beverly Hills, was torched by arson in 1975. Schilling had a history of labor problems and had friends in organized crime, such as his close friend and backer Ben Kees.

The deed of the Beverly Hills property tells the story.

In 1943, it was transferred from Pete Schmidt to Sam Tucker, a member of the Cleveland Four gang. In 1951, Tucker transferred it to Boulevard Enterprises of Las Vegas, a Moe Dalitz front company. In 1967, it was sold for $10 to Hyman Ullner by A.E. Giesey—the accountant for the Moe Dalitz/Cleveland Four mob.

Ullner sold the club to Dick Schilling in 1967, then sold him another parcel of land on the hilltop in 1974 for $130,000. That property adjoined an interesting neighbor: Sam Schrader, who had first set up the Cleveland gang's Arrowhead Club in Loveland, Ohio in the 1930s, then moved into Northern Kentucky as one of the owners of the Beverly Hills Country Club.

The mob was not gone in 1977. It had just gone underground—still brazen, but more sophisticated.

In 1976, the *Louisville Courier Journal* reported that eight Northern Kentucky Clubs were burned in the 15 years, with six in the previous five years. "We've proved some were arson," said Newport Fire Chief Ralph Quitter. "We've just never been able to prove who did it. You practically have to see a guy running away with a gasoline can to prove arson."

Nightclub fires were as regular as the Fourth of July in Northern Kentucky. Among them:

1970: The Beverly Hills and the Galaxie Club, formerly the Stork Club.

1971: The Cabana Club.

1972: The White Horse.

1973: The Lookout House.

1974: The Brass Ass.

1975: The Pink Pussycat.

For Kentucky State Police investigators and Governor Carroll to arrive on the scene of the Supper Club fire in 1977 and not immediately suspect arson by organized crime is obtuse or suspicious. It was as if detectives found the bullet-riddled corpse of mobster Sam Giancana, shot in the face in his kitchen in 1975, and immediately declared it was a suicide.

Kentucky's Beverly Hills was a crime scene from the first 1936 arson, to illegal gambling, to the 1970 fire that burned Dick Schilling's club before it opened. But like police, judges and prosecutors who were blinded by "Newport Eye" during the syndicate days, the governor and the state police could hardly wait to tell the public, "Nothing to see here, move along."

As the saying goes, "Those who ignore history... are doomed to repeat it."

Epilogue
The Last Reunion

**Former Supper Club busboy David Brock and his
collection of tableware, china, cigarette cases,
scorched cash, matchbooks and menus.**

David Brock returned to the Supper Club at 3:30 p.m. on May 28, 2020 the same way he reported to work there 43 years before, almost to the minute. But instead of setting up tables in the Cabaret Room and Zebra Room, he set one up at the bottom of the hill to display his remarkable reliquary of Beverly Hills artifacts: matchbooks, plates, menus, postcards, silverware, cigarette lighters, swizzle sticks, photos of celebrities and guests...

For survivors who were there during the fire or lost their friends and loved ones, it was more than nostalgia. Those menus and matchbooks were tangible proof that the club and its victims were not forgotten. For Brock and a few others, the items were swizzle-stick symbols for all the documents, photos and bits of evidence they have collected over four decades to prove the Supper Club fire was no accident.

As Brock hooked up a public address system, the parking lot in front of the South Hill Professional Center gradually filled with cars, pickups, SUVs and TV news trucks. About a hundred people and a dozen reporters gathered for "The Last Reunion of Supper Club Survivors," before the site would be cleared for a housing development.

Brock introduced speakers, who stood near a gate across the old driveway. Nearby, a gold-painted angel watched the entrance where signs once announced the Beverly Hills Country Club and the Beverly Hills Supper Club. Nearby, a small memorial of flowers and crosses was enclosed by a white picket fence.

A historical marker along the side of Alexandria Pike was the only official evidence of what happened there, placed about a hundred yards away to discourage the curious from exploring the top of the hill.

But for the 2020 reunion, the mayor of Southgate had granted special permission for access to the hilltop where the Supper Club once lit up the nights in all its electric glory.

Just a few weeks before, Southgate City Council had unanimously approved a $65 million development including apartments, homes and an assisted living center on the hilltop.

Some said 43 years was long enough. It was time. Others shook their heads and wondered who would want to live on such a cursed piece of ground. Brock said he only hoped to get a look when the developers started digging in the basement below the Zebra Room, where evidence of arson might still be found.

According to plans, the new neighborhood would be named "Memorial Point," and would include a cenotaph listing the victims and their families, and honoring the first responders.

Dotty Paeltz came to the reunion—her first time back since the night of the fire. She was there that night for the John Davidson show, seated in the Cabaret Room with her husband. "When I saw that young man Walter Bailey come down the aisle so fast, I grabbed my husband and said, 'Let's get the hell out of here. Something is wrong.' We were in the back so we headed right for the exit. We went out a hallway in back next to the Garden Room. It was my mother-in-law's 80th birthday. We all got out okay. We were among the last who got out through that exit before the smoke rolled in."

Donald Hurd held a bouquet of spring flowers to honor his good friend and fellow musician Richard Pokky, a graduate of the University of Cincinnati College Conservatory of Music who played in the Beverly Hills house orchestra. "He had a brand new trombone," Hurd recalled. "He got out but went back in to get it and never came out again." Like most of the crowd at the reunion, Hurd listened to a few speakers, then made his pilgrimage up the long, overgrown driveway to the top of the hill. Winding through arching arcades of sunlight-dappled honeysuckle, he found the place he was looking for and placed the flowers at the base of a tree that marks the southeast exit of the Cabaret Room, where his friend's body was found. A small picture of a trombone was attached to the bouquet. Hurd's eyes misted as he stood for a moment of silence.

Gina Parry came back to see what was left of the place where she was a waitress. She was supposed to work on the night of the fire but took the day off. She would have been in the Cabaret Room, and might have died there with other waitresses and guests.

"I was there in 1977," former Fire Chief Richard Reisenberg told the crowd. "We were there for ninety-three hours. According to the FBI, we saved 2,000 people who didn't know how to get out. We were always proud of that. Many were already dead when we arrived. Many were injured. We had people with burns. We had broken legs, from missing a step in the dark.

"In 2012 the Southgate Fire Department was given a Medal of Valor, the highest medal a firefighter can receive. I go to sleep knowing we got a medal, that we did a good job. But I am always troubled by the 165 people we lost."

Then he choked up as he told about a woman who asked him to help her find her husband. "I didn't have the heart to tell her that if he was not out there among the survivors or among the bodies on the lawn, he was still inside. I didn't have the courage to tell her and it has always bothered me."

On the way up the driveway, the wild tangle of bushes and undergrowth that shrouds the hill allows glimpses of unidentified objects, pieces of the past that have rusted beyond recognition.

Handmade signs sealed in clear plastic mark the trail where the front entrance would be, then the Zebra Room, the main dining room and the grand lobby where a red-carpeted spiral staircase echoed palaces and plantation mansions.

More signs mark the sad spots where congregations of the dead were found, many within just a few feet of fresh air and safety.

For 40 years the earth has been heaving up the remains of the Supper Club and the personal belongings of its victims, as if the ground itself gags on what happened there. Shoes, broken dishes, cocktail glasses, melted silverware, chair legs, a serving cart bent and rusted, wine bottles, watchbands, pieces of jewelry, parts of a kitchen mixer, wrought iron railings, broken water glasses, the metal bones of a table for eight...

Black cables loop out of the ground like phone lines to the underworld.

Under a plush carpet of dead leaves, the floor of the Garden Room can be found near the partial remains of an aqua-painted fountain pool, peeking through 40 summers of moss and memories.

In 2010, Tom McConaughy met a woman who told him she was a medium who could communicate with the spirit world. He told her a little bit about the fire and invited her to visit the hilltop.

McConaughy had been fascinated by the Beverly Hills since he worked as a manager of Dick Schilling's next big restaurant and nightclub on the downtown Cincinnati riverfront, Oodles, opened in 1978. Modeled after New York City's famed Studio 54, Oodles was part of a sprawling nightclub trio at Second and Plum that included 1950s-themed Porky's and formal January's, which seated 900 and had a nightly orchestra.

When he asked the Schillings about the fire, they shut down. "The Schillings would never, ever talk about it," McConaughy said. "Their father told them not to."

But coworker David Brock told him stories. After they attended the 30th reunion of survivors together, McConaughy was hooked. As he joined the scavenger hunt for clues, he battled the Kentucky State Police to pry loose a buried treasure: 30 boxes of files and photos that he still keeps in his basement.

"I would bring up one or two boxes at a time into my living room, go through them, make notes about what workers said, what the firemen and experts said. I started to realize, 'There seems to be a pattern here.' It was pretty blatant. A cover up."

In 2010, Brock and McConaughy led a team of investigators who spent hundreds of hours searching through documents and photos that had been mothballed in the National Archives in Atlanta, Georgia. They found that many items listed among the contents of each box were missing—especially photos of the basement under the Zebra Room. The search also revealed that none of the previous investigations had found any trace of aluminum wiring that was blamed by the paid, expert witnesses in civil court.

"We found that in fact the Kentucky State Police were told about and knew about these men in the Zebra Room." McConaughy said. "They knew they were there doing things they shouldn't and didn't pursue it. I said, 'You guys knew about this and did not follow up?' You could see (in photos) where someone removed fuses and put in copper pipes" to jump the fuse box circuits, he said. "And yet the Kentucky State police said there was no damage to the basement. They wouldn't let the insurance companies go down there, wouldn't let NFPA go down there. They said it was too dangerous."

The evidence made him even more determined. "It's about justice. Especially for Keith Holliday."

Keith Holliday, 5, went missing seven months after the fire, on December 20, 1977. His mother was Judy Holliday, who was the waitress with Shirley Baker when she overheard two men threatening the Shillings about selling the Supper Club. Her son's tragic disappearance became one of the biggest stories of 1977 and 1978, making headlines all over the U.S.

More than 1,000 volunteers searched for the boy for two days, on horseback, on foot, in helicopters, in cars and jeeps, scouring the area near his home.

Lakes were dragged. A nationwide search was launched and came up with nothing. There was no ransom demand, no clues. A $10,000 reward was offered. Pictures of the cute, blond, friendly little boy were posted in airports and bus stations all over Indiana, Ohio and Kentucky. Keith's brother, Kevin, 11, spent a whole day writing a letter asking President Jimmy Carter for help. The brush-off reply from a White House assistant was almost more than the family could bear.

The only lead was two men seen in the family's Alexandria, Kentucky neighborhood the morning Keith disappeared, driving a van that had primer covering a sign on the driver's door.

Three months to the day after he went missing, on March 20, 1978, Judy Holliday glanced out her kitchen window and saw the blue knit cap her boy was wearing when he disappeared. His body was found in their backyard, floating in a small above-ground swimming pool that was only four feet deep. An autopsy showed the cause of death was drowning.

But firemen had searched the pool several times. It's almost inconceivable that 1,000 searchers dragged nearby lakes without looking in the backyard pool. "I talked to at least three or four people who searched that pool," McConaughy said. "They all said he was not in there."

Wayne Dammert, who lived nearby and knew Judy Holliday from the Supper Club, was one of the searchers. He remains certain that the boy's body was not in the pool until it was put there in March.

Shirley Baker was still getting threatening phone calls when she heard about the missing boy. "When I found out her little boy disappeared it literally scared me to death," she said. "I felt like it was my fault that Judy's son was murdered. I had an awful time with that. I was afraid that they killed her little boy thinking she was me and he was my son. That's an awful burden to carry. I woke up in the middle of a dream one night, hollering. All I could see was that little boy.

She wept for the family and thought, "Until this is proved they won't get their peace."

Voices from the underworld

McConaughy had heard all about that story. Nobody who lived in Cincinnati or Northern Kentucky could have missed it. So when he met the medium, they made plans to visit the hilltop with David Brock to see what she might be able to tell them about the Supper Club fire.

"She had never been there but she identified every room," he recalled. "She identified people by name who came up to ask where they could get out. She said, 'Two men who did this were in a white van parked near the caretaker's house and sat there and watched.' We went back and looked at pictures taken on the night of the fire, and there was a white van right where she said it would be."

"It was surreal. It gave me goosebumps. I believe there are souls still trapped on that hill. She would say, 'Here's somebody coming up to me. They know that I can communicate.' She would tell us what they were looking for or trying to do. Some were looking for a spouse. Others were still trying to get out."

Ten years later, a second medium was drawn to the 2020 survivors' reunion by her curiosity and the rare access to visit the hilltop. Tammy Nolan introduced herself as a "paranormal investigator." She carried an electronic device called an EMF, about as big as a TV remote, black with colored lights to indicate electromagnetic frequencies. According to ads, EMF devices are popular with ghost hunters as "a top instrument for both detecting spirit activity and for finding potentially harmful high EMF levels in your home or work environment." Meaning it's a "smoke-detector" for ghosts, to find out if your home is haunted.

Nolan said she found the Supper Club site to be unusually haunted with voices that ghost hunters call EVPs (electronic voice phenomenon). "We've only been up there one time, for about four hours of audio. Usually when we go into a case, within four hours we might get six EVPs. If anything comes up on the recorder we can pull it out and see what it was.

"Up there we got sixty-something EVPs. At least sixty separate voices. It was very active. What we found has been incredible. Some of the sentences we've gotten are just amazing."

Using her latest equipment Nolan and two friends set up a grid of laser lights. "We can see the lights flicker as they are shaded out. We could see them coming through the lights."

She took a geophone that could detect movement of the ground, and a temperature gauge. "If a spirit comes through, you get a drop in temperature that you can feel, a cold front. The EMF picks up their magnetic field and flickers to blue. The geophone will actually show me if there's something on the ground wherever it's placed.

"We got a tremendous amount of hits. Usually five or six investigators would work eight hours through the night and maybe get six actual recordings. We got sixty in four hours."

She also used flashlights. "The spirits can turn them on or off. We saw that happen that night. I'd say, 'Go ahead and turn it off.' And then we saw it dim and flicker, and eventually it turned off."

Her companions had been there before, but she asked them not to tell her anything about the fire or the layout of the club on her first visit. They set up their equipment near what had been the southeast exit of the Cabaret Room, where 31 bodies were found.

"One part I remember: To you and me it looks like a long trail in the woods. But I see it like a long hallway. I see a lot of red. Everything in this hall was red. I see like two, then one, then two people coming through the hallway, pointing to the front door. Later I asked why they were pointing to the front. I found out that's where the fire started. It all made sense when I listened to the voices we recorded.

"There were a lot of feelings. I was standing there and went to turn around and I had to grab a tree to hold myself up. I saw a woman in this hallway trying to hold herself up. I felt what she was feeling. She tells me to go back. Like she's left somebody. Some of the wives got out and husbands didn't—I felt like, 'Maybe I need to look for whoever she was with.'

"I heard a lot of names. A lot of victims' names. There were so many different sentences. Some don't make sense. There's a little boy up there, screaming. Babies crying. There's a lot going on in that area up there. I have had dreams about that red hallway. It's haunting me and won't stop."

She said some of the contacts felt threatening. "I warned the people with me that a few were not-so-good men. Two are not very nice at all. I can visually see this one man. He's pointing his finger at us, like, 'You need to stop.' Physically threatening. I make it clear, 'We're not here to harm you.' But a few get very aggravated.

"Some can be pretty powerful. They can actually attach themselves to a person. I tell them they can't go home with me. I asked if there were any messages. I got a loud and clear 'Thank you.' Thank you to the people who have kept their spirits alive. A lot of calls for help. Different names. It was almost overwhelming. There were some whispers, but I can't understand what they are saying. But one clear female voice said, 'John Davidson.'"

The spirits that were there aren't necessarily victims of the fire, Nolan said. They could be spirits who have been attached to that site by what they did while they were living. Such as, "He's passed on and that was a major part of his life," she explained. The arsonists, for example.

Nolan said she has been able to communicate with the spirit world

318

since she was 15. "I was in the hospital with spinal meningitis. I had a 'visitor' come to me, a spirit who told me I would have gifts to help people. Since then I can feel and sense things before they happen. It's not always a good feeling.

"People think I'm crazy. But I use it to pass on messages. Things like that. I do readings, but I don't charge because it was a God-given gift. I want to help people."

At the Beverly Hills site, "My goal is to help some of the spirits move on to the light. Once they move ground up there (to develop the property), they will be lost. It concerns me that they are planning to put a nursing home up there. There is spiritual stuff that could attack weakness, and the elderly are not strong enough to resist it. That's not a good idea at all."

Nolan said she has hunted ghosts at famous sites such as a haunted penitentiary in West Virginia, Waverly Hills Sanitorium in Louisville, Kentucky and Ashmore Estates Sanitorium and Poor Farm in Ashmore, Illinois. "But this was the most activity I've ever gotten out of any case."

Scientists and skeptics call ghost hunting "pseudoscience" that has no credibility and no scientific method. They say mediums are hoaxers or people with overactive imaginations, who "hear" voices that are really just background noise or static. Attempts to scientifically confirm the presence of spirits have consistently failed.

But the same "experts" and scientists have insisted since 1947 that UFOs were "swamp gas" and didn't exist—until one day in April 2020 when the Pentagon confirmed UFO sightings by Navy pilots and released videos of encounters recorded by flight cameras.

"Those are demons'

There's another answer from a book the scientists and ghost hunters have overlooked: the Bible. It says the spirit world is as real as the Dead Sea Scrolls and as old as Creation. "Ghosts" and "spirits" do exist, but they are not what most of us think. They are not spirits of the dead, but imposters—fallen angels, demons that wage spiritual warfare on mankind.

Leviticus 19:31 says, "Give no regard to mediums and familiar spirits; do not seek after them, to be defiled by them: I am the LORD your God." Leviticus 20:6: "And the person who turns to mediums and familiar spirits, to prostitute himself with them, I will set My face against that person and cut him off from his people."

An ordained reverend who has battled evil spirits to free victims from demon oppression or possession explained the voices and contacts on the Supper Club hilltop:

"Those would not be spirits of people. They are not the individuals who died there. What she is hearing is legitimate. She is not making this stuff up. But what she's doing is communicating with a demon. Or many demons. It could be one. It could be 60."

Bible scholars say demons can disguise themselves as people we knew and loved. They are fallen angels who rebelled against God and were cast out of Heaven with Satan. They are evil, deceptive and dangerous. A popular Bible study website, Crosswalk.com says:

> The ghost might appear to be a familiar spirit impersonating a departed family member (but) is certainly not a returned-family member. Once we die, there exists no possible pathway to return to the land of the living. This fact rules out the return of a dead person as a "ghost" to haunt a house or place of their death—or wherever. ... The apparition could be an actual demonic manifestation.

"When you die, you die," says the reverend. "You are not a ghost. We are not seeing Civil War soldiers, our grandmother or our grandfather. Those are demons and their goal is to draw people as far away from God as they can."

Most world cultures are open and aware of the spirit world, he said. But Western culture is wrapped in the security blanket of science.

He warns that dabbling in the occult or communicating with "spirits" gives them permission and authority to move into your life, your family, your home—what Nolan described as "an attachment." And the Supper Club site would give demons a place of authority because of what has happened there over the years. "The enemy can have strongholds. They have control in these areas. They have a right to be there because it's a place of so much darkness and evil, where so many people have sold their souls to the devil for fame, fortune, popularity, sex, whatever they thought they had to have. This is where the enemy is going to dwell.

"We live on a battlefield. But let's not go overboard," he said. "There's not a demon behind every bush. Don't give the enemy too much credit. There is no power conflict between God and Satan. Satan's power is an inch from the ground. God's power goes to the end of the universe. The battle is for the truth. The victory is ours."

Nobody knows the crime, cruelty and evil that was been done at the Beverly Hills. Could spirits there claim the names and anguish of victims, going as far back as the first fire in 1936—even clues such as the white van?

"Absolutely," the reverend said. "The demons could have been there. They could have observed and experienced it. They could be getting all kinds of information."

But some questions are better unasked, he says. "Remember that demons are liars. It is very hard to discern what is truth and what is lies. They have an ulterior motive, to give you things that drive you closer to them, to have more control, manipulate you more."

Ephesians 6:12 warns, "For our struggle is not against flesh and blood, but against the rulers, against the authorities, against the powers of this dark world and against the spiritual forces of evil in the heavenly realms."

Who will pick up the cross?

While others climbed the driveway to the hilltop in small groups, Wayne Dammert, one of the heroes of the Supper Club fire, stayed put. "I'm done with that," he said. "I'm not going back up there again."

Wayne Dammert became the unofficial custodian of the overgrown hilltop where the Beverly Hills Supper Club once drew thousands. He made signs to show where the original rooms were.

For years, he was the caretaker of the hilltop when it seemed as if everyone else had forgotten. He went up alone or with anyone who would help, to keep the trails clear and put up handmade signs and pictures, sealed in plastic, that showed where rooms were located, where people died. Little by little, he rebuilt the Supper Club he loved in the woods of his imagination.

He constructed a cross made from PVC pipe and lumber, erected it on the hilltop and attached an American flag. It could be seen from the highways below, standing at the top of a cliff that drops almost straight down to Alexandria Pike. It was his memorial to the dead.

Then on October 2, 2019, it nearly killed him. The survivor and witness to so many accidents, crashes, deaths and Kentucky's worst tragedy, almost became another number on the list of people killed there.

The memorial installed by Wayne Dammert for 165 who were lost in the fire could be seen from the highway below and was lit at night. Local 12 News

"It was braced by four-by-fours and set in concrete. But one day I looked and it was broken and laying on the ground," he said. "I don't know how that happened. Draw your own conclusions."

The day he went up to raise the cross and the flag again, he took along a young student who was working on a report about the fire, accompanied by his mother.

"I was trying to straighten the flag. I really don't like to go up there anymore. I pulled the guy-wire—the line back to the edge of the slope, right at the crest. Suddenly the line broke at the base and I went flying down the hill screaming, 'I'm dead!' Just as I was ready for the first tumble, my head hit this shrub, and it stopped me. 'Okay, I'm stopped,' I thought. Then BOOM, the flagpole came down and hit my head. Oh, that hurt."

Somehow, the boy and his mother got him up and helped him to the crest of the hill again. "I still don't know how they did it," he said. "But all I could think was, 'God's with me.' If I kept falling down that hill I would be dead for sure."

A rescue team from Southgate Fire Department and EMS responded to the call. Dammert had a bad cut on his head that left a visible scar—struck by the cross he put up for the victims.

He decided to leave it there on the ground. "I've had enough," he said. "I'm not going back."

But in a figurative sense, he wonders who will pick up the cross for the victims and carry on the search for the truth.

It's long past time to hold anyone accountable or get justice. Brock and his team identified two men as the most likely perpetrators. They worked for a heating and air-conditioning company in Cincinnati that was the favorite contractor for the mob in Newport, according to their interview with Johnny TV Peluso.

But they are long dead. So is Peluso, the last of his kind from the wild Sin City days. And the tireless survivors who have worked so hard over the years—Brock, Dammert, McConaughey and so many others—are not getting any younger. Even the ones in their teens at the time of the fire, such as Brock and Walter Bailey, are now in their 60s.

What was the motive?

An aerial view of the Supper Club after the fire wreckage was sifted and cleared away. The foreground to the right was the Cabaret Room.
Courtesy of Tom McConaughy.

Anyone who has watched *Perry Mason* or *Law and Order* knows the classic elements to prove guilt in a criminal case are means, motive and opportunity. The "prosecution" for arson has proved two categories beyond a reasonable doubt.

Means. Organized crime arsonists had already burned dozens of nightclubs by the time the Beverly Hills Supper Club went up in flames. They used accelerants and had even burned the Supper Club twice before, in 1936 and 1970. Setting an incendiary device to go off on a Sunday morning when the club was empty would have followed the mob's typical *modus operandi.*

Opportunity. The arsonists would have no need to break in. In such a busy, hectic place, it would be easy to walk in boldly, impersonating maintenance workers. Eyewitnesses saw two men in maintenance uniforms, others working below in the basement, and a crew applying some substance to the walls in the Hall of Mirrors. And they may have had an insider, according to the FBI report in which gangsters talked on a plane about burning the Supper Club and mentioned a college student who worked there.

Motive. The problem with motive is not a lack of theories, but too many.

After the 1970 fire, the fire chief said he suspected Schilling's use of non-union labor may have been a motive. Mob affiliation and control of unions was brazen in the 1970s, and Schilling had already had union trouble at the Lookout House, which also was burned.

Tom McConaughey believed the mob wanted Schilling's property because it adjoined land owned by mobster Sam Schrader of the Cleveland Four, who wanted to control valuable parcels in advance of a new highway interchange that was soon to be built. "Governor Carroll had a relationship with Sam Schrader," McConaughey said. "Johnny Peluso said Carroll went to Sam Schrader's Christmas party before the fire. Schrader had tremendous acreage around there. The reason the mob got pissed at Schilling was because the Schillings were going to develop property that the mob wanted."

If he's right, that could explain the connection to the governor, who could influence routing of the new interchange and might have been easily blackmailed to cooperate because of his closeted homosexuality. Fire investigator Clell Upton said it was Carroll who refused to consider the possibility of arson and ordered the Zebra Room destroyed the day after the fire.

Brock believed it was the original mob boss Moe Dalitz who was behind the takeover, just as he took the club from Pete Schmidt in 1936. "Mr. Schilling was a very strong man, the kind of man who would command your attention when he walked in a room. When he went to Vegas, Moe Dalitz and the others, they all knew him. He took no crap from anybody."

He says Dick Schilling once told him, "That Jew burned me down," meaning Dalitz. "I was told they burned it down because they wanted the business back."

At first glance, it's hard to believe Dalitz, who had become Mr. Las Vegas, would take such a risk. But Dalitz was a Picasso of crime, building cubist schemes that nobody could figure out or trace back to him. The Beverly Hills was the place where he learned everything he needed to build an empire in Vegas. It was his sentimental first love.

Once a gangster, always a gangster. As the authors who interviewed him for their 1963 expose of the mob in Vegas, *Green Felt Jungle*, wrote:

"He was a sanctimonious little mobster from Cleveland. He is still a hoodlum in conscience and mind."

Moe Dalitz became 'Mr. Las Vegas' and was lauded for his philanthropy before his death in 1989.

At about the time Dick Schilling was planning his new hilltop expansion, Dalitz was planning a new Las Vegas Convention Center, which he said in 1983 was his greatest achievement. The mob was also pushing legalized gambling, which may have been on Schilling's radar as well.

A national commission studied legalized gambling in the early 1970s and found that 80 percent of Americans were in favor. States were urged to permit casinos as revenue sources. That report was issued in 1976.

It would be no surprise if Dalitz wanted to be among the first to pioneer legal casino gambling at his favorite club near a new highway interchange in Kentucky. If so, the strong-arm takeover backfired horrifically.

Atlantic City, New Jersey opened the first legal casino outside Nevada in 1978, followed by dozens more. Today, more than 30 states have casinos run by the "gaming" industry, sporting names such as Harrah's and Bally's. Compared to the dirty 30s, they are as clean as a new bar of soap. Their "bosses" are governors, not gangsters.

And the man who became known as the King of Casinos and the "Father of Gaming" in Mississippi was Dick Schilling. Following their success with the Oodles/January's complex on the Cincinnati riverfront, the Schillings opened a popular riverboat restaurant-nightclub in Newport called The Islands and Splash. In 1986 they moved it to Louisville, then down the Mississippi River to Tunica, Mississippi in 1992, where it became the first of two Schilling casinos. The second was Harlow's in Greenville, Mississippi, valued at $75 million. Schilling died in 2010 at his retirement home in Fort Lauderdale, Florida.

Not even the boom years of syndicate gambling at Beverly Hills could make a drop in the Mississippi River of profits from legalized gambling. Yet ironically, Kentucky remains an island surrounded by casino states. Ohio, Indiana, Missouri, Illinois, West Virginia and Tennessee all have casinos. But Kentucky has repeatedly rejected ballot proposals.

Some blame the Bible Belt. Or maybe Kentucky has learned from other states that followed the hooker's wink of casinos to chase empty promises that gambling revenues would "fix" public education.

Or perhaps it's the painful memories of Sin City that keep Kentucky free of casinos.

The buried past

"You should see Newport now, Myron," Knuckles said. "You wouldn't know it. Thousands of people come over the river from Cincinnati on the weekends, but it's nothing like the old days. They're bringing their *kids.* There's a whole new place they call Newport on the Levee, down by Riverboat Row where Dirty Helen's and the Sportsman Club used to be.

"They even opened a Newport Aquarium, with alligators, penguins, and big turtles. I saw a shark in there that smiled like Screw Andrews. You wouldn't believe it."

He looked up through the red and gold leaves at a gray wintry sky and thought, I wonder why the prettiest trees seem to grow best in cemeteries?

"Sorry I can't stay long, Myron. These old knees can't take it. Between that and my emphysema, sometimes I think you're the lucky one, going fast that way with a heart attack. What was it you called it?

'Cardiattack infartshun.' See, you're still making me laugh."

He paused and looked across the rows of graves toward the old section, where round-shouldered headstones swayed and leaned, their carved names smoothed away by time. "You'll be glad to know I visited Jimmy over there near the Civil War soldiers, and put a new set of flags next to his headstone. His MIA flag was getting ragged. And you have a new flag too. They're all over the place here at Evergreen for Veterans Day.

"I guess we did our share. Nothing everyone else didn't do, I guess. Maybe that will be good for something against some of the other stuff we did. God forgive me, I miss those wild old days sometimes. The Alibi. Slowfoot Bill. Gus the bookie. Even Breck Girl Steve. You'll be glad to hear he finally got a haircut. He's an anesthesiologist at St. Elizabeth. You wouldda had some fun with that. Maybe he was just practicing the pain-killing trade on us.

"But most of all I miss you, Myron." Knuckles brushed his cheek with the back of a trembling big hand that looked frail, bony, tattooed with age spots on wax-paper skin.

He glanced back to the car where his son Jake was waiting, the exhaust making a thin little cloud as he kept the heater going. Then he gave a last look at Myron and raised his shaking hand in a final salute. "Say hi to the gang. Wherever they are."

Sources and Further Reading

Books

Barker, Thomas, et al. *Wicked Newport: Kentucky's Sin City*. History Press, 2008.

Best, Richard. *Reconstruction of a Tragedy: The Beverly Hills Supper Club Fire, Southgate, Kentucky, May 28, 1977*. National Fire Prevention and Control Administration and National Bureau of Standards, US Commerce Department, 1977.

Burbank, Jeff. *Las Vegas Babylon: The True Tales of Glitter, Glamour, and Greed*. M. Evans & Company, 2008.

Carr, Howie. *Kennedy Babylon: A Century of Scandal and Depravity*. Frandel, LLC, 2017.

Denton, Sally. *The Bluegrass Conspiracy*. iUniverse, 1990.

Elliott, Ron. *Inside the Beverly Hills Supper Club Fire*. Turner, 2010.

Goldfarb, Ronald. *Perfect Villains, Imperfect Heroes: Robert Kennedy's War Against Organized Crime*. Random House, 1995.

Goldsmith, Jack. *In Hoffa's Shadow: A Stepfather, a Disappearance in Detroit, and My Search for the Truth*. Farrar, Straus and Giroux, 2019.

John, Cathie; Celestri, John. *Little Mexico: An Original Sin City Novel*. John and Cathie Celestri, 2000.

Lawson, Robert G. *Beverly Hills: Anatomy of a Nightclub Fire*. Commonwealth Book Company, 2016.

Messick, Hank. *Syndicate Wife: The Story of Ann Drahman Coppola*. Amereon House, 1968.

Mouldon, Stuart. *The Kefauver Organized Crime Hearings: Abridged*. Amazon, 2013.

Newton, Michael. *Mr. Mob: The Life and Crimes of Moe Dalitz*. McFarland & Company, 2009.

Pinger, Dan. *A Reporter's Memoir: When the Mob Ruled Newport.* Amazon, 2019.

Reid, Ed; Demaris, Ovid. *The Green Felt Jungle: The Truth About Las Vegas Where Organized Crime Controls Gambling – And Everything Else.* Ishi Press, 2010.

Webster, Robert D., et al. *The Beverly Hills Supper Club: The Untold Story behind Kentucky's Worst Tragedy.* CreateSpace Independent Publishing Platform, 2016.

Williams, Michael L. *Sin City Kentucky: Newport, Kentucky's Vice Heritage and Its Legal Extinction, 1920-1991.* University of Louisville, 2008.

Documents

Best, Richard. *Tragedy in Kentucky.* Fire Journal, 1978.

Bright, Richard. National Fire Prevention Association Report on the Beverly Hills Supper Club Fire. NFPA, 1979.

Comparing the Club with the Code. Fire Journal, 1978.

Dunn, Cecil. *Report of the Special Prosecutor: The Beverly Hills Supper Club Fire.* Commonwealth of Kentucky, 1979.

FBI records, wiretaps, memos, obtained by FOIA request, 1960s to 1970s.

Investigation of organized crime in interstate commerce. Hearings before a Special Committee of the U.S. Senate to Investigate Organized Crime in America. Official Record of the U.S. Senate, 1950.

Investigative Report to the Governor: Beverly Hills Supper Club Fire, Commonwealth of Kentucky, 1977.

National Archives: Declassified Kennedy papers and documents related to the assassination of 1963 and investigations.

Report of Beverly Hills Supper Club Fire Review, Office of the Inspector General, Commonwealth of Kentucky Labor, Public Protection, and Energy and Environment Cabinets, 2009.

Report of the United States House of Representatives Select Committee on Assassinations, Congressional Record, 1979.

Robert F. Kennedy Assassination Records, California Secretary of State, State of California Archives, 1987.

Sin City Revisited: A Case Study of the Official Sanctioning of Organized Crime in an "Open City," Matthew DeMichele, Gary Potter. Justice and Police Studies, Eastern Kentucky University.

Swartz, Joseph. *Human Behavior in the Beverly Hills Fire.* Fire Journal, 1979.

Warranty Deeds, Beverly Hills Supper Club and Beverly Hills Country Club property transactions. Campbell County Clerk archives.

When Vice Was King: A History of Northern Kentucky Gambling 1920-1970. Jim Linduff, Roy Klein and Larry Trapp, May 23, 2012.

Williams, Michael. *Sin city Kentucky: Newport, Kentucky Kentucky's vice heritage and its legal extinction, 1920-1991.* University of Louisville, 2008.

United States Senate Select Committee to Study Governmental Operations with Respect to Intelligence Activities (the Church Committee). 1975.

Newspapers, media, etc.

The Cincinnati Enquirer, 1930s to 2020.

The Cincinnati Post, 1930s to 2020.

The Cleveland Plain Dealer, 1930s to 2020.

The Hamilton Journal, 1960s to 1970s.

The Louisville Courier Journal, 1930s to 2020.

The Lexington Herald Leader, 1930s to 2020.

The Miami Herald, 1960 and 1970s.

WCPO TV archives, Cincinnati, 1961.

The Mob Museum: National Museum of Organized Crime and Law Enforcement. 300 Stewart Avenue, downtown Las Vegas, Nevada: https://themobmuseum.org

FBI Records: The Vault. https://vault.fbi.gov

Kenton County Library, Faces And Places (photo archive).

Northern Kentucky Views (photo archives). http://nkyviews.com

Acknowledgments

Menu from the 1950s signed by Ozzie and Harriet Nelson.
Northern Kentucky Views

Special thanks to Librarian Cierra Earl of the Kenton County Library, Bernie Spencer of Northern Kentucky Views, Supper Club historian and researcher Shane Goins and the excellent librarians at the Chase College of Law Library at Northern Kentucky University, especially

Carol Bredemeyer. Cretia Kuhl, assistant chief deputy in the Campbell County Clerk's office, helped dig out the original deed to the Beverly Hills property.

First Amendment and media law attorney Jack Greiner reviewed the manuscript, graphic artist Andy Melchers designed the cool cover and the rest of the book, and proofreading was done by Jane Wenning and my wife, Kathy, who has devoted many years to the thankless task of trying to correct my mistakes.

Special appreciation to the survivors who have devoted years of research and perseverance to keep digging for the truth about the Supper Club fire. Among them: David Brock, Wayne Dammert, Tom McConaughy and Shirley Baker. Thanks also to authors who graciously consented to quote from their books: Ron Goldfarb, David Brock, Tom McConaughey, Michael Newton and Howie Carr.

First-person stories make history come alive. This book would not be the same without stories told by survivors and family members of the victims, including Pam Ford, former Fire Chief Richard Reisenberg, Jeff Ruby, Wayne Dammert, David Brock, Shirley Baker and others.

My sincere apologies to anyone I missed.